Rutherford's Ladder

The Making of
Northumbria University, 1871–1996

Joan Allen and Richard Buswell

R J Buswell

Published by Northumbria University Press
Trinity Building, Newcastle upon Tyne NE1 8ST, UK

First Published 2005
Copyright © Northumbria University

British Library Cataloguing in Publication Data. A Catalogue Record for this book is available from the British Library.

ISBN 1-904794-09-2

Designed by External Relations, Northumbria University
Printed by Graphicom, Vicenza, Italy

Typeset in Garamond BE

Illustration acknowledgements

A large number of the illustrations were taken from the University archives. We gratefully acknowledge Simon Veit-Wilson, Jim McAdam, the employees of the University who took many of the photographs, Hong Kong Polytechnic University and Newcastle Chronicle & Journal Ltd. The Editor also wishes to thank Richard Bott, Derek Webster and Sean Figgis for allowing use of personal archives and to the authors and the many University employees for all their help in sourcing illustrations. Every effort has been made to obtain permission from copyright holders. The Editor apologises for any inadvertent breach of copyright convention.

Cover image: Stained glass window in Ellison Building foyer commemorating John Hunter Rutherford, founder of Northumbria University. Photographed by Simon Veit-Wilson.

Northumbria University is the trading name of the University of Northumbria at Newcastle. ER–111697/K/6/05

The University of Northumbria at Newcastle Ceremonial Sword

Lord Glenamara, Chancellor of Northumbria University (1983–2005)

Dedication

EDWARD SHORT, LORD GLENAMARA OF GLENRIDDING, PC, CH, LLB, Freeman of the City of Newcastle upon Tyne, Hon FCP, Hon DCL (Dunelm), Hon DCL (Newcastle), DUniv (Open), Hon DLitt (CNAA), Chancellor of the University of Northumbria at Newcastle (1983–2005).

This history is dedicated to Lord Glenamara, a unique and special man, whose wise guidance and friendship have been so readily conferred upon countless numbers of the University community for more than two decades. As Secretary of State for Education and Science, he presided over the formation of the then Newcastle upon Tyne Polytechnic in the late 1960s. In 1992, by then as its Chancellor and member of the Board of Governors, he oversaw its transition to the University of Northumbria at Newcastle.

Throughout this period until he announced his retirement in December 2004, Lord Glenamara was mentor and counsel to three Vice-Chancellors, three Chairmen of the Board of Governors, and to many other staff – senior and junior alike – and governors. He has been the inspiration of generations of students, their families and friends, who attended Academic Awards Congregations to hear his memorable and rousing speeches.

The development of the University of Northumbria at Newcastle, in the latter half of the twentieth century and the beginning of the twenty-first, would have been infinitely the poorer without Lord Glenamara's gentle but firm guiding hand. The University gratefully acknowledges our debt to this best of friends.

Contents

Professor Kel Fidler, Vice-Chancellor of Northumbria University

Foreword

THE APPEARANCE of this first edition of *Rutherford's Ladder* is very timely, published in July 2005, when the University is embarking on the most ambitious expansion project in its history, with the investment of more than £100 million, to obtain a City Centre Campus in Newcastle upon Tyne worthy of the University's status, its staff and student body.

When I was appointed as Vice-Chancellor of the University in 2001, I knew something of the recent history of the University and the city because of my own previous, very happy graduate and postgraduate university studies in Newcastle. I also knew of the University's potential, and my personal aspiration, then as now, was to lead the University into the twenty-first century, with a new Northumbria University Vision. This is, '*...to become one of the World's leading teaching and learning Universities, renowned for its innovative and research-based practice and exercising its regional, national and international role through an extensive network of locations and partnerships*'. The University Mission encapsulating our approach to meeting this Vision is, '*...to meet the diverse needs of an international learning community and to contribute to society and its economic development through research, excellent teaching and high-quality student support*'. These two statements encourage us to look forward to the new century but are firmly grounded in the attainments and achievements of the past.

Even so, it is a lesson in humility for me to read this history of my University, and to realise that I am 'standing on the shoulders of giants', to quote the famous phrase of Isaac Newton from 1676. *Rutherford's Ladder* highlights the contributions of my distinguished predecessors, the large personalities without whom institutional development is impossible. My admiration for them is immense, and here I pay my own homage to their greatness. However, none of these distinguished forebears could have attained anything without the countless numbers of loyal staff, students, mentors and benefactors who helped to realise their aspirations, but who inevitably cannot be named in one volume. If it were possible, all would have their names engraved on every stone of our buildings, for us all to appreciate.

If modern vice-chancellors are permitted aspirations, then mine is first to prove a worthy successor to many eminent forebears, and to carry the torch first lit by Rutherford, after whom this history is named. Next, and even more difficult, it is to realise the destiny of Northumbria University as an international and national institution of higher education, in a time of unparalleled change and challenge, but without being imprisoned by the past.

Like my predecessors, I cannot achieve anything without the strong and unstinting assistance of academic and non-academic colleagues, as well as lay governors, and numerous other supporters. I am fortunate, as were Rutherford and others in the past, in being able to rely upon an incredibly able and energetic cadre of such supporters. Amongst these I must pay particular tribute to a magnificent Chancellor, Lord Glenamara, who has just retired from office after many decades of contribution to the University at national, regional and local level. I also pay tribute to Gavin Black,

Chairman and Pro-Chancellor for his support and wise guidance, which will continue to be forthcoming as we face the next exciting phase in the University's development

This is what I would call a *real* University history. Although beautifully produced, it is no 'coffee table' book. As its authors point out in the Preface, it presents their picture, as distinguished scholars, and they have had complete freedom to write it, unfettered by any University requirement other than to tell the story of the institution as they saw it. Northumbria University deserves nothing less, and in *Rutherford's Ladder* much can be learned of the development of higher education in Britain in the last century, and earlier. The authors, in producing a magisterial and challenging portrait of an amazingly energetic institution, have directly challenged me and my successors not to lose sight of the enduring objectives of 'our sort' of University. I trust we will not fail them as we take the institution into the second decade of this century and beyond.

Here I am pleased to thank the authors for what has clearly been a labour of love to each of them. In a very real sense, Joan Allen and Dick Buswell are products of Northumbria University, and there can be no better advertisement for the institution than this volume, full of perspicacity and insight. It is essential reading for anyone interested in higher education, and particularly for those who seek to find the essence of a great university.

There is no doubt, as the authors hope, that further volumes will follow – and will perhaps inspire personal memoirs from those who have been part of the University's history, to add depth and breadth to the picture of a complex institution. If it causes debate and discussion, and alternative interpretation, so much the better: all the best histories do just that. Of course, I also look forward with eager anticipation, as to the judgements which will be made about the current period.

Finally, I pay my own tribute, alongside those of the authors, to those within the University and its Board of Governors who have seen the University history project through from its conception to realisation and in particular Richard Bott, University Secretary, for his tireless enthusiasm. Such is the pace of change in higher education today that most of us are, and have to be, obsessed by current and future developments: hence, we spend insufficient time and investment in recording past achievements.

Nonetheless, in our heart of hearts, we all recognise that nothing is achieved from nothing: the determination of future direction is impossible without knowing where we have come from. In this history, the origins of Northumbria University have been firmly recorded, and future generations like myself, will for the first time be able to refer to a definitive source when we need such guidance.

I am delighted to see *Rutherford's Ladder* appear in production as a distinguished contribution to the list of Northumbria University Press.

Professor Kel Fidler

Preface

THE IDEA of writing the history of Northumbria University was first mooted in the 1990s when a number of newly-appointed governors began to ask questions about the origins of the institution. Despite their initial enthusiasm little came of this until the appointment of Professor Gilbert Smith as Vice-Chancellor in 1995. Richard Bott, the University Secretary, was extremely supportive of the idea and it was largely due to his determined advocacy that a small working party was set up in 1997 to consider what form such a history might take and, most importantly, who might want to read it. The committee invited Professor Norman McCord (Emeritus, University of Newcastle) and Professor Robert Colls (Leicester University) to act as academic advisors to the project. Thereafter, the School of Historical and Critical Studies were asked to put forward proposals and, as a result of that process, Dr Joan Allen was appointed to research and write the history. With a millennium fast approaching the ideal target date was set for summer 2000 but these plans suffered a setback in 1999 when she left Northumbria to take up a new appointment at the University of Newcastle. Although considerable research had been undertaken by then, the pressure of new commitments made it difficult for further progress to be made and for a time the completion of the history was effectively stalled. Professor Buswell, who had always had a strong interest in the history of the institution, became involved at this point. A chance enquiry in the autumn of 2003 as to the progress of the book revealed that the work was 'on hold' and he generously volunteered his assistance. His research record in the field of local historical geography and his long service to the Polytechnic and the University for more than 30 years[1] was a powerful recommendation. The complementary disciplinary strengths of the two authors certainly indicated that by combining their academic expertise, and their knowledge of the institution, a more comprehensive history might thereby be produced. This history spans 130 years of educational progress from the institution's origins in 1870 to its first steps as a 'new' university for the city of Newcastle and the North East region. In her capacity as a modern British historian[2], a 'division of labour' was agreed whereby Joan Allen would write the Introduction and the first half of the history up to 1966 and Richard Buswell would produce the remaining three chapters and the Epilogue which concentrate on the polytechnic years and more recent developments. For the purposes of this book, the history concludes in 1996.

The original remit was to produce an academic history written in a readable style for the enjoyment of staff and students alike, but with sufficient academic rigour to be of interest to educational historians and theorists. Above all, the authors were charged to produce a serious history, which located the institution's development within its broader social and political context. Armed with this brief the authors set out to uncover the complex history of Northumbria University from its origins in the last quarter of the nineteenth century. It is not altogether surprising, then, that research for this history has involved delving into national educational movements, policies and legislation. For this we have been able to draw upon the work of numerous historians, political scientists, journalists and biographers whose work constitutes our secondary sources.

The primary material has mainly been drawn from two sources: the official records of Bath Lane Schools and the colleges which developed from them are held by Tyne and Wear Archives Service, Blandford House; these have been supplemented by material held in the Local Studies Department of the Newcastle Central Library, most particularly the records of Newcastle City Council, its Education Committee and various associated sub-committees. In addition, the authors have plundered the records held by the institution itself and which comprise a vast collection of meetings, minutes and policy documents. Of these, the most valuable sources have been the papers and minutes of various academic boards and the Council or governors' papers. As with any history the more recent records are much more plentiful than those for the period 1870–1945. Regrettably, despite the publicity which has been given to the project in staff newsletters and the local newspaper, the attempt to uncover more personal ephemera such as letters, memoirs, and diaries has only been partly successful. We were, however, fortunate enough to locate a large scrapbook of cuttings which related to the modern history of the School of Art and Design and another two volumes which charted the history of Northern Counties College; both sources have greatly illuminated our appreciation of the institution's rich history.

The availability of sources has inevitably acted as a constraint on the scope of the book and like all such histories, what follows, of necessity, offers only a partial view. The emphasis here is very much on the colleges, the Polytechnic and the University as institutions. We have concentrated on analysing relations between locality and centre, the way that national policies were modulated by local government aspirations, the process of merger, the evolving curriculum, internal structural relations and their frequent changes, and physical expansion and financial imperatives. In the process, some significant individuals have emerged: educational pioneers such as J.H. Rutherford and Joseph Cowen; key members of local government, such as T. Dan Smith, Cyril Lipman and Derek Webster, and those officers who helped to shape the institution in the post-war period, most notably Professor Laing Barden. Some sections of the history have relied very heavily upon the good offices of a long list of individuals (see Appendix I) who gave lengthy interviews and helped us to 'flesh out' the history in a more textured and grounded way. It is fair to say that in this history of Northumbria University individual staff members and students do not figure very prominently. We would hope that when our successors come to update this history, as they surely must, they will remedy this omission. We do not expect this to be the last word on the subject but rather that it will in some small way encourage others to take an active interest in what was a truly remarkable educational development.

Acknowledgements

THE AUTHORS owe a debt of gratitude to a large number of people who have assisted in a myriad of ways with the publication of this history. First and foremost, we would like to thank Richard Bott, the University Secretary. From its inception he has been the driving force behind the book, resolving any and all difficulties and providing unstinting support. Professor Gilbert Smith, who was Vice-Chancellor of the University from 1995 to 2001 gave the history his official backing and chaired the University History Advisory Committee which included Professor (Emeritus) Norman McCord of the University of Newcastle and Professor Robert Colls of Leicester University.

In the early stages the School of Historical and Critical Studies provided an intellectual home for the project and, later on, both the School of Mathematics and Computing and the Social Science Research Centre provided much-needed office space. The porters were kept busy transporting files backwards and forwards from the University's archive to the NERU office in North Street East. As ever, they displayed considerable patience and good humour, a reminder, if one were needed, of the essential contribution that the support staff make to the life of the University.

Professor Owen R. Ashton (Staffordshire University) and Dr Richard C. Allen (Northumbria and Sunderland Universities) cheerfully read drafts of the early chapters and gave invaluable and constructive advice. Their input has greatly improved the final manuscript; any surviving shortfalls remain the responsibility of the authors. Andrew Peden Smith of Northumbria University Press has provided excellent editorial guidance throughout, exercising commendable patience while the authors resolved the occasional overlap and stylistic inconsistency and making helpful suggestions about illustrations and editorial structure.

Many present and former members of staff generously gave up their time to be interviewed by us and their recollections have helped flesh out our text. They are listed in Appendix I. Professor John Rear gave useful guidance to the archive of the institution covered by his term of office. He also took time out from his retirement to set down some of his thoughts in writing.

We are grateful for the cheerful and unfailing assistance of staff at the following libraries: Northumbria University Library, Robinson Library (University of Newcastle) and Cardiff University Library, the Literary and Philosophical Society of Newcastle upon Tyne, Newcastle City Library and the British Library. Many of our primary sources were unearthed for us by staff in the Tyne and Wear Archives and the Local Studies Collection of Newcastle City Library, and we would like to acknowledge their expert assistance. The difficult task of accessing the archives of the Polytechnic and the University was made easier by the intervention of Marianne Milton and Andrew Sutton of the University Secretary's department, and by Tricia Reed of the Registrar's department. Andrew McKirgan provided valuable statistical information.

Inevitably, this institutional history has drawn heavily upon the work of others who are listed in the select bibliography. We would nevertheless, like to register our indebtedness to Eric Robinson's early work on the 'people's universities', John Pratt's magisterial work on the history of the polytechnics and Harold Silver's important work on the Council for National Academic Awards, as well as his contribution generally to our understanding of British higher education in the twentieth century.

We would also like to thank the following individuals for their support: Kate Adamson, Sandra Chilton, Hilary and Ian East, Aled and Louise Edwards, Hilary Fawcett, Sean Figgis, Jeremy Gregory, Alan Harvey, Jonathan Hugman, Tim Kirk, Bill Lancaster, Malcolm Gee, Roger Newbrook, Stephen Regan, Sam Ripley, Patrick Salmon, Jane Shaw, Jill Steward, Ian Stone, Amy Sumner, Paul Usherwood, Andrew White and Rosie White. As one of the authors is no longer resident on Tyneside, travel arrangements and accommodation while undertaking research were important considerations. Marianne Milton provided excellent assistance while Dr Roger and Olive Hogg and Dr Michael and Vivienne Barke were more than generous in their hospitality. Their valuable reminiscences have added colour to this story, not all of it printable. The staff in Claude Gibb Hall of Residence were as warm and welcoming as only Geordies can be.

Most of all, we would like to thank Richard Allen and Hawys Pritchard, who have been a constant source of strength and support. They have tolerated our enforced absences and the long hours away from home spent in libraries and archives, especially in the final stages of completing the book.

We have both had a longstanding connection with Northumbria University. Joan Allen completed all of her undergraduate and postgraduate studies at Newcastle Polytechnic before taking up a lecturing post in the School of Historical and Critical Studies; Richard Buswell was a member of the academic staff for 30 years. We owe a great deal to the University. In addition to the dedication to our Chancellor, Lord Glenamara, we would like to dedicate this history to all of the students and staff of the University, and its predecessor colleges. *Floreat Northumbria.*

Yours truly

Jos: Cowen

Introduction

HIGHER EDUCATION provision has been the focus of considerable sustained reform since the end of the Second World War. No longer regarded as an elite activity, the modern university sector is the product of a series of restructuring processes designed to promote the effective delivery of high quality mass education. The foundation of the polytechnics in 1969 marked an important staging post: for the first time, access to higher education courses was made a realistic option for all who were 'qualified by ability or attainment to pursue them and who wish to do so'.[1] It was not the egalitarian reform which the Robbins Committee so ambitiously envisaged[2] and, initially at least, Anthony Crosland's conversion to a binary policy – that 'rough mixture of logic and irrationality'[3] – seemed destined to strengthen the old structural divide. Crosland's determination to provide a viable alternative to the traditional university reflected his belief that they simply could not deliver the necessary expansion. Consequently, while the university sector continued to be regarded as the repository of the nation's scholarly endeavours, the new polytechnics were expected to deliver a measurable return on the public investment in the shape of a highly skilled and technologically sophisticated workforce. Robbins' disappointment and frustration at the time was acute:

> *I just cannot understand what has happened... They are deepening the existence of lines of division in higher education and actually announcing... that these divisions are to be permanent.*[4]

Fortunately, as it turned out, the educational objectives of the thirty new polytechnics in England were never so precisely defined.[5] While policy was undoubtedly driven by both explicit and implicit utilitarian expectations, in the absence of an unequivocal charter of limitation, the inherent potential for 'academic drift' proved irresistible.[6] The aspirations of staff, who seized the opportunity to enhance their careers, coupled with a rising demand, determined that the academic parameters of the polytechnics were stretched to embrace ever more degree level work and a wider curriculum, eventually forcing a fundamental reappraisal of higher educational provision.

By the middle of the 1980s the binary system, which had been an article of faith for a generation or more of theorists and reformers, had come to be regarded as a serious 'obstacle to further progress'.[7] The ensuing debate on the need for reform pushed education firmly to the top of the political agenda until new legislation was cast to unify the system, largely by introducing appropriate funding arrangements and permitting existing polytechnics to apply for university status. Reorganisation on this scale was always bound to be tricky, given the conflicting claims of different interest groups and, even now, as we move further into the twenty-first century, the academic community and the wider public continue to wrestle with the changes which the new framework put in place. Arguably, the newfound university status of the former polytechnics has still not been accepted by all sections of the community: the acquisition of new titles, coats of arms and other perquisite rites of passage have not served to breech the cultural divide and there remains a stubborn reluctance to dispense with the long established and, in some quarters, much-cherished educational hierarchy. Official assessments based on key performance indicators for the sector have not helped this protracted assimilation process either. 'League tables' are published with a subtext which indicates that, at some subliminal level, the binary system is still firmly in place.[8]

Realistically, legislative reform of higher education, however radical or progressive, was never going to dispose of such deeply-embedded elitist attitudes overnight and the likelihood is that the present specious distinctions will continue to undermine the best efforts of the reformers. Intense competition for students and the aggressive cultivation of external sponsorship has been driven partly by the new marketplace ethics, and partly by inadequate funding arrangements. The imposition of fees which are intended to address the latter may, in the end, serve only to complicate matters further as students seek to secure the competitive advantage and 'trade upwards'. In a cultural climate in which image is all, institutions such as Sheffield Hallam, Manchester Metropolitan and Northumbria University are all earnestly engaged in reclaiming the premiership credentials they fought for as polytechnics and, to all intents and purposes, relinquished when they applied for redesignation. The benefits that flow from university status are undeniable but there have been palpable losses too: once again, as in 1969, they find themselves having to contend against public perceptions of their newcomer status and prove their worth. There is, self-evidently, a profound misunderstanding at work here. Most new universities, including those mentioned above, have been at the cutting edge of progressive educational initiatives for a century or more, albeit in a different institutional guise. Each can stake their own legitimate claim to having a wealth of experience and a history that is as long and as illustrious as their supposedly more established competitors.

This history aims to trace the origins of Northumbria University back to the foundation of Bath Lane Elementary School in 1871, one of many Board Schools provided for under the 1870 Education Act. The inspiration and driving force behind this new educational venture was Dr John Hunter Rutherford, a local Congregationalist minister, educational reformer and leading philanthropist. While the Bath Lane School benefited from the usual financial support and the extended provisions of the new legislation, the cost of both buildings and equipment were borne by the Bath Lane Congregational Church and the generosity of local people. This combination of collective endeavour and individual initiative is an important feature of the way that the institution developed over time and is still enshrined in Northumbria's commitment to serve the region's community of scholars, young and old.[9]

Bath Lane School was a dynamic institution which quickly expanded its provision on Tyneside with the establishment of a number of branch schools and the foundation of successive institutions of secondary and further education. In turn, the School of Science and Art (1879), and Rutherford Memorial College (1892) worked with the grain of democratic ideals, which lay at the heart of the pioneering initiatives of Rutherford, and offered an integrated framework through which young people of ability could progress and develop their knowledge and skills. Rutherford was supported in his development of an educational 'ladder'[10] by the radical, MP Joseph Cowen Jnr. They were men of vision who shared an absolute faith in the principle of education for all, accessible on the basis of ability not class; education, they believed, 'begins with the cradle and ends with the grave'.[11] Cowen and Rutherford were not the only advocates of change in the North East of England at that time. Robert Spence Watson, a prominent Quaker and educationalist, and William Armstrong, both gave generously of their time and money, though it is fair to say that Armstrong's great investment in technical education sprang from more mixed impulses. Notwithstanding the conspicuous generosity that underpinned the creation of his own Elswick Works' School, his involvement in the Northern Union of Mechanics' Institutions, and subsequent endowments to the College of Physical Science, a measure of that investment ultimately flowed back into his vast business empire in the shape of his workers' technical prowess.

The tension between the principles of 'useful' and 'liberal' education emerges as a perennial theme in this history. While educational provision in Newcastle and its environs was enlightened and remarkably generous in the nineteenth century, not least because of the prevailing radical political consensus, there remained many who still maintained that 'further education was necessary only for the very few'.[12] As W. B. Stephens observes, there was a fear that providing the working classes with anything more than basic literacy skills 'would make the poor dissatisfied and unfit for their natural occupations and introduce them to undesirable religious and political ideas, threatening the existing social order'.[13] Such fears resonated in the North East of England as much as they did elsewhere and, to a large extent, the pace of educational development has to be viewed within the context of these competing ideologies and beliefs.

One of the surprise discoveries in researching the history is the way that adverse circumstances, at certain key moments, acted as a drag on the pace of progress. For example, as early as 1856 the Northern Union of Mechanics' Institutes had debated the possibility of setting up a 'Northern University', which would draw together all of the institutes and Literary and Philosophical Societies in the Union, but the proposal was effectively blocked by Durham University. Later, in 1881, the Bath Lane Schools' Committee set up a 'University Club' in Higham Place, as part of the move towards establishing a Newcastle upon Tyne Technical College, and with a view to offering degree level courses. By 1887, the planned institution had been reconfigured as 'Newcastle upon Tyne University College' and its development had been formally approved by the Bath Lane Committee. Unfortunately, the timing was less than auspicious: at that time the College of Physical Science was also engaged in bringing its own ambitious plans for expansion to fruition and, as a consequence, Rutherford was pressured to 'drop' the word university from the title of the proposed college. These early attempts to establish what would have been Newcastle's first university were mostly thwarted by the prevailing culture of deference and social snobbery. Much later on, in the middle of the twentieth century, progress was frustrated by an unhappy combination of economic, political and cultural factors. In the 1950s, Rutherford College of Technology was a prime contender to be designated as a College of Advanced Technology (CAT). As we now know, the award of CAT status then would have placed the institution in a strong position in the 1960s when the other Colleges of Advanced Technology were upgraded to universities following the Robbins Report.[14] In the aftermath of the failed designation bid the possibility of Rutherford College amalgamating with what became Newcastle University was mooted, debated and then dropped when King's College finally seceded from Durham. Whether this was fate or serendipity, Rutherford's dream of creating a university, as the final rung on his educational ladder for the working classes, proved to be tantalisingly elusive.

Financial constraints proved to be a perennial problem, not just because the institution's growth and development rested upon charitable endeavour in the earlier period, but because stresses and strains in the national economy impacted negatively upon the availability of funds for buildings and equipment. War inevitably exacerbated these difficulties, though it is interesting to note the extent to which the constituent colleges (Rutherford, and the College of Commerce) responded creatively to the challenges this posed. During the First World War, for instance, the colleges' direct links with local industry and emphasis upon technology and design innovation provided unique opportunities to recruit trainee munitions' workers; interestingly enough, this placed Rutherford College at the cutting edge of providing new working and training opportunities for women. Similarly, the demand for new technologies in the Second World War helped to embed specialist programmes such as nuclear and reactor physics and radio chemistry into the rapidly expanding curriculum.

The period from the mid-1960s constitutes an important period in the institution's development. The foundation of Newcastle Polytechnic in 1969 brought three local colleges together to form a national institution which offered, for the first time, access to higher education outside of the traditional university framework. The 'polys', as they soon became affectionately known, represented a completely new departure. Fortunately, Newcastle had a highly accessible site of 26 acres in the city centre, thanks to the foresight of the charismatic chair of the city's planning committee, and later Leader of the Council, T. Dan Smith. From the beginning local politicians of all parties strongly supported the 'mewling infant' and gave it sufficient latitude to develop in its own way. Its first Director, George Bosworth, brought stability rather than radical progress to the Polytechnic but he was succeeded by a man of much greater ambition and dynamism, Laing Barden. Once he had established his authority, Barden displayed notable leadership and entrepreneurial skills which, during a 25-year term of office, transformed Newcastle Polytechnic into a successful and thriving national institution, regarded by many as one of the foremost in the country.

The mergers with the colleges of education in the 1970s consolidated the Polytechnic's vocational mission by including the training of teachers. This also added to its considerable real estate, making land in the east of the city available for the later expansion in the 1990s. During the 1970s and much of the 1980s the curriculum steadily expanded from it original focus on engineering, business and design to include fine art, law, social sciences, modern languages, humanities and applied sciences. Although the Polytechnic became a more comprehensive institution with a noticeable growth in full-time numbers, it still retained its earlier commitment to part-time and evening classes. During this period, the institution gradually secured greater autonomy from the Council for National Academic Awards (CNAA) who were impressed by both management and curriculum.[15] Moreover, this new found independence was further enhanced by the negotiating skill of the governing council who persuaded the local authority to allow them a greater measure of self-determination.

The election of the Conservative government in 1979, and its domination of British politics for most of the following two decades, heralded the arrival of a new and quite different political ideology. In time this impacted upon all aspects of life in Britain and higher education was no exception. New phrases and key words made their way into the educational lexicon such as 'value for money', 'accountability', 'market forces', 'quality management', 'monetarism' and 'public sector borrowing requirement', but unfortunately the drive towards greater expansion was not matched by any real increases in resources. Newcastle Polytechnic, like most comparable institutions, reeled from one financial crisis to another. At the same time successive secretaries of state for education appeared eager to devolve ever more powers to the funding bodies, the National Advisory Body and the Polytechnic and Colleges Funding Council. In reality, by controlling the revenue available for higher education, their authority over the sector was, if anything strengthened. These new management structures included the imposition of a marked restriction on capital investment in buildings and equipment; as the numbers of students rose rapidly, pressure on space, on laboratories and studios, became almost intolerable.[16] 'More' was beginning to mean 'worse' but not quite in the way that Kingsley Amis had originally intended. One unforeseen outcome of the controlling interest of Tory governments, especially under Sir Keith Joseph and Kenneth Baker, was the need for polytechnics to develop new bureaucracies and technocracies to plan, manage and administer the educational process. Academic staff in higher education relinquished more and more of their autonomy as the curriculum was modularised, the teaching year was semesterised and, in response to the new 'quality management', programmes of study became increasingly standardised.

From the 1988 Education Reform Act onwards Newcastle Polytechnic, like so many similar institutions, had to find strategies for coping with an unprecedented expansion in student numbers without any commensurate increase in teaching staff. The immediate casualty was the staff-student ratio which, on average, doubled from 10:1 to 20:1. This in turn brought about a revolution in teaching and learning to which staff and students had to react with remarkable speed. By the mid-1990s the delivery of mass higher education rested on the assumption that students would become more independent learners. Unitisation of the curriculum and the semesterisation of the academic year were introduced to improve the efficiency of teaching and learning; both demanded an enormous investment of time and energy by academic and administrative staff. Naturally, many of these changes were fiercely resisted. While much of the resentment this aroused was directed at the senior management the hard reality was that this new style of delivering higher education was being adopted in other institutions as a standard feature.[17]

The 1988 Act also put in place more extensive quality assurance mechanisms, yet another government-inspired initiative intended to ensure that higher education delivered 'value for money'. It began with the direct observation of teaching by academic peers but after the further reforms of the 1992 Act, and the implementation of more widespread institutional audit, the costs increasingly seemed to outweigh the benefits. The separation of research funding from teaching monies was a parallel move. Northumbria's reaction to these funding arrangements was initially quite optimistic and its policy objectives were carefully modified in a bid to share in the benefits which they believed would follow. The research culture of the older universities gave them the advantage and it soon became apparent that only a handful of institutions would be able to compete. Nevertheless, even though only a small amount of research money was gained, it proved to be a useful injection of cash to research-active departments.

As students poured into Newcastle at the beginning of the 1990s, the Polytechnic struggled to deal with the pressures on space. Relatively small additions to the real estate were made in close proximity to the city centre site but the reality was that another large site had to be developed. Although a number of alternatives were considered the only practical solution was the development of the Coach Lane site. Earlier attempts to resolve the crush on space by the acquisition of property located some distance from Newcastle had proved fraught with difficulties despite their initial potential. The two-centre University located in the conurbation eventually became a reality when the College of Health merger in 1995 brought with it over 1,000 student nurses.

In the midst of all these changes none was to be as profound as the 1992 Education Act which enabled polytechnics to adopt a university title. Newcastle upon Tyne Polytechnic with its simple trident logo became the University of Northumbria at Newcastle with a coat of arms and a Latin motto. Most of the staff welcomed the redesignation, believing that at long last their years of steady investment in the delivery of high quality education were about to be appropriately recognised. As for the students, they too were enthusiastic about their new status and pleased to be members of a University with all the advantages that would bestow. There was, however, to be no

Royal Charter and relatively little increase in autonomy. Control remained vested in the governing body and the creation of the office of Vice-Chancellor to replace that of Director did not alter lines of responsibility. Becoming a university was destined to raise the status of the institution but nonetheless, finding a new mission suited to its new place in the world was to preoccupy the executive for much of the decade.

As educational professionals look with some trepidation at the swelling numbers of university students, which will undoubtedly take the sector into a further period of change and development, this might be considered an opportune moment to appraise the history of a major institution. In itself, celebrating earlier and more recent achievements is no mean objective for there is much to celebrate and be proud of, but the main purpose in recovering the past must be altogether more serious. As Brian Simon noted in 1994:

> *If schools, colleges, universities and teaching and learning institutions of all kinds are to flourish, and so realise their purpose of empowerment, we need to understand what circumstances hinder or encourage such a situation.*[18]

The events of the last decade find their mirror image in the early years of polytechnic provision. By the end of the 1970s the leaders of the polytechnic sector had begun to seize the initiative and capitalise on the readiness of the Council for National Academic Awards to facilitate innovation; as they matured they emerged as markedly different institutions from those which the reforming legislators had originally envisaged. There is a need to evaluate this process of change critically, to understand the prevailing influences and the socio-political climate, local and national, in which key decisions were taken. Although there are undoubted pressures to do so, the newer universities do not necessarily have to mould themselves strictly in accordance with the existing educational tradition, nor do they have to abandon the applied courses that have proved to be such a successful component of their academic portfolio. From its earliest beginnings as a modest elementary school with suitably immodest ambitions, Northumbria University has epitomised the ideal of liberal education. At every stage of its development it has embraced that ideal and made strenuous efforts to widen its community of scholars to include non-standard and mature students. The challenge now, and in the future, is whether Northumbria can uphold its reputation as a progressive institution, and to instigate the kind of radical change that will deliver an education designed to meet the needs and expectations of future generations.

Chapter One

Men of ideas:
education and the people
in Newcastle upon Tyne, 1850–1890

NORTHUMBRIA UNIVERSITY has a long history, traceable back to the nineteenth century and the educational initiatives of the reformer and evangelist, the Revd Dr John Hunter Rutherford[1] who founded Bath Lane School in 1870 to deliver much-needed elementary schooling to the city's poor children. Rutherford was a Congregationalist preacher, who played a leading role in Tyneside radicalism from 1849 onwards, following his arrival in Newcastle from Kelso. The Temperance Movement was only one of many social and political causes he championed and yet, strangely enough, it is his lifelong campaign against drink rather than his contribution to education which is memorialised by the Rutherford fountain that still stands in the city's Bigg Market.[2] The university of which he was the founding father still displays the three-panelled stained glass window that was commissioned by Bath Lane Church after his death in 1890, and which portrays Rutherford as the Good Samaritan.[3] It must be questionable, however, whether any of the thousands of staff and students who pass through Rutherford Hall fully appreciate its provenance or indeed recognise the organic connections between the present modern university and the modest school of which he was so proud.

Rutherford's experiences of gaining his medical degree at the relatively mature age of forty-one may constitute part of the explanation for his dedication to educational reform and innovation, but undoubtedly his high profile involvement in working class organisations such as the Co-operative Movement, and his work for the Newcastle upon Tyne Poor Law Union, also gave him powerful insights into the needs of the working classes.[4] Just as Rutherford's work with the Northern Reform League in the 1860s and 1870s was informed by his commitment to the creation of a more democratic society, so his pioneering ventures into the world of working class education were prompted by the same political vision. Throughout the 1850s he was a regular speaker at gatherings of Nonconformists, Radicals and Chartists in the Nelson Street Lecture Rooms and it was in this forum of progressive intellectualism that he explored the possibilities of developing a more egalitarian educational system. This system visualised educational provision as a 'ladder' or staged process whereby all children of ability would be given the resources and facilities they needed to steadily progress in their studies up to, and beyond, degree level. It was a vision which insisted, against the prevailing orthodoxy, that the education of working children should not be limited by anything other than their own intellectual capacity.

His progressive ideas about religion, charity, temperance and education were published in his own weekly journals, the *Bible Defender* and, later, *Truths for the People*.[5] Occasionally, when the subject matter was considered particularly important, the articles were also sold as cheap tracts. In 1856, for example, he published his tract *How Should the People be Educated* which, among other things, argued that the government should not interfere in education. Rutherford believed that the voluntaryists should 'work harder to fill the vacuum' and he was opposed to compelling children to go to school.[6] At this stage at least, Rutherford did not advocate state intervention but rather sought to encourage the educational initiatives of the voluntary organisations. Nonetheless, when Forster's Education Act was finally passed in 1870, Rutherford moved quickly to secure a place on the first Newcastle upon Tyne School Board.[7] He seized the opportunity to put his ideas into practice. With the help of voluntary subscriptions Bath Lane Elementary School was officially opened on 8 April 1872 and quickly established a notable reputation for its high academic standards. The central argument here is that the generous and innovative educational provision which Rutherford put in place for working class children and young people, and the ideological principles which underpinned it, left behind a belief in equality and progress that lived on in the schools and colleges which followed.

Education in the nineteenth century

Prior to 1870, when the landmark Education Act was passed, successive governments had resisted the growing clamour for a legislative commitment to compulsory mass education. Revenue was not the principal obstacle for, ironically, government grants to schools based on the principle of payment by results had been spiralling throughout the 1860s, and the public coffers were already being plundered for educational purposes.[8] Official reticence owed more to the prevailing *laissez faire* tradition of British politics and the thorny problem of satisfying the competing claims of denominational interests.[9] As D.G. Paz has observed, 'education was at its heart a religious issue'.[10] From the early nineteenth century onwards, the radical press had argued the case for educational reform but involvement in the debate extended far beyond the relatively narrow concerns of the nation's cultural community. The social function of working class education was a matter of great concern to those with the money and the inclination to be beneficent. Most studies of the early history of education, up to the closing decades of the eighteenth century, conclude that schooling for the poor was sponsored and paid for by philanthropic individuals and associations eager to inculcate a work ethic which would eradicate idleness and dependency; 'social cement' rather than social mobility was the desired outcome of their educational master plan.[11] Throughout the nineteenth century and beyond, notwithstanding the relatively ambitious provisions of the 1870 Elementary Education Act, education was destined to be the site of deep ideological conflict. The potential for instituting a more generous system was seriously undermined by a blinkered influential minority who believed that 'there must be nothing to pamper self-indulgence, to raise the child in his own estimation above his natural position in society'.[12] To a large extent, the currency of such prejudicial attitudes reflected the stranglehold which religious bodies had traditionally exercised over both formal and informal schooling. While a broad spectrum of religious charities sought to give poor children some rudimentary reading, writing and mathematical skills – the 3'Rs' – the overriding concern was to equip them for work and to instil in them an unquestioning acceptance of their place in society.

The Sunday School movement which was initiated by Robert Raikes' experiment in Gloucester in 1780, undoubtedly served to buttress this value system. Raikes was concerned that local children should not fall into 'idle and disorderly' ways and to that end he decided to provide some classes in his local church.[13] Initially such schools catered for children of the lower middle as well as the working classes and, inspired by an evangelical mission to promote Bible reading, dedicated their efforts to the delivery of that moral imperative. After the turn of the nineteenth century, Sunday schools quickly took root in most of the large urban cities and towns and were established as a major presence in the countryside. Arguably their role in providing education was more significant than that of the charity schools, not least because initially adults as well as children were able to attend the classes.[14] Whilst their target constituency became perceptibly more working class, the sabbatarian lobby resolutely resisted any attempt to broaden the curriculum beyond basic reading skills and religious education, and many children were still refused admission if they were dirty or unkempt. By the 1820s almost all working class children had spent at least some time at Sunday school,[15] but the educational benefits are more difficult to assess. In Nottingham, the 1842 Children's Employment Commission reported that reading standards were depressingly low and pupils displayed the 'most awful ignorance' of religious knowledge.[16] Nevertheless, by 1851 over 2.4 million pupils attended Sunday schools in England and Wales with a further 300,000 pupils in Scotland.[17] Lacquer's comprehensive study reveals that there was rather less take up of Sunday schools in Northumberland and Durham than in other similar northern counties.[18] Yet he also points out that Durham had one of the highest literacy rates in the country and links this to the availability of excellent weekday provision. The schools were officially hailed as a great success in the 1854 *Census Report*, compiled by Thomas Mann, who confidently estimated that the behaviour of some 2,400,000 of the nation's children had been 'conspicuously improved as a result.[19] The emphasis on 'behaviour' rather than education is significant, gesturing as it does to the prevailing moral panic of the Victorians.[20] Day provision had expanded too, particularly with the advent of industrial schools, but, as 2 years was the average period of attendance in 1851 for most working class children, many left school with only the most rudimentary education.[21] Overall, most historians would concede that while Sunday schools had a positive impact upon literacy the decision not to teach writing skills was a significant failing.

Educational provision on Tyneside

Provision for North East school children entirely conformed to this model of limited provision. There were fee paying institutions such as St Nicholas School which charged parents 1*d.* per week and, after 1810, a number of Jubilee Schools and Dame Schools offered tuition to poorer children, some attracting sufficient local sponsorship to be able to offer free tuition.[22] Robert Spence Watson, a prominent Quaker solicitor who later in the century became a founding member of the Newcastle College of Physical Science, took a keen interest in the education of Tyneside's poor children.[23] The Ragged School initiative of the 1840s, whereby the poorest children from slum areas were educated and often fed by volunteers, found a willing advocate in Spence Watson and his wife Elizabeth. By the 1850s Ragged Schools were being encouraged by the government to become recognised providers of craft training. Those which satisfied the criteria received financial support and were certified as Industrial Schools under the auspices of the Home Office. More crucially, such schools functioned as reformatories under the existing penal code.[24] In the 1850s and 1860s the Spence Watsons were both actively involved in managing the Newcastle Ragged and Industrial School, providing food and clothing as well as reading and writing materials.[25] According to Spence Watson's biographer, the school which housed and taught girls and boys separately was 'not a prison but a preventative institution where the children were boarded, lodged, educated and industrially trained'.[26] It remains the case, however, that certified 'industrial' schools were motivated more by the need to reduce juvenile delinquency and provide craft training than they were to cultivate a thirst for knowledge.

Although the primary focus of philanthropic largesse was to educate children, the needs of young adults, who had not gained previously from improved educational investment, were also met by charitable donations and activities. Benefactors were often drawn from an aspirational and increasingly large business class who had one eye on their continuing profits and the other on their own status in the community. Then, as now, such conspicuous generosity was regarded as an essential attribute of all those who sought political power at Town Council and parliamentary level.

Tyneside stood in the vanguard of industrial progress in the early decades of the nineteenth century and investment in technical education had long been earmarked as a priority by a number of prominent local citizens. The Mechanics' Institute movement, which was established by George Birkbeck and other radicals in London in 1823 rapidly took root in the northern counties by the 1830s.[27] In 1824 Newcastle upon Tyne was one of the first to establish a mechanics' institute. By 1848 membership levels across Durham and Northumberland were considered sufficiently buoyant to warrant the foundation of a parent organisation, the Northern Union of Mechanics' Institutes, to direct its activities in a more uniform, cohesive manner. Some, though by no means all, of the member institutes subscribed to the rigid hierarchical ethos that pertained elsewhere in the country. Typically, they tended to be run by wealthy, paternalistic management committees who loudly proclaimed their commitment to the dissemination of 'useful knowledge' whilst expressly prohibiting the circulation of political and religious materials which they feared might inculcate dissent rather than subservience.[28] The democratic structure of the Blaydon Mechanics' Institute, as devised by the leading Radical and entrepreneur Joseph Cowen Jnr,[29] represented a new departure in that its members were given every opportunity to read and discuss controversial literature, and to embrace a panoply of radical and reform causes which ultimately aimed to challenge the *status quo*. By 1855 the Union's twenty-four constituent branches had 2,443 members, including sixty-three women and, as a number of institutes were modelled along similar lines to the Blaydon Institute, the preponderance of deeply conservative views was gradually leavened.[30] Even though Cowen never quite succeeded in turning the Northern Union into a radical organisation he was able to influence many of the decisions that were made, and their annual meetings became a regular forum for airing and implementing progressive policies.

In the past, the Mechanics' Institute movement has been judged and found wanting by historians, who claim that it failed to meet the educational needs of the working classes, but, latterly, more stress has been placed on the way that individual institutes were shaped by their immediate communities.[31] This was certainly the case in the North East of England: in the rural villages and towns of Northumberland and Durham members were offered an esoteric programme of activities, with lectures on botany, astronomy and the classics, for instance. The demand for science and art classes was naturally a higher priority throughout urban Tyneside where technical skills were at a premium and institutes targeted their resources accordingly. The quality of technical educational provision was officially recognised in 1856 when the Department of Science and Arts began to provide certificated examinations for the members.[32] Unfortunately, as the Northern Union executive admitted, working class members had neither the time nor the money to travel to London and so were unlikely to avail themselves of the opportunity.

In spite of the obstacles, what is most striking about the activities of the Union in that period is the sheer scale of their ambitions. Addressing the assembled delegates that same year was J. P. Dodd, a solicitor from North Shields, who delivered a lengthy paper outlining his plan for a 'Northern University'. He acknowledged the practical problems of setting up a sufficiently distinguished board of examiners in the region, but insisted that this could be satisfactorily resolved by approaching Durham University for their assistance – 'if they should be disposed to encourage such an institution'.[33] As for other academic establishments in the region, he believed that 'its operations would light upon a field totally disregarded and uncultivated by them', and consequently he thought that they were unlikely to raise any objections:

> *Our University would thus consist of the Central Board of Examiners assembled in Newcastle, having for its departmental colleges all the mechanics' institutes and Literary and Philosophical Societies in the Union… It would interfere with none of the established institutions… but perhaps give an impulse and be a complement to them all… Ours would be a University for self educated men, affording them stimulants and honours to encourage their unrecognised but meritorious labours.*[34]

Inevitably, given the prevailing culture of snobbery and privilege, his grand scheme failed to secure the necessary backing and, despite the progressive work of the Northern Union, a northern university of the kind he envisaged failed to materialise. Undaunted, the Union continued to provide a challenging curriculum and to publicize their student's successes in their annual Exhibition of Art and Science.

From the 1830s onwards, the efforts of the Tyneside business class to extend the technical skills and knowledge of their workers, as well as their basic literacy, were undoubtedly spurred on by a natural concern to retain their strong position in the industrial hierarchy and remain competitive, particularly as the manufacturing output of France and Prussia began to grow and develop. Equally, at the national level, the government of the day had its own anxieties about the buoyancy of trade and the future stability of the British economy. A report by the Select Committee on Arts and Manufactures set up in 1835, which stressed the key role which art played in industrial design, finally persuaded the government to act. Adopting the continental model of state education, albeit selectively, appeared to offer some advantages and this competitive, defensive climate was the immediate context in which the London School of Design was set up in 1837.[35] Similar institutions founded in the provinces were mainly financed and promoted as the optimum means of ensuring the acquisition of essential technical skills. The Nottingham School of Design, for example, was set up in 1843 as a result of strenuous lobbying by local manufacturers determined to match the superior design expertise of French lace makers.[36]

In the North East, there was a ready awareness that design education was of crucial significance to a city and a region at the forefront of industrial innovation and change. Sir William Hutt, who was then MP for Gateshead, highlighted the fact that in the mid-1830s Bavaria had thirty-three schools of design and claimed that British workmen were 'deficient in the application of ornament and design'.[37] As part of a concerted attempt to tackle the perceived advantages of European manufacturers, the Newcastle School of Design was established in 1844, with premises in the south east corner of the new Central Exchange Building and under the mastership of the acclaimed artist, William Bell Scott.[38] In 1851, even as the Great Exhibition was being hailed as a runaway success, and each medal secured a lasting testimonial to British and indeed Northern industrial prowess, fears of foreign competition continued to preoccupy entrepreneurs and politicians. The post was not exactly conducive to an artist of his talents, more a means of acquiring a stable income: having failed to secure a commission to decorate the new Houses of Parliament, Scott had very little choice but to accept the vacancy.[39] Given the London Board ruling that 'no one intending to follow any of the fine art professions was admissible as a student', and that there was to be no life drawing, the post was indeed challenging. As Christopher Frayling has observed far too much energy was expended in quarrelling over the curriculum and the self-imposed limitations created more problems than they solved.[40] Scott was, understandably, less than sanguine about the task that lay ahead. His express remit in setting up the Newcastle School of Design was, according to his autobiography, to 'teach the working class, who could not hold a pencil, to create new decorative designs and to begin new trades'.[41] A tour of local manufactories in order to appreciate the remit of his position depressed his spirits even more and, gloomily, he concluded that there was 'no scope for individual handiwork... at the time I felt myself painfully in a false position'.[42]

For much of the 1840s and 1850s the Council of the School of Design were caught up in defending their commitment to training, as opposed to the formal art education espoused by Ralph Wornum[43] and others. And in 1853, the Department of Science and Art (DSA) was created at South Kensington. This was to have a major impact upon the development of technical education for the DSA was to pursue quite different policies from the Education Department.[44] As it turned out, in Newcastle the majority of students were middle class women not local industrial workers and, as a result, provision had to be made for the teaching of fine art. Scott was, moreover, heartened to discover that, after a period of relative decline, Newcastle's arts culture had begun to pick up and there was a regular calendar of cultural events supported by the North of England Fine Art Society. In due course, and with the backing of the Trevelyan family and other prominent local patrons,[45] Bell Scott was able to take a more independent line and successfully expand the curriculum. At long last he was able to satisfy the requirement to promote and develop the industrial arts in the North East and indulge his own idea of what art education could, and should, be. It is, perhaps, not entirely whimsical to see in Scott's famous painting, *Iron and Coal*, which dramatically foregrounds a handful of labouring men, an artist who, by 1861, had not just come to terms with his provincial posting but one who had come to appreciate the essential dynamism and creativity of northern industrialisation. As far as technical education was concerned, statutory and voluntary provision, as delivered by both the School of Design and the various mechanics' institutes, served the region's army of industrial workers well enough. What neither institution could do was to compensate for the continuing poor levels of basic literacy and numeracy. Inevitably, the uneven quality and distribution of elementary schools across the region was bound to hinder even the best efforts of local philanthropists and social reformers such as William Armstrong.

Altruistic motives notwithstanding, local businessmen whose disposable income largely derived from their commercial and manufacturing profits were naturally alive to the advantages to be gained by facilitating the acquisition of industrial and technical knowledge. Beyond his sponsorship of local mechanics' institutes and a raft of other good causes, William Armstrong, the largest engineering employer in Newcastle in the 1860s and subsequently knighted for his services to industry and charitable works, opened his own Elswick Works' School in 1866.[46] Providing a measure of elementary instruction in works' schools had been something of a tradition among philanthropic employers from the late eighteenth century onwards.[47] Typically children would attend school for a few hours during the week or at weekends, though by the time that Armstrong set up his works' school it conformed to the government 'half-time system'.[48] The School was an exemplary model of this kind of benevolent self-interest. Nominally funded by his own workers' one penny or two penny contributions, payable on a sliding scale according to the level of wages and deducted at source once a week, Elswick Works' School turned out boys who were literate and numerate *and* most likely to be employed subsequently as one of Armstrong's team of disciplined workers.[49] It is worth noting that the School also catered for girls, in a separate building and with a modified curriculum favouring domestic skills.[50] The detailed School log-books show that Armstrong and his wife were proactive in the School's management, making regular visits and providing annual prizes and treats.

In 1871, the School's educational standards attracted favourable comments from the government inspector, H. E. Oakley, who enthusiastically declared that there was 'not a better boys' school in the whole of my district'.[51] Nonetheless, given the connection between Armstrong's Elswick works and the School, problems were bound to arise. Attendances at the School fluctuated whenever workers left to take up alternative employment and in 1871, when the engineers went on strike for a shorter, 9 hour day, large numbers of children were absent from their studies.[52] The ill effects were all too apparent to the Inspector whose Report drew attention to the fact that the examination 'candidates have not been so well taught'. More importantly, he noted the great disparity between the numbers on the register and those entered for graded examinations.[53] It was not uncommon for schools to select only their strongest candidates for examination as a large number of failures could only impact unfavourably on the size of government grant.

The foundation of Bath Lane School

The long-awaited Reform Act of 1867 not only ushered in working class representation but a raft of other reforms too, including changes in the sphere of education. However, despite the groundswell of supporters who had campaigned tirelessly over many decades, and the general consensus that reform was urgently needed, the passage of the 1870 Education Act was protracted and fraught with problems. It has often been referred to as an 'untidy compromise' and it is certainly the case that the dual system of control, whereby some schools were controlled by democratically elected School Boards and others by the existing voluntary providers proved to be highly contentious.[54] Debate raged over the thorny issue of compulsion, with the voluntary schooling lobby led by the Church of England battling to retain their dominance of existing provision; some parents, especially those living in rural communities where child labour was required at key moments in the agricultural calendar, feared that the plan to compel children to attend school would greatly impact upon the family's earning capacity. As ever, there were also those who regarded education 'on the rates' as not just wasteful but unhelpfully calculated to give workers ideas above their station.

Rutherford and Cowen had shared interests in democratic initiatives, particularly mechanics' institutes, public libraries and non-sectarian schooling, stretching back over many years and both men were closely involved in the events which followed. As a sturdy advocate of the 'knowledge is power' lobby, Cowen had long been a prime mover in promoting working-class education and he had consistently argued that, once franchise reform had been secured, 'the first use they would make of it would be to establish a system of education'.[55] The Reform Act of 1867 had ushered in not only working-class representation but a raft of other reforms including that in the sphere of education. In November 1869 the first education conference was convened at the Newcastle Literary and Philosophical Society, and an unseemly row broke out when the National Education League put forward their proposal for secular education. In 1870, Cowen had accepted an invitation from the Birmingham radicals to serve on the executive of the National Education League which was then at the forefront of the demand for a rate-supported system of education.[56] One of the League's leading lights, Joseph Chamberlain, was determined to publicise the parlous state of British education.[57] At the first School Board elections,[58] which were instituted under the new legislation, Rutherford, Cowen and Spence Watson decided to present themselves to the electorate as 'Unsectarian candidates' on the grounds that:

> We cannot establish schools in this country that will be universally acceptable until they are made absolutely unsectarian. In schools supported by the rates there should be no doctrine peculiar to any church taught, and the unsectarian candidates go for the Bible being read, with any rational explanation of its contents; but we are opposed to any denominational teaching... While others battle for special sects, we will battle for the common good.[59]

Elsewhere, sectarianism was destined to become a key issue in School Board elections, notably in Liverpool 'where the sectarian card remained the ace of trumps right to the end of the School Board's history'.[60] In Newcastle, the radical consensus prevailed and in the elections held on 25 January 1871 the 'Unsectarian' lobby secured the seats of more candidates than any other single group.[61] Although the volume of support for the Roman Catholic candidates was relatively strong, neither they nor the Secularists succeeded in gaining representation on the Board.

With the backing of the Tyneside people, plans could then proceed for the establishment of new Board schools, based on democratic principles and in line with Cowen's mandate that the education they provided should be free of sectarian influence:

> *You cannot drive religion into children by three feet of cane, a birch rod, or a leather strap. Religion is not a system of manners… It cannot be whipped into children any more than it can be beaten into men. Some of our methods of instruction are radically defective. Instead of teaching children what to think, we should teach them how to think. We should strive to improve their minds so that they could think for themselves.*[62]

Critics of the legislation included the influential Liberal MP John Morley whose polemic, *The Struggle for National Education*, was first published as a series of articles in the *Fortnightly Review*.[63] Morley complained that the 1870 Act had been 'almost worthless'. Singling out the Church of England schools as particularly ineffective he argued that the reforms had conspicuously failed to drive up standards. The narrow curriculum, he claimed, would take working children 'no further than the gates of civilisation'.[64]

Rutherford's educational plans were calculated to achieve exactly the opposite. As a Nonconformist minister he naturally expected his pupils to be God fearing, but it is clear from his writings and speeches that expanding their minds and their horizons was an even greater priority. The Sunday school associated with Bath Lane Church had been flourishing since 1862, and thus the elementary school that Rutherford and his fellow Congregationalists established in 1871 had no difficulty recruiting its first pupils. The foundation stone was laid by Lord Amberley in a lavish ceremony attended by all of the local civic dignitaries to mark the importance of the event.[65] Addressing a large fundraising gathering that same evening, Rutherford reaffirmed his commitment to non-sectarian education, arguing that they were to be 'nationalists in education'. Even at this early stage of development Rutherford expounded upon the ambitious curriculum he intended to put in place. It would, he said, include the 'essential science': human physiology.[66]

The single storey 'very pretty gothic' building located in Corporation Street was designed by the architect, Thomas Oliver, to complement the existing church building to which it was connected by a small corridor.[67] At a cost of £3,000 the Bath Lane Elementary School comprised two classrooms and a large hall with a view to accommodating up to six hundred senior and junior pupils. Rapid progress was made and it was quickly apparent that the premises would have to be extended to cope with the expanding numbers. Rutherford taught the physiology class himself and seems to have acted as school physician too! The evangelical work of the Bath Lane Church took them to all parts of the city and inevitably they were called upon to assist in the development of other branch schools. The first of these, Camden Street School, opened its doors in August 1874 to the working class children of Shieldfield and the surrounding areas. A mere 2 years later, a second school was set up in association with Gateshead Congregational Church in Bensham Road, and Rutherford and his committee were asked to take charge of this school's management.[68] This was to set the pattern for the future and the surviving records show that Rutherford was the key driving force behind the provision and success of non-sectarian education on Tyneside in this period.

The scholars at Bath Lane School responded well to Rutherford's adventurous and stretching curriculum, and the Management Committee (hereafter the Committee) were soon obliged to consider how best to provide a more advanced syllabus. Financial provision had recently been made under the new code for 'special subjects' and so the answer was found in the development of a School of Science and Art. The keynote speech by Joseph Cowen to the assembled sponsors, when the foundation stone was laid in Corporation Street in November 1877, was in keeping with Joseph Cowen's notoriously radical views; his combative rhetoric was entirely appropriate for the foundation of an institution which represented such a radical step forward in education provision. He referred to the remarkable progress which the Bath Lane School had made, claiming that while some schools in the north of England had enjoyed equal success, 'none has had greater'. Most of all, Cowen urged his audience on to further efforts in the cause of educational reform:

> We have had one fight to get our schools; we are having another to fill them. When filled, we must strive to raise the tuition to the loftiest standard. Let us reverse the old and illiberal maxim that because a man is poor he only requires a poor education, and act upon the opposite doctrine, that as knowledge is both power and wealth, the poorer a man is the greater the need for his having the best education he can secure.[69]

Rutherford predicted that the new building would soon be full to capacity and he urged the Committee to consider rethinking the original plans before the roofing stage was reached. He argued that if another storey was added this would accommodate 200 more pupils and, in the long run, this would be cost-effective. It is interesting to note that at the time he claimed that these modifications would not have any implications for staffing or for running costs! His calculations were based solely on the estimated additional building costs of £470.[70] Whatever else he may have been, Rutherford was no businessman and he had already had his fingers burned over the spectacular collapse of the Ouseburn Engineering works in 1875.[71] Nevertheless, the Trustees were readily persuaded that this made good sense. New plans were drawn up and provision was made to connect the two schools by means of a gangway, a practical feature which made manifest Rutherford's ambitions for his pupils. Staffing needs were managed by making it a requirement for new appointees to teach two evenings per week in the new School of Science and Art (SSA) in addition to their other duties. Concern that the expenditure on education in Newcastle was in excess of other towns prompted government officials to make an unexpected visit in March 1878 and the Committee were greatly relieved when the inspectors reported that they were 'perfectly satisfied'.[72] Meanwhile, Bath Lane School continued to go from strength to strength. When the Northumberland and Gateshead Schools' Association made five scholarships available in open competition they were all secured by Bath Lane candidates.[73]

In the months preceding the official opening of the SSA Rutherford worked tirelessly to recruit new pupils. Part of his strategy was to secure a raft of scholarships and to that end he introduced ten Science and Art Scholarships, each worth £10, available to all students in the neighbourhood. The government officially sanctioned the SSA's management and scholarship scheme, and agreed to support an Art and Industrial Exhibition which was to be held at Christmas by making available some important artworks from the national collection.[74] The Exhibition meant more to the Committee than just an opportunity to display the student's talents and achievements. With an overdraft standing at £866 the School fund was 'temporarily embarrassed' until the government grant came through; it was hoped that ticket sales and sponsorships from the Exhibition would help to bridge the gap. Rutherford persuaded the bank to advance £500 for 6 months but this was immediately swallowed up by the building contractor's bill.[75] These financial problems proved to be an ongoing source of difficulty, partly because Rutherford's system of accounting was notoriously cavalier, but mostly because he seemed to scarcely register the need to trim back on his plans. While he pressed ahead and began to prepare some students for the London University examinations the greatly enlarged Finance Committee was left to wrestle with the rising costs. The Committee agreed that school fees should be brought in line with other science and art classes in the district and chased more government grants for equipment and materials. Such measures would have gone a long way towards putting the Schools' finances on a more stable footing had Rutherford not pushed immediately for twenty free scholarships for night classes. In the autumn of 1878 the frustrations of the Treasurer were self-evident and he promptly resigned.[76]

In anticipation of the grand opening ceremony, the SSA opened its doors in September 1878 with a capacity of 615 pupils. By then, some strategic teaching appointments had been made, in Naval Architecture, Metallurgy and Science. The auguries were good, save for the growing dissatisfaction with the management style of Mr Lindsey, the Headmaster. Matters came to a head following an adverse inspection, and although his departure in June 1879 was presented publicly as a cost cutting measure in reality there was a consensus that he would have to be replaced. Chaos ensued when he not only left them in the lurch but also took the school keys with him![77] Financial difficulties continued to dog the Committee as the overdraft grew ever larger and they found themselves liable for rates and taxes. The guarantors of the original loan withdrew their support and Rutherford was forced to secure an additional mortgage on the school buildings. Inevitably, it fell to Rutherford and his two colleagues, James Blakey and William Walker, to pledge their own money against a further loan of £500.[78]

The School of Science and Art

After many months of planning the School of Science and Art was formally opened in September 1879 by the Liberal leader, Lord Hartington. It was a prestigious gathering which brought together all of the region's civic dignitaries and twelve members of parliament, including Joseph Cowen.[79] The existing awards and bursaries were renamed the Hartington and Cowen Scholarships on order to acknowledge their support. The October prize-giving reveals how adventurous the curriculum was, with awards in acoustics, magnetism and electricity, animal physiology and applied mechanics as well as the standard range of arts and science subjects. At the beginning of 1880 the School's achievements were officially recognised by London University when it was selected as the Northern District Centre for science and art examinations.[80] Although the overdraft was now running at £1,039 the Committee were still making new plans. In particular, Rutherford was eager to move forward with his scheme to set up the 'Newcastle upon Tyne Technical College'.[81] As part of this new venture, Rutherford wanted to establish a university club. A house in Higham Place was rented at a cost of £50 per annum and the Committee were obliged to appeal to the Town Improvement Committee for a subvention of £35 to cover the costs of altering the building. In March 1881, the Stephenson University Club was officially opened at 8 Higham Place and the Committee began to look for a teacher capable of taking students to degree level and another who could prepare students for Civil Service appointments.[82]

By 1882, the student intake of 1,235 had more than met Rutherford's original target and as the government grants began to flow into the school coffers the financial burden eased, albeit temporarily. Pressure was mounting on other fronts, however, for the demand for places at Bath Lane School far exceeded its capacity. Rutherford thought the best solution would be to raise the roof by two storeys and to secure other premises, in Swinburne Place, as a temporary overspill. In addition, science and art classes were established at North Shields, Blaydon and Hebburn. Rutherford's idealism was arguably a key factor behind this seemingly relentless expansion but he was also painfully aware that government grants could be reduced or withdrawn if the facilities failed to meet official guidelines. For example, when laboratory facilities were judged too small for the existing numbers in April 1883, the Department of Education reduced the grant by 50 per cent.[83]

As 1883 dawned plans were being drawn up to convert No. 9 Higham Place into a Teachers' College, and Rutherford made visits to a number of training colleges to consider how he might best secure the approval of the Education Department. He was destined to be disappointed. The Department refused to award a grant for the new College unless he could procure 'a suitable new building free of debt' which conformed to their exacting specification.[84] This was not entirely unexpected for they would have been well aware that the Bath Lane Schools' finances were not in very good shape. Undaunted, Rutherford lobbied MPs with a known interest in education for their help and began to pack out the Committee with influential local politicians and businessmen. Fortunately, the success of the schools progressed in proportion to the scale of the debts, and educational provision, especially at elementary standard, continued to attract favourable comment. When the latter was judged to be 'excellent' and awarded additional government grant the Committee called upon the Education Department to recognise Bath Lane as an Advanced School.[85]

Rutherford's plans to build a new college were constantly frustrated even though he used every possible influence to try to secure the necessary approvals. A meeting with A. J. Mundella MP failed and he was further thwarted by the Town Council who refused to allow the erection of new buildings in Higham Place. In 1885 the administration of the schools passed into the hands of a newly constituted Property Committee which by that stage was managing and maintaining schools in Camden Street, Heaton Road, Diana Street, Bath Lane and Shields Road, as well as the Higham Place properties. On paper at least the Committee was solvent, for while their liabilities stood at £10,670 their property portfolio was an estimated £16,350.[86] It availed them very little, however, for they had no reserves and various applications for funds were turned down. When the opportunity arose to secure sufficient land to build a college on the Bowling Green site the decision was made to sell the Higham Street properties for £1,700. In the interim, fundraising began in earnest with appeals to the county families and to the British and Foreign School Society.[87]

Rutherford, meanwhile, was already rethinking his plan for the technical college and his proposal that the title be changed to Newcastle upon Tyne University College was duly approved by the Committee on 30 December 1887. Persuading his own committee was not quite the same as winning over Professor William Garnett who was then Principal of the Durham College of Science. The College of Physical Science, as it was originally called, had been established in 1871 largely in response to public demand and some energetic fundraising on the part of Joseph Cowen, Robert Spence Watson, Isaac Lowthian Bell and William Armstrong. Crucially, Durham University promised to assist them by suspending some fellowships and using the savings to provide an annual grant of £1,250 for the first 6 years.[88] By 1888 when Rutherford's dream of creating a working class university college seemed just within his grasp, the College of Physical Science was embarking on a new phase of its history and development. After years of depending on *ad hoc* facilities, such as the cellar in the Nicholas Wood Memorial Library, rooms in the Coal Trade building and in the School of Medicine, the College had finally acquired their own premises. In the past, the College of Physical Science and the School of Science and Art had collaborated successfully on a number of projects and had usually negotiated any overlaps in provision quite amicably. By the late 1880s, with the backing of the state and educational authorities across the region for the new College, Professor Garnett was in strong position. Quite naturally, he had his own plans for the future and he seems to have been determined to assert his seniority. Suffice to say that, following a meeting with Professor Garnett in January 1888, Rutherford agreed to drop the name 'university' and revert to the original title.[89] The School of Science and Art nevertheless had a good reputation in the locality and when the Newcastle Library's Books and Education Committee decided that they could no longer offer classes they engaged in discussions with Garnett and Rutherford.[90] Shortly afterwards, it was suggested that the two colleges could broker a formal association and a meeting with Theophilus Wood Bunning, the Registrar of Armstrong College, was duly arranged. Nothing came of it for there were concerns on the part of the Bath Lane Committee that the Schools would simply be taken over and 'our Chairman's personality would be lost'.[91] It is notable that it was to take another century and a major piece of legislation before the university of which Rutherford dreamed was finally realised.

At the end of the 1880s the Bath Lane Schools were flourishing, as evidenced when pupils picked up four prestigious Whitworth scholarships in August 1889. This was no mean feat for they were hotly contested. These DSA scholarships had been set up by Joseph Whitworth of Manchester in 1868 and many of the award holders went on to become distinguished academics.[92] The School of Science and Art even had its own magazine, full of sporting fixtures as well as exhortations to work hard at the annual examinations. Much had changed since the first school was founded as one writer to the magazine observed:

> *I sometimes wonder what good it is going to do a girl to know about the construction of Ruhmkorf's coil, or the manufacture of sulphuric acid… it won't be any consolation to the grumbling victims if, when the pie crust is burnt to a cinder, she is able to inform them that it is only slightly carbonised.*[93]

Not everyone coped well with the progressive changes that had taken place in education. Even William Armstrong who had ploughed a good deal of money into various projects, especially the foundation of Armstrong College, proclaimed in a high profile journal article that 'education remains a mysterious process; we are sure neither of how best to achieve results, nor of what results we want to achieve'.[94] Rutherford had no such difficulties and his plans for the new college were at an advanced stage, not least because the schools now had 2,500 pupils at elementary level and a further 1,300 in the secondary schools. Bath Lane was the chosen location and the new college was to have its own library and an observatory at an estimated cost of £10,000. Fundraising had begun in earnest when Rutherford died suddenly in March 1890. The next phase of his educational work was carried forward by others and in 1894 when the College finally opened it became a fitting memorial to his work.

The Rutherford College building in Bath Lane, Newcsatle upon Tyne. Source: The Story of Rutherford Grammar School *by W. Maw (1964) (from a drawing by T. R. Davison, 1887)*

Chapter Two

Learning and Living:
developments in education, 1892–1939

IN THE 50 year period which elapsed between the dawn of the 1890s and the end of the Second World War, education in Britain was substantially transformed. To a certain extent, some of those developments must be attributed to various government initiatives which delivered reforming legislation in 1902, 1918 and 1944, all aimed at widening access and extending the scope of existing provision. Any assessment of the piecemeal achievements of those years must first acknowledge the difficult climate in which these changes were made. The financial constraints posed by the First World War and its aftermath, the global economic depression that cast a long shadow over the thirties (especially in the North East of England), and the onset of war once again in 1939 inevitably limited the scope of national investment.

The dynamism of educational progress in the 1890s stands in marked contrast to this and thus assumes a particular significance, not just because of developments in the provision of technical education but because of the important role played by the school boards and key individuals in establishing higher grade schools. For many years historians regarded the Board of Education as 'the broker of progressive policy', and made rather less of the enterprising initiatives sponsored by school boards who, as democratically elected bodies, were directly accountable to local parents and ratepayers.[1] Their attempts to create 'an alternative and democratic system of schooling' which was 'forward looking and forward moving' has not always been fully recognised; instead, historians have tended to stress the radical character of the 1902 Act, which sought to rationalise provision and introduce a greater measure of uniformity.[2] Such views presuppose that the inherent diversity of the existing educational provision was a negative factor which needed to be remodelled and standardised if progress was to be achieved.[3] These ideas were challenged recently by Brian Simon whose revisionist work has stressed the 'modernising work' of school boards which he claims was not compromised by their geographical variation. Local initiatives on Tyneside, most notably those connected with the development of Rutherford College and its satellite schools and colleges, would seem to add another dimension to Simon's analysis. Arguably, the Bath Lane Schools set a progressive educational agenda to which the Newcastle School Board was bound to respond. This is particularly likely given that Rutherford was a founding member of the School Board, serving as Vice-Chairman for more than 10 years and as Chairman of the Schools' Committee for 13 years.[4] As this chapter will show, the providers of secondary education in Newcastle responded creatively to the challenges posed by adverse economic circumstances and the dislocations caused by two world wars. In a curious way adversity itself proved to be a powerful agent of educational progress and development.

Rutherford Memorial College

The sudden death of Dr Rutherford on 21 March 1890 did not bring to an end his ambitious plans to build a new college; if anything, his friends and supporters were even more determined to carry the project forward to fruition and they resolved that it should be called Rutherford College in his memory.[5] The funeral procession was led by 2,000 children from Bath Lane Schools and, as a mark of respect, the College of Medicine and the Public Library were closed while workers at Armstrong's factory in Elswick stopped work at noon so that they could join the 100,000 local people who lined the route.[6] Afterwards, an appeal was launched to gather subscriptions for the Memorial College and the Bath Lane Committee (hereafter the Committee) set themselves the daunting task of finding someone to act as College President. Rutherford's old friend, Joseph Cowen, was approached as the obvious successor but, as he had already withdrawn from political life at that point and was not in good health, he declined. James Blakey,[7] who had been Hon. Secretary of the Committee for many years, stepped into the breach and it fell to him to oversee the new development.

Finding a suitable plot of land for the College was equally problematic. Just months before he died, Rutherford had finally secured a 60 year lease on 4,224 sq. yards of land in Bath Lane from Newcastle Council at an annual rent of £100. Unfortunately, the Department of Science and Art (DSA) refused to provide a grant of £1,000 towards the cost of the building because the lease was less than the required 99 years. Protracted negotiations ensued until, finally, in April 1890, the Council agreed to extend the lease subject to the fulfilment of certain conditions: they insisted that the Committee spend

£10,000 on the building and reserved the right to appoint up to one third of the College's Management Committee. Furthermore, they advised that 'the building shall not be used as a private adventure school or for personal profit', and called upon the Committee to make a large number of bursaries available.[8]

The North East District Co-operative Society with whom Rutherford had been closely connected for so many years was one of the first and most generous subscribers.[9] Meanwhile moves were afoot to press the City Council to release money that had been made available under the provisions of the 1889 Technical Instruction Act (which allowed local authorities to increase the rates by one penny in order to pay for technical education), and the 1890 Local Taxation Act. The latter was an adroit piece of legislation which permitted some of the revenue raised by customs and excise to be reallocated to local councils; for their part, they were positively encouraged to spend this 'whisky money' on technical education. This new stream of funding was overseen by new Technical Instruction Committees who were themselves answerable to the DSA at South Kensington.[10] A special meeting of the Rutherford Schools' Committee was held to consider whether they ought to cooperate with Durham College of Science and make a joint bid to the Newcastle Council. A number of 'amicable' meetings were indeed held between the two institutions but in the end it was agreed that there was little to be gained from any coordinated effort.[11]

Finances were, by then, a little healthier as revenue flowed in from the sale of property in Higham Place, and additional funds were forthcoming from both government grants and Durham and Northumberland County Councils.[12] There were still residual problems, however, for the adventurous curriculum of the School of Science and Art (SSA) included subjects such as mechanical engineering and shorthand which were not officially recognised for grant aid. After the tenders for the building of the new College were submitted it was agreed that some modifications would have to be made in order to prune back the costs. The Committee agreed to settle for a less elaborate architectural style, to use ordinary bricks and to sacrifice the central hall, thus saving £2,000; the tender was eventually awarded to Alex Pringle of Gateshead at a cost of £13,961. The Memorial College was not the only development in the pipeline for the Committee had also invested heavily in the establishment of a new elementary school, North View, in Heaton. Hard decisions had to be made and, in the event, salaries were pegged back so that school fees could be reduced to a reasonably low level.[13] Fundraising efforts continued apace and a Prospectus for the College, published in November 1892, made much of the achievements of the SSA. The School had been listed as the best in the UK in the 1891 Official Report, ahead of Leeds Central, Manchester Central, London People's Palace, Glasgow School (Allan Glen's) and Birmingham Municipal School, and the promotional literature described the SSA as a veritable 'People's College'. At that stage only £5,500 had been pledged and even allowing for the government grant this still left a shortfall of £8,500 to be raised.[14]

In November 1891, Northumberland and Durham County Councils officially recognised the Saturday classes for teachers provided by Bath Lane Schools. In time this proved to be quite lucrative when Bath Lane staff were seconded to teach in Northumberland centres. Although Rutherford College was nowhere near completion the Bath Lane trustees were already anxious about whether the accommodation would be large enough. In the end, they agreed that the plans would have to be modified to add an additional storey. North View School was opened ahead of schedule on 26 September 1892 and the following month Joseph Cowen laid the foundation stone of Rutherford College. In a lengthy speech to the gathered dignitaries, Cowen observed that it had been Rutherford's great objective:

> …to establish an educational ladder for deserving students of the industrial classes connecting the elementary school, by means of the School of Science and Art, with the university… There is scarcely a cottage in any murky pit row or breezy village on Tyneside which has not its tender ties with Bath Lane.[15]

Despite problems with the design, a strike by building workers, and the perennial problem of raising money, Rutherford College was finally opened on 5 April 1894 in a lavish ceremony presided over by HRH Duke of York. The festivities, which included a fund raising bazaar and art exhibition, were truly a community enterprise with donations from local firms such as Newcastle printers, Mawson, Swan and Morgan, Robert Sinclair and Pumphreys.[16] South Kensington Museum donated some handsome artwork and artefacts from Egypt, India and Japan, while an army of helpers provide an endless supply of food and refreshments to the thousands of visitors who attended the bazaar during the 3-day jamboree. The opening was a great success and raised a further £950 from ticket sales, donations (including £100 from Lord Armstrong) and other fundraising activities. The monies raised went some way towards meeting the final cost which now stood at £24,000, including furnishing and fittings for the laboratories and lecture rooms.[17]

Rutherford Memorial College, with its thirty-seven rooms and laboratories, was well-equipped to teach both day schools and evening continuation classes. The day school catered for pupils beyond VI or VII grade and provided a broad syllabus in art, science and humanities subjects until the third year when pupils were encouraged to specialise. The primary aim was for the most able students to study for the matriculation, intermediate and final BA and BSc external examinations of London University. The evening school offered science, art, technical and commercial classes specifically aimed at the Elementary, Advanced and Honours examinations of the DSA. Students were able to study for the qualifications of the City and Guilds of London Technical Institute and could choose from an extensive portfolio of vocational subjects: mining, mechanical and electrical engineering, naval architecture, building construction, brickwork and masonry, carpentry and joinery, photography and cookery. The Fine Art Department was open to all pupils and included classes in architecture and mechanical drawing. The Commercial classes were equally adventurous, offering a raft of European languages, shorthand and book keeping, all certificated by the Society of Arts, London. In addition, Saturday classes catered for teachers entered for Queen's Scholarships and the Certificate of Education (Whitehall) as well as local teachers from Northumberland and Durham who wished to undertake further study. To all intents and purposes the advanced work of the College curriculum 'was mapped out and defined by the Senate of the University of London'.[18] While the primary aim was to provide an intellectually challenging curriculum, this was underpinned by the ethos of 'muscular Christianity' and pupils were encouraged to take part in an extensive range of sporting and recreational activities. As the magazine, *Ours*, reveals they could join the football, cricket, cycling and athletic clubs, the literary society or play in the SSA orchestra.[19]

With an overdraft now standing at £7,588, and the Treasurer threatening to resign, it was agreed that a larger and more able management committee was needed. The balance of power shifted with the appointment of eleven representatives of the Newcastle Corporation and a further two from Newcastle School Board to the newly-constituted Rutherford College Council (RCC). Although the Chairman, Dr Vickerman Rutherford (Rutherford's second son), could still count upon the nine members of Bath Lane Congregational Church for support the old Committee no longer had the controlling hand.[20] This certainly marked a transitional moment in the management of the College. However, these new organisational structures appear to have had little effect on finances and the overdraft continued to rise steadily until August 1894 when an unsecured loan was obtained from a local firm of solicitors. One of the problems was the time-lag between the submission of attendance registers and exam results, and the receipt of grants from the DSA, especially when school and college rolls were rising so rapidly; the other was that the amount of 'whisky money' they might receive was difficult to estimate with any degree of accuracy, as was the annual grant from Newcastle Council.[21] Yet, despite the constant cash flow crisis, the Committee continued to allow local firms to use the premises at minimal cost. The Master Painter's Association is a case in point: they conducted classes in the College for their own apprentices at a cost of just £5 per annum.

At the end of 1894, Vickerman Rutherford deposited £6,000 in the Committee's accounts to reduce the escalating interest charges on the overdraft and purchased a silver cup for the Athletics Prize. The architect's bill had still not been paid when the overdraft finally reached over £10,000. Instead, the Treasurer paid Oliver and Leesom the accrued interest on the debt each month and only settled other accounts when absolutely necessary. Those members of the Committee who had stood guarantor for the original loan were clearly concerned by the ongoing financial crisis. An attempt was made to resolve matters by securing a mortgage on the College from, first of all, the British Empire Insurance Company and, when that failed, from the Friend's Provident Institution. As one member, Mr Cooke, demanded to be released from his guarantee, and subsequent mortgage applications were repeatedly rejected,[22] it looked as though the long-term viability of the College might be in jeopardy. Nevertheless, the commitment to the educational aims of the College remained an absolute priority and ten scholarships were still allocated to Newcastle Council. In August 1895, the exorbitant cost of the College rates bill (£437. 10*s*.) generated a public outcry and an appeal was launched. Given all that the Bath Lane Schools had contributed to the education of local children, it seems extraordinary that Newcastle Council was not prepared to assist by waiving the payment of rates.[23]

In 1896 the RCC tried to increase their revenue by renting out laboratories and rooms to Central Newcastle Girls' School and holding the University of London final BA examination in the College rooms at a cost of 2 guineas per entrant. Following yet another rejection from the North East Coast Institute of Engineers and Shipbuilders, who said they had given all that they had to spare to Durham College of Science, the RCC were forced to contemplate the possibility of handing over the elementary schools to the Newcastle School Board. The desire to retain the independent character of the Schools was clearly very strong. On 1 April a letter was received from the bank demanding that the £12,441 overdraft be reduced to the agreed limit without delay and yet the RCC continued to vacillate over whether to relinquish control over their schools. Inevitably, the introduction of woodwork to the curriculum (which was due to be a compulsory subject in 1897–98) was deferred as it was 'not advisable to incur the expense this year'.[24] As they struggled to find £125 for the ground rent, the Schools' solicitor, Mr Youll, finally secured an advance of £6,000. It was small comfort that that with 528 pupils on the day school register they had been awarded the maximum grant in all subjects.[25]

At a special meeting of the RCC it was agreed that some radical steps would have to be taken to put their finances on a firmer footing. As the elementary schools had been running at a loss for some considerable time they explored the possibility of selling off North View, Camden Street and the SSA to the Newcastle School Board. It was thought that once the mortgage on those buildings had been paid off, they could invest the surplus in Rutherford College. In addition, they considered leasing Bath Lane Hall to the Newcastle School Board for £25 per annum.[26] These negotiations took some time but by March 1897 some firm proposals were ready to be presented to the School Board. Undoubtedly, the chief priority was the future development and success of Rutherford College but there was also great concern that the Board might close some of the schools and that staff might lose their jobs. In response to dissenting voices on the RCC who argued that they had failed to carry on Rutherford's legacy, the Chairman retorted that Bath Lane School was not established:

> ...to relieve the ratepayers, still less for sectarian purposes. He [Rutherford] was always an urgent advocate of unsectarian education and devoted administrator of Board Schools. His aim was to raise an educational ladder for the deserving poor.[27]

Making this decision was all well and good; persuading others to accept it and the School Board to agree to the transfer of assets was to be an extremely protracted process. For those who did not wish to see the Schools pass into the hands of the School Board there was a small victory when Bath Lane Church took over the management of the SSA and all existing debts in September 1897. The School Board, for their part, were unwilling to take over Camden Street School with its falling rolls but secured Diana Street School for £6,850.[28] In this climate of rationalisation, the old symbiotic relationship between Bath Lane Church and the Schools was recast. For whatever reason, the Church decided that 'the connection should now cease' and it was agreed that the Church should purchase the Bath Lane Hall for £1,000.[29]

The first official inspection of the College was reportedly 'very satisfactory' in terms of attendance and results; there were 594 students registered for the day school; 789 for the evening classes and 208 attending the art school. But the College ran into difficulties with the DSA over the statutory maximum class size. Two new teachers were appointed in a bid to placate the DSA but without additional classroom space they could not easily meet the requirements.[30] Newcastle Council was asked to lease the site of the 'old Fever hospital' so that purpose-built premises could be made ready for the projected woodwork class. When the DSA representative, Dr Hoffert, threatened to reduce the grant the RCC paid two members of staff to provide additional classes and arranged to curtain off a section of the hall to provide the additional space. Sir Joshua Fitch,[31] who was appointed by Newcastle Corporation in November 1896 to assess the technical education delivered by all schools in receipt of a grant, declared himself to be 'highly pleased' with standards at Rutherford College. His official report raised concerns that the building was 'unsatisfactory' but nevertheless Fitch argued that Rutherford College was 'unique' for it 'fulfils functions which neither the School Board on the one hand, nor the College of Science in the other, would be able to discharge'.[32]

As Newcastle Corporation was unwilling to pay grants to both Rutherford College and the Durham College of Science,[33] he urged them to negotiate a division of labour. As a result, a joint sub-committee was set up to consider how best to proceed. Durham was represented by the Dean of Durham, Dr Merz, Robert Spence Watson and Revd Henry Palin Gurney (Principal), while Dr Vickerman Rutherford, Hugh Crawford Smith (Treasurer), J. Ainsworth and Andrew Murray Ellis, represented the interests of Rutherford College.[34] They met in June 1897 and drew up a plan whereby the two institutions might be 'drawn more into line with one another' and agreed to meet at regular intervals to monitor any overlaps.[35]

Less than 3 years after it opened, Rutherford Memorial College had become the victim of its own success. Three further Whitworth scholarships and four national scholarships had been awarded to Rutherford students and yet the DSA continued to pressurise the College to drastically reduce class sizes. They were, it seems, determined to apply their rules even though there can have been little doubt about the quality of the teaching. Accommodation in the College was, by then, at such a premium that the woodworking class had to be conducted in a large shed on some adjoining land. In October 1897 the RCC appealed to the Corporation to allow them to develop the adjacent land, so that they might have dedicated space for technical subjects but, once again, the Corporation's response left a good deal to be desired. The Town Clerk informed the RCC that the land could only be leased at 'its fair market value'; in other words, they would make no special concessions to the College.[36]

The steady increase in degree level work offered by Rutherford College was viewed with some disquiet by Durham College of Science and this points to the existence of some tension between the various local providers of higher and further education. When the annual calendar of activities for Rutherford College was produced a formal protest was raised in a joint report at one of their regular meetings. Somewhat disingenuously, Durham College claimed that they had no wish to prevent Rutherford College from offering such courses but objected to their being advertised 'in such a glaring manner as if these classes were the main feature' of their work. The RCC was called upon 'to cease to make any further public pronouncements' about classes or examinations for London University degrees at a level higher than matriculation.[37] The RCC, which had gone to great lengths to employ suitably qualified teaching staff to support this work,[38] was not willing to accept such intrusive directives without a fight and sought an urgent interview with Revd Gurney. While he was happy to reaffirm that Durham had no wish to prevent the continuance of London University work, Revd Gurney declared that the joint report had been formally agreed at the meeting and therefore could not be rescinded. A stand-off ensued as the RCC insisted that 'they could not see their way to abandon any part of their work'. In the interest of co-operation they agreed to advertise their degree level work 'without any undue display'.[39] It seems clear that Durham was concerned about losing potential students and prepared to take steps to outmanoeuvre the perceived competition; on this occasion, however, they did not succeed.

As already noted, the future success of Rutherford College hung in the balance as their debts continued to rise and they failed to acquire sufficient additional accommodation to expand their delivery of technical subjects. Discussions with the Newcastle Corporation were still ongoing and they called upon them to 'reserve the land for educational purposes'. The RCC were fully aware that the government was planning to create a tier of Local Education Authorities 'in whose hands the College would be entrusted, and this authority would probably be the Corporation'.[40] At that stage, this legislation was still far from being worked out much less approved; the attempt to effect a reform in 1899 failed as had previous attempts in 1896.[41] Nevertheless, it is interesting to note that independent institutions, such as Rutherford College, were already preparing themselves for precisely those changes which the 1902 Act would eventually bring. Meanwhile, they tried to secure the use of the Bowling Green Club House from the Corporation in order to teach dressmaking and dress cutting which was recognised by the DSA as a suitable *(sic)* subject for girls.[42]

Raising enough revenue to keep apace with all of the innovations they wished to make was a perennial problem and one which became increasingly difficult in this period. The Northern Counties Association of Voluntary and other Schools which, in the past, had distributed grants to support independent elementary schools withheld the grant aid at the beginning of 1899 on the grounds that North View School was due to be transferred to the School Board.[43] The transfer had certainly been agreed but until the sale was complete the RCC was still liable for the costs of running the school. The situation was exacerbated by the fact that Durham County Council Technical Instruction Committee (TIC) refused to pay the fees due for 1897–98 until the College had been independently examined. Although the RCC protested that the Department of Education inspection was extremely thorough and any additional inspection would be superfluous, the Durham TIC was not prepared to negotiate, even though a more detailed report was obtained from HM Inspector. Durham University were duly called upon to inspect the College at a cost of £15. It is all the more surprising that having made such excessive demands, and burdened the College with further costs, Durham County Council should then decline to pay any grant at all the following year.[44]

The appointment in 1899 of several high profile local dignitaries to the RCC may well have been part of a careful strategy aimed at encouraging those with influence to take a special interest; while Lord Grey was appointed President, the Chairmen of Durham and Northumberland County Councils, and the Mayor of Newcastle, were all invited to be Vice-Presidents. It appears to have had little immediate effect, however, for shortly afterwards Northumberland County Council claimed that they, too, were unable to pay the College any special grant at all in 1899 even though they accepted that the work of Rutherford College was 'deserving'.[45] Whatever financial benefits were supposed to flow from the improving legislation of 1889 and 1890 appears to have been effectively circumvented by the local councils. In Newcastle, the Public Libraries Committee had been charged with administering the 'whisky money' and their accounts for 1900 show that they regularly kept back more than £1,000 of the money available to qualifying institutions under the scheme[46]. Inevitably, resolving the complex resourcing arrangements for schools and colleges was to pose a major challenge for the legislators in 1902.[47]

Yet more friction with Durham College of Science arose over the minimum age of scholarship candidates. Newcastle Corporation, who awarded scholarships to both institutions, called upon RCC to raise the age of their applicants to fifteen to bring them into line with Durham. The RCC discussed this carefully but decided against making the change as many Rutherford students reached standard VI by the age of twelve or thirteen. The Newcastle Corporation appears to have accepted the logic of this argument and there is no evidence that Rutherford students were disadvantaged when the annual allocation of awards were made.[48] Rutherford students continued to distinguish themselves in national competitions, carrying off one National Scholarship, one Royal Exhibition in Science and a Whitworth Scholarship as well as several art medals in the summer of 1899. Dancing classes and callisthenics made their way on to the crowded curriculum on a self-funding, experimental basis, though how space was found is a mystery. By then a Special Estates sub-committee had been set up to try to resolve the accommodation crisis.

As the new century dawned, the RCC finally reached an agreement with Bath Lane Church and was relieved of the remaining £2,000 mortgage on the elementary schools. Once the charity commissioners had given their approval, the proceeds from the sale of North View School would further reduce the outstanding debts. One of the casualties of these years of unstable finances was, of course, teachers' salaries. The Principal, Mr Ellis, was paid £360 per year but other teachers might receive anything from £85–£160 depending upon their initial terms of contract. There was no Burnham scale at that time and so teachers were obliged to appeal to the RCC on an individual basis. Salaries had been so low that in 1899 several teachers had 'defected' to the Board Schools.[49] This gave the RCC some pause for thought but they were extremely unwilling to introduce any standard system of payments. Citing financial constraints as the chief obstacle, they agreed that the customary arrangement of individual contracts and discretionary rises (usually 'performance related') would have to remain in place for the foreseeable future. There was a tendency to reward science masters rather better than other subject specialists, with mining lecturers being paid more than twice as much as language tutors, as well as having their travelling costs met. While the average increase in teaching salaries was somewhere between £10–£15 in 1900, some teachers received no increase at all.[50]

By then, it is noticeable that levels of interest in the College Council's activities were declining: meetings were very thinly attended and in 1901 they agreed to meet only on a quarterly basis. It may be that the members were anticipating the forthcoming legislation and were already beginning to feel disenfranchised; or it may just reflect the reduction in the RCC's sphere of activity. The Victorians' display of conspicuous philanthropy was waning then too and, to some extent, the social pressure to dispense charity and good works had long since given way to the new pragmatism whereby the population increasingly looked to the state to provide.[51] A bequest included in Joseph Cowen's will of £1,000 was the exception at a time when such generosity was becoming increasingly rare. Local working-class organisations such as the Co-operative Societies and trade unions remained the best source of additional funding and, although the amounts were very small, collectively the money that was raised helped to keep Rutherford College afloat. Rutherford College finally became solvent at the end of 1901 but still owed the bank almost £5,000 on the Bath Lane Schools' account while they awaited settlement of the transfer of assets. It seems ironic that in 1902, just as the College's accounts registered a credit balance for the very first time, of more than £2,000, the legislation that would effectively divest them of all control was finally being brokered.

New beginnings

The provisions of the 1902 Act were strongly contested and in some quarters hostility translated into substantial resistance once it passed into law.[54] The Act swept away 2,568 School Boards and replaced them with Local Education Authorities (LEAs); voluntary institutions such as Rutherford College, which had precariously existed on 'grants, endowments, ping-pong tournaments, whist drives and jumble sales', were to be supported in future from the rates.[55] Whatever criticisms have been levied at this legislation – not least that it established 'an elitist and selective system of secondary education… catering essentially for the middle and lower middle class' – it remains the case that it rescued those voluntary schools which had striven to provide a progressive, democratic alternative.[56] The transitional period was one of confusion and stasis. While, on the one hand, Rutherford Council continued to extend the curriculum with evening classes in elementary steam, applied mechanics, advanced mechanical drawing, mine surveying, gas manufacture and mining engineering, on the other hand, they were not able to make any progress on the planned extension until the full ramifications of the Bill were revealed.[57]

In April 1903, RCC was invited to send a representative to a meeting to consider the establishment of the new Education Committee and Mr Ellis was elected to sit on the Secondary and Technical Education sub-committee. As the Education Committee worked slowly towards establishing a uniform system for the city, steps were taken to bring Rutherford staff salaries broadly into line with those in the Board Schools. The last meeting of the Newcastle School Board on 28 September 1903 was reported in detail by all of the local newspapers, who all hailed its 'great work' and contribution to education on Tyneside.[58] The transfer of Rutherford College was to take rather longer. It was not until March 1905 that agreement was reached to hand over the management of the College to Newcastle's Education Department. The transfer proposal included the following crucial clauses: the name of the College was to be retained as a memorial to J. H. Rutherford; no religious teaching should be allowed and no religious test imposed upon the teaching staff.[59] The transfer documentation powerfully sets out the reasons why the Council felt they had no choice but to relinquish the institution which they had nurtured, against the odds, for so long:

We have tried to discharge our trust and may claim to have done so with a measure of success. With our present source of income we are not afraid of our financial obligations, but we feel that we are unable to keep abreast of the educational demands of the district and the requirements of the times. We are in a chronic state of overcrowding, notwithstanding that the present building was regarded ten years ago as somewhat too large. We have recently had to provide temporary classrooms at the rear of the College at a cost of £500. We have had to make provision in various places outside the building, some of them not particularly suitable, for such subjects as wood, metal work, dress cutting, painting and decorating, practical brickwork and masonry, boot manufacture etc. If we continue as managers we shall require not only greater financial support to meet current expenses but a considerable capital sum for an extension. An advanced physical laboratory, technical workshops and special classrooms are urgently needed. Lastly, and an equally important reason for transfer, we consider that the time has come when semi-private enterprises in all national education should not only be supplemented but supplanted by the Public Authorities.[60]

The LEA acquired considerable assets as a result. The building was valued at £22,659 including furniture and fittings and, according to the *Northern Echo*, this represented a 'good bargain' for the city.[61] At the point of transfer, Rutherford College had 2,133 pupils on its rolls with more than half that number attending in the evenings or on Saturdays.[62] Fees for the secondary school were charged at £4. 10s. per annum but poor children were admitted on half fees; evening classes were charged by the session and ranged from 5 shillings to 2 guineas depending upon the level of the course. Rutherford was, moreover, operating as a truly regional college, drawing students from County Durham (20 per cent), Northumberland (30 per cent) as well as from Newcastle, Gateshead, Tynemouth and South Shields.[63]

Inspections, valuations and a full audit of the College finances all had to be completed before the transfer could be finalised and formally approved by the Board of Education. It was truly the end of an era. Three members of the College Council withdrew as they became more politically active and, after 28 years service, Mr Ellis retired. He was succeeded by John B. Gaunt, a graduate of Durham College of Physical Science who had previously been the Principal of Newcastle upon Tyne Teacher Training Centre.[64] Money was extremely tight. The rising cost of teacher's salaries forced a freeze on any new appointments and some classes had to be dropped. The reduction in grants, because of a new scheme of assessment, constituted a loss of £1. 3s. 6d. per head and an urgent appeal was made to the Board of Education to have the College rated at a higher level, under Section 37. Eventually, at the end of March 1907, and 5 years after the 1902 Act passed into law, Rutherford College was transferred to the Newcastle Education Committee. It was, said the *Newcastle Journal*, 'willingly offered and willingly accepted… a sure and certain step of perpetuating the memory of John Hunter Rutherford'.[65] A major restructuring of the College was an integral part of the transfer deal and consequently a separate girl's school was established in the former Royal Grammar School premises in Rye Hill; establishing a separate secondary school for boys took another 2 years. Other branches of the College were to be called respectively Rutherford College School of Art and Rutherford College Technical School.[66]

From then onwards, the affairs of the College were managed by a sub-committee of the Newcastle Education Committee, the RCC, consisting of ten representatives of the various interest groups, including Armstrong College,[67] who met in the Town Hall every month. These new administrative arrangements greatly alleviated the stresses and strains of constantly trying to make ends meet but, aside from the disappearance of the honorary positions of President and Vice-Presidents, the business they conducted appeared to be largely the same as before. In keeping with the LEAs remit to 'develop technical education in response to industrial demand and in close co-operation with industry', a conference was swiftly convened between local employers, RCC and the Education Committee.[68] As the rationalisation of provision had significantly reduced the number of students at the College it was agreed that responsibility for classes in building construction, typography and telegraphy should be transferred to Rutherford from Armstrong College.[69] The most noticeable feature of this period is the turn away from that earlier democratic ethos and a shift backwards to the stress on functionality that had defined attitudes to working class education for so much of the nineteenth century. While the Corporation pressed ahead with the planned building extension, RCC explored the possibility of expanding its commercial education provision. An appeal to the Chamber of Commerce to provide an advisor yielded nothing but regrets and the plan was temporarily shelved. On 23 November 1909 the foundation stone of the new Technical wing of Rutherford College was formally laid by Sir Ernest Shackleton CVO, and this two storey building essentially became the home of the evening continuation classes when it was opened by Professor Michael Sadler in September 1910.[70]

On the eve of the First World War students enrolled at Rutherford Technical College had reached 3,379, including 197 registered in the School of Art. An extension was urgently needed and the architect W. S. Knowles was asked to draft some suitable plans, including a bedroom for the caretaker![71] As ever, such work could not be progressed without the assent of the Board of Education; in this case, the Board called for full costings and asked for major changes to the plans.[72] A large portion of the College's work was, by then, being tailored to the needs of local employers, such as the North East Railway Company, Parsons Marine Engineering Company, Clarke Chapman & Co., Consett Iron Company, Swan Hunter and Wigham Richardson. This was something of a mixed blessing for, on those occasions when contracts had to be completed, work took precedence and the attendance rolls slumped, with a concomitant loss of grant. However, the relationship between the College and these firms was mostly co-operative for each party recognised that the benefits of working together were significant.[73]

The troubled relationship between Rutherford College and Armstrong College stands out in marked contrast. As the evidence has shown, previous attempts to demarcate spheres of operation had only been partially successful. In March 1914, Armstrong College once again tried impose restrictions on the Rutherford curriculum by demanding exclusive rights to teach naval architecture. In addition, the Rutherford School of Art was asked to discontinue their classes in fine art on the grounds that 'more suitable provision' had been made in the Art Department of Armstrong College; instead, Rutherford College was invited to retain applied art as a technical subject. Naturally, Armstrong College could not simply impose their will for such matters were subject to the approval of the Board of Education; and there was no good reason why Rutherford should accept this dictat, given that the inspection of the School of Art had been 'satisfactory'. Nevertheless, the Board called upon Rutherford College to document the precise nature of the art classes they wished to offer. Driven, no doubt, by the pre-war emphasis upon industrial and technical strength, and 'South Kensington' utilitarian views, the Board of Education decided that Rutherford College should concentrate its efforts on applied art and any preparatory classes that would provide foundation knowledge for such work.[74] At the same time, they announced that Armstrong's King Edward VII School of Art would be officially recognised as 'the central Art School of the city and district'. This enshrined Armstrong College's exclusive rights to teach art work 'of an advanced character other than that associated with technical subjects'.[75] The judgement was very harsh for it also required Rutherford College to transfer any student who displayed 'exceptional ability' to Armstrong College. Rutherford's senior art master, Mr Easton, engaged in lengthy discussions with Richard Hatton to try to find an acceptable compromise but to no avail. HM Inspector of Art Schools was duly called in to mediate and clarify the delimitation of art subjects in the two institutions but events overtook all of the contending parties.[76] When war was declared such disputes had perforce to give way to more accommodating relationships and to more radical curriculum changes.

The impact of war, 1914–1918

The most immediate problem for Rutherford College was the falling rolls with the numbers of attending students less than half the 1913 level in October 1914. As some day classes were no longer viable, Armstrong College was called upon to teach those boys whose courses had been discontinued. Thus it was that Armstrong College began to 'borrow' the laboratories in Bath Lane and the two old adversaries were obliged to coordinate their activities for the duration of the war. Agreement had still not been reached about art provision and correspondence between the two institutions and the Board of Education overshadowed the new climate of *détente*. In November 1914, the Board reaffirmed that Armstrong College was to control 'all advanced work, including the preparation for examinations and classes for teachers', indicating that Rutherford College should concentrate upon industrial design and other technical arts subjects. To avoid any confusion and further conflict, the parameters of the new curriculum were precisely delineated: elementary and intermediate drawing, geometrical drawing and elementary design were all permitted, whereas life drawing was embargoed; practical typography was allowed but not book decoration or illustration; there was to be no stone modelling or carving from heads or full figures, and no architecture, apart from basic courses related to the building trade. Finally, suitably able candidates in arts subjects were to be transferred to Armstrong College at the age of sixteen.[77]

The initial concern at government level with the nation's technical, industrial and imperial prowess forced an urgent reappraisal of the educational initiatives that had been mooted before the outbreak of war. There were particular concerns, too, over the inadequate supply of drugs, explosives and lethal gas, prompting state investment in industries such as the British Dyestuff Company.[78] When new research confirmed that the German chemical industry was vastly superior the government accepted that education was the key: they would have to provide 'an educational ladder by which the ablest boys in the country may climb through the secondary schools or technical colleges to the Universities'.[79] Unfortunately, the chief proponents of these reforms, J. A. Pease and (Lord) Haldane, both lost their seats in the Cabinet when the War Coalition Government was set up in May 1916. The new government were rather more concerned with the deployment of labour, economic retrenchment and winning the war.

Once the initial shock had begun to subside, Rutherford College coped quite well with the disruption of studies caused by the wartime crisis. Munitions' work became a major feature of the College's activities during those years, encouraged as they were by the Ministry of Munitions,[80] who supplied specialist equipment, and by local firms such as Armstrong Whitworth and Company who needed dedicated training for its army of young unskilled employees. Delivering this training was not entirely unproblematic. The shortage of transport, particularly in the evenings, was a significant obstacle and firms were not always cooperative. For example, they would not allow engineering workers to leave work early at 4 pm, a concession that would have enabled them to complete their evening classes, and catch the last tram home.[81] The other aspect of the curriculum that expanded during the war years was the training of women workers who, under dilution schemes, had replaced men engaged in military service. It is ironic that the heavy industrial economic profile of Tyneside, which had for generations kept a large percentage of women out of the workplace, and anchored the ideal of the family wage, proved to be the source of such good opportunities for work, education and training after 1914.

The training of women fell under a branch of the Ministry of Labour, the Central Committee on Women's Employment, which had been set up in 1914.[82] To begin with, Rutherford College scheduled four classes of twenty students: two providing training in routine clerical work and two offering higher level work in shorthand and typing, at a cost of 30s. per 10-week course. The courses immediately attracted forty students and their enthusiasm was viewed as 'very encouraging'.[83] The next step was to persuade Swan Hunter and Wigham Richardson to allow women to be trained as semi-skilled munitions workers. Financial support was sought from the Ministry of Munitions, not least because specialist facilities were needed that would require an extension to the College. In February 1916, the Ministry approved the plan to add another storey to the Technical College wing at a cost of £1,450. In the interim, Parsons engineering firm asked Rutherford College to train women tracers to take on the role of draughtsmen; in return, they agreed to provide the accommodation, apparatus and all material, and to pay 20s. per lecture. These new industrial training demands produced a raft of outreach programmes for security restrictions on the handling and moving of explosive materials, and the pressure on accommodation, meant that staff mostly had to conduct their classes *in situ*.[84]

Other parts of the syllabus suffered as teaching staff volunteered or were called to active service. Of course, the College was eligible to apply for exemptions but, in practice, they did not deter those who wished to enlist. In June 1916 the evening classes in science had to be closed, primarily because part-time students with work commitments did not have the time to dedicate to independent study. Mr Gaunt resigned himself to the fact that the standards would have to be lowered for the next academic year, especially in the engineering trades.[85] The RCC acknowledged that 'dilution of skill' was in its initial phase on Tyneside and that this would continue to grow. Notwithstanding the exigencies of war, or perhaps because of them, building work at the College had progressed rapidly and in July the Lord Mayor was called upon to open the new extension.

By the end of 1916, student numbers had begun to stabilise and then pick up, with 3,528 studying science and technology and seventy-six studying art subjects. A new course in wireless telegraphy also helped to boost the numbers and was sufficient to warrant a £2,000 investment in specialist equipment for the Marconi, Telefunken and Poulsen systems. As it assumed ever greater priority on the curriculum, the School of Wireless telegraphy was inaugurated.[86] The Ministry of Munitions was highly satisfied with the training of women munitions workers at Rutherford College but still requested that a full-time supervisor should be appointed to oversee the work. This work became so important that a Supervisory sub-committee of the RCC was set up to monitor the work and make further suggestions for training. The response to the new army of female industrial workers was not wholly positive, despite their proven capability. The Supervisory sub-committee conceded that only a small number of women were suitable for training as fitters and turners, and there were perennial difficulties in placing trained workers in employment because of the prevailing chauvinism of certain trades. Elswick workers, for instance, prevented women from working as 'screw cutters' because of restrictive trade union regulations. In such cases, the Ministry was often asked to intervene but overturning trade union decisions was not something to be entered into lightly, especially at a time when the preservation of trouble-free labour relations was a given.[87] Such problems apart and the move to return women to their traditional role as homemakers after the war, the inherently progressive character of the training schemes eroded some, if not all, of the entrenched attitudes to what constituted women's work during the wartime period.

At the end of 1917, the emphasis had begun to shift to the needs of disabled soldiers and sailors and the RCC began to anticipate the educational provision that would be needed after the war ended. Student rolls were buoyant and growing, particularly in commercial and technical subjects. With money forthcoming from the Local War Pensions Committee, approved courses for the disabled in motor mechanics, wireless technology, and watch repairing were introduced, once hostel accommodation had been secured.[88] For the remainder of the war, this new work sustained the College and indeed energised certain aspects of the curriculum. However, the economic constraints of the immediate post-war period, and the onset of global depression that followed, were to pose new and exacting problems for the College as it moved into the next phase of its development.

The inter-war years

While classes for ex servicemen kept Rutherford staff busy after the war, the declining demand for wireless telegraphy forced retrenchment in other areas.[89] In the inter-war period there was precious little money available for new equipment and the accommodation problem that had been present before the war began had still not been resolved. With 2,000 evening students and another two hundred on the registers of the day schools the case for new premises was irresistible. In April 1921, the Board of Education accepted the Education Committee's proposal to acquire a plot of land on Northumberland Road and progress began on securing temporary buildings on the site. At a special meeting on 30 April, the Education Committee took out a 5 year option on the site and agreed to pay £2,000 per annum until the option lapsed in 1926. The purchase price was fixed at £41,232, which some thought was too high, and the Charity Commission insisted upon a new evaluation.[90]

Meanwhile, the demand for commercial education grew apace. By 1922 the Education Committee were providing evening commercial classes in seven separate sites across the city. In 1923, when a report from HM Inspector questioned the quality of the teaching and the suitability of the teaching accommodation, it was agreed that classes in commercial subjects would be withdrawn until suitable premises could be found. The Chairman of the Board of Education suggested that either the Northumberland Road site could be used as a temporary site for the proposed College of Commerce, or 'alternatively and preferably' given a permanent home as the Commercial wing of the new Rutherford Technical College. One of the obstacles that stood in the way of progressing these ambitious developments was the City Council's longstanding commitment to provide a new secondary school at Heaton. Ultimately, the education of school children was judged to be a greater priority and the Board of Education insisted that the development of Rutherford Technical College should not jeopardise this.[91] The Education Committee was forced to rethink its plans and it was suggested that Dame Allan's School should be used as an evening College of Commerce until some more permanent solution could be identified. At a cost of £175 for 32 weeks, and some additional payment to the caretaker for working after hours, this was considered to be a workable solution. The rather grand-sounding Central School of Commerce, as it was then called, was duly based in Dame Allan's School in College Street and a Principal was appointed in August 1924, at a cost of 25s. per evening, even though its 420 students were as nothing compared with the 1,070 local students who were being taught in small units elsewhere.[92]

At the close of 1924, the Board of Education was asked to approach the Ministry of Health to sanction the raising of a loan of £41,732 for 60 years for the purchase of Northumberland Road.[93] As student numbers at the College of Commerce reached almost 600, four rooms were secured in the School of Medicine but even this was not enough. The demand for commercial education and training was a particular feature of the inter-war period as the numbers of white collar workers grew at an unprecedented rate, reflecting the growth in local as well as national government administration and that required by the 'lighter manufacturing' firms.[94] By the end of the 1920s, the College of Commerce had more than doubled its original intake but was no nearer to securing permanent premises.

Rutherford's reputation as a centre of excellence continued to grow as it was recognised as an approved institution by the Institute of Chemistry in 1927 and as a centre for the National Certificate in Electrical Engineering in 1928.[95] Yet, these achievements were made against a backdrop of economic stasis: the long awaited development of Rutherford Technical College had effectively been mothballed and, even though the Committee continued to make plans and the city continued to pay the interest on the original lease, no progress was made. The only significant developments on the Northumberland Road site were the activities of the Allotments Association who rented some of the land at £1 per allotment and put it to good use.[96]

One parallel aspect of educational provision that deserves attention in Newcastle in this period was teacher training. In the nineteenth century, the emphasis had been upon the monitorial system and in 1880 pupil teachers made up more than 50 per cent of the entire service. In 1888 the School of Science and Art and the Durham College of Science were both eager to be accepted as official centres but following the outcome of the Cross Commission teacher training was managed thereafter by the universities.[97] After 1902 the LEAs assumed responsibility for training colleges while the universities retained control over the education of secondary school teachers.[98] After the end of the First World War student teachers in Newcastle, who were educated at Kenton Lodge Training College, had to enter into a covenant with the Board of Education which stated that for 5 years after their training they would remain as teachers in the service.[99] Given the earlier discussion about expanding opportunities for women, perhaps a more interesting development in teacher education was the further expansion of Northern Counties College of Cookery and Household Management, which had been established on an independent basis in 1880 to promote training in domestic economy. In the 1890s it had been located in a private house in Eldon Square, first of all under the auspices of Newcastle and Northumberland County Councils, and then, after 1895, as part of a regional partnership which included Durham County Council.[100] In 1903 the College relocated to 54 Northumberland Road with some overspill catered for in 13 Osborne Road.[101] The falling numbers of domestic servants during the First World War prompted a more expanded curriculum with more emphasis on technical expertise and on the training of domestic science teachers.[102] Afterwards, recruitment grew until 1934 when the Education Committee explored the possibility of finding a new greenfield site for the College, alongside its other plans for further education in the city.[103]

Building developments finally began to move forward once more in the mid-1930s when a local firm of architects, Marshall and Tweedy, were appointed to draw up plans for the proposed new colleges. Student numbers in what was now called the Municipal College of Commerce had reached 1,340 at the end of 1934 and Rutherford's evening classes were nudging 2,000. The increase undoubtedly reflected the wider remit of the College of Commerce's syllabus which, by then, embraced elocution and economic history.[104] The Director of Education visited technical colleges in Prague, Germany and Holland in 1935 in a bid to marry the City Council's plan to the supposedly superior continental model. In 1936 the Education Committee considered a number of possible schemes for resolving the accommodation crisis in both colleges. These included locating both Commerce and Technology on the existing Northumberland Road site enlarged by Ellison Place, the Union Cold Storage and Lockey's properties; using the Ravenswood Road site; locating Technology only on Northumberland Road without any additional land/buildings and relocating the College of Commerce in the existing Rutherford College premises.[105]

As ever, the final decision would rest with the Board of Education. Thus it was that the Committee found themselves no further forward in the middle of 1936 and contemplating yet another site: this time, 5 acres of land in the Exhibition Park. The plan was never likely to succeed because the Freemen who controlled Newcastle's ancient Town Moor had successfully fought off encroachments since the eighteenth century. The architects fees had mounted to £7,845 and other costs involved in developing the plans had reached £12,058 when, on the eve of yet another war, and just following the final approval of the scheme, the Board of Education wrote to say that it would be necessary to 'postpone for an indefinite period all building projects'.[106]

On balance, the period between 1890 and 1939 was one of piecemeal development and it appears that most of this progress was made in the 1890s, which emerges as the most dynamic decade. The difficulties posed by two world wars and the constraining effects of economic retrenchment and depression in the inter-war period were always bound to hinder the development of purpose-built premises. Even so, Rutherford College still managed to innovate, expand its curriculum and increase its student rolls. Pragmatism may have replaced civic philanthropy as the twentieth century progressed, yet there were still many who were willing to dedicate their time and their energy to the education of the young. Unfortunately, the belief that working class education should be functional and driven by industrial and economic imperatives prevailed, and this was to remain a defining feature of the post-war period.

Northern Counties Training College of Domestic Science, 6 February 1939

Chapter Three

The long revolution:[1]
stability and change, 1939–1966

THE OUTBREAK of war in 1939 was to have a profound affect upon educational development. Retrenchment in the late-1930s had already taken its toll, with resources in schools and colleges stretched to the limit, and all building projects on hold for the duration of the war. In addition, the 1936 Education Act which should have been implemented in September 1939 had been suspended until further notice. Children's education was not only disrupted by the large scale evacuation at the beginning of the war but by the bombings, which rendered families homeless, or prompted a move to those parts of the country which were perceived to be safer.[2] Some historians have argued that the suspension of the 1936 Act, which embodied 'the political hesitancies and chilled steel financial climate' of the 1930s, was a blessing in disguise.[3] According to G.A.N. Lowndes, it would have produced 'administrative chaos'.[4] Yet, even though educational progress became a central plank of the wartime reconstruction programme, the 1944 Act has been regarded as an inherently conservative measure which did little to address the prevailing inequities in the system.[5]

In 1939 the Rutherford College Council (RCC) had more pressing matters to deal with. Rutherford College had lost half of its usual intake of students and air raid precautions and blackout curtains had replaced the building programme on the agenda.

The College of Commerce had been even more badly affected and had only 880 students in January 1940.[6] In the spirit of cooperation and collectivism which prevailed, some short courses were provided for locally stationed troops, such as the 42nd East Lancashire Division Signals Regiment. The College of Commerce offered free first aid classes and Rutherford College offered domestic science courses for housewives in wartime cookery and catering.[7] The Principal and one of the assistant lecturer's received their call-up papers in December 1939 but the RCC successfully fought off their recruitment to the forces on the grounds that Rutherford College was 'continuing on a full-time basis'. This was not entirely true for Rutherford College was not operating at full strength, even with the return of many of the evacuees. However, by the middle of 1941, the delivery of special courses for the troops and subjects, such as first aid, English conversation (for Polish refugees) and wireless telegraphy, were beginning to have a positive impact upon the attendance rolls.[8] By the end of 1941, the building programme once again became the focus of attention when 13 Ellison Place came up for sale. It was thought that the purchase of the property would allow RCC to expand its holdings in that part of the city and make the move to Northumberland Road a more viable proposition. The Education Committee subsequently secured the 380 sq. yards site, including the house and a dentist's surgery, for £3,000. The move itself, however, was still far from certain.

Student rolls climbed steadily from 1942 onwards and Rutherford fought hard to keep its staff, even retaining its married women by allowing them to return to duties as temporary wartime appointments.[9] For their part, the Board of Education continued to support courses in food education, fuel economy, and the care and repair of household effects. Of course, those who benefited most from these initiatives were women.[10] By January 1944, the College of Commerce had 1,050 evening students and 139 day students. When the opportunity arose to purchase the premises in College Street, that had been temporarily occupied by the College of Commerce for some years, the Education Committee agreed to offer the vendors £2,000. It was in this upbeat atmosphere that Rutherford began to expand the curriculum to include classes in wig making, hairdressing and perfumery,[11] and the Education Committee convened a special meeting in March 1945 to consider the building programme. In all, £9,022 had been spent on architects' fees and other costs but, as the war drew to a close, they were no nearer to securing the new premises they so badly needed.[12]

Education in the post-war period

It is all too easy to be critical of the slow progress that was made but, to a large extent, the piecemeal provision that characterised educational policy in the post-war period was determined by the political and economic difficulties which beset Attlee's Labour ministry (1945–51). Understandably, Attlee was extremely reluctant to commit surplus capital at a time of enforced retrenchment and ministers regarded their own initiatives as little more than an interim solution. In this make do and mend climate only the most pressing project was financed and while the Manchester College of Technology finally secured its long overdue building extension countless other institutions were unable to modernise their provision.[13] School-based education was an enormous national enterprise but further education, on the other hand, was something of a Cinderella service, usually poorly regarded by town hall and Whitehall alike. Yet it would be wrong to assume that the period between the 1944 Education Act and the Robbins Report (1963) was a time of stasis and inaction. Even though the pressures on resources acted as a significant constraint on educational reform, the intellectual debate about how to tackle the problem of industrial decline continued to gather momentum. In the closing stages of the war, politicians busied themselves with plans for post-war reconstruction and, in the 'White paper chase' which characterised 1944–45, educational reform was a notable priority.[14] More than ever before, young people were perceived to be 'the greatest national asset'.[15] Industrialists and policy makers, too, devoted considerable time and energy to exploring ways of improving the quality and quantity of technological training. Gradually, a more coherent education policy began to emerge.

The Percy Report, which published the findings of the Special Committee on Higher Technological Education in 1945, had concerned itself with the need to support 'appropriate collaboration between Universities and Technical colleges'.[16] Led by Lord Eustace Percy, who was then Rector of King's College, the Newcastle offshoot of Durham University,[17] its recommendations raised the profile of the colleges and allowed for the designation of a small number of technical colleges as Colleges of Advanced Technology (CATs).[18] Most significantly, the Report proposed that the unwieldy administration of technical education should be streamlined by the setting up of regional advisory bodies. In turn the regional councils were to be accountable to a National Advisory Council on Education for Industry and Commerce. The latter organisation subsequently acted as a powerful pressure group throughout the 1950s and beyond, and played a key role in designing a new raft of technical awards.[19] They hoped that this would circumvent any damaging competition between courses and colleges. While the Percy Report was broadly supported, there were some dissenting voices on the Special Committee who were reluctant to endow the proposed CATs with degree-awarding powers. This was a highly sensitive issue for, as they acknowledged, the 'power to confer degrees is the distinguishing mark of a university'.[20]

The Barlow Report (1946) which was published the following year had been commissioned to investigate scientific manpower. The Report focused on technological provision in the university sector and put in place advantageous funding arrangements to enable the universities to double the numbers of science graduates as quickly as possible. It is interesting to note that in making their recommendations the Scientific Manpower Committee were concerned that 'the quality of our graduates must not be sacrificed to quantity'.[21] The Universities were, quite naturally, supremely confident of their role as the primary providers of science and technology degrees and were thus well placed to become the key players in the newly formed Advisory Council on Scientific Policy (1947).[22] From this position of strength, they were able to press for those innovations which would strengthen their control over higher education. But it was not all plain sailing. The money to finance a technological university, the plan favoured by the University Grants Committee (UGC), simply was not available and the controversy surrounding the establishment of Keele University undoubtedly served as a cautionary tale.[23] In some respects the decision not to include applied science and technology on the new curriculum at Keele University looks perverse, given the stated priorities of the policy makers at that time. But, by the time Keele took in its first batch of students in October 1950, the findings of the Percy Report had begun to be implemented and other providers had taken on the challenge of widening access outside of the university sector. As for the universities, after 1951 they were able to exploit their influence with Churchill and the incoming Conservative government who agreed to fund the expansion of the Imperial College of Science and Technology. The award of a Royal Charter formalised its newfound status as a university.

During what was to be his final term of office, Churchill resolved to 'bring back all of our true glories' and restore Britain to 'its true strength' but his vision of regenerating imperial and economic strength was essentially Utopian.[24] Few could have foreseen the successive political crises that beset the post-war governments – devaluation, the Korean War (1950–53), East-West conflict over Berlin – and it is hardly surprising that so little was achieved during the decade which followed the end of the Second World War. With characteristic conceit, Churchill was not at all sanguine that his successor was capable of reversing the trend towards decline, and he greatly underestimated the mood of the times and the government's commitment to reform. Educational progress was made a central tenet of the government's new programme when parliament convened in June 1955, and the case for change was cogently expressed by Sir Anthony Eden at a meeting he addressed the following January. The size of the labour force, he explained, would no longer, of itself, guarantee economic success:

> *Those with the best systems of education will win. Science and technical skill give a dozen men the power to do as much as thousands did fifty years ago. Our scientists are doing brilliant work, but if we are to make full use of what we are learning, we shall need more scientists, engineers, and technicians. I am determined that this shortage shall be made good.*[25]

Whilst the finer points of this policy were being thrashed out in the respective education committees, many of the regional colleges had put their own strategies in place and begun to make real progress towards tackling the anticipated demand, primarily by developing new courses in partnership with local industries. Sandwich courses, later regarded as one of the National Council's 'most important achievements',[26] had been on offer to Scottish students since the 1890s and at Sunderland Technical College from the turn of the century.[27] Unfortunately, neither the staff nor the students at the time had any clear understanding of how the industrial component of such courses was meant to function; connections between theory and practice were rarely other than makeshift and, when the viability of the sandwich course was first mooted, there was broad acceptance that a more structured approach would have to be implemented. The new applied studies which were put in place following the Percy Report, and the establishment of the National Council for Technological Awards (NCTA) in 1955, combined theoretical and practical competencies co-ordinated by the Regional Advisory Councils. According to Harold Silver, the NCTA 'delineated a set of purposes and procedures that were to act as guidelines for development outside the universities for more than a quarter of a century'.[28] The National Council's chief objective was to secure rational provision tailored to specific manpower targets. The NCTA announced that in future, a new award, the Diploma in Technology, would be available to students who had been 'educated partly in an academic and partly in an industrial environment'[29] and, moreover, official approval would only be granted to those colleges whose courses conformed to the new guidelines. Great care was taken to draw a distinction between the Diploma and the Bachelor award which was exclusive to the universities. With these provisos in place, both structure and objectives were substantially reconfigured, ensuring that all industrial training was fully integrated into the teaching programme, and offering students the opportunity to choose from a range of 'thick' and 'thin' sandwich courses.

Once sandwich courses were made the linchpin of the strategy for meeting the demand for technical education, attention automatically turned to the desirability of locating them in an optimum learning environment. Until after the Government's White Paper, *Technical Education*, was published in 1956 there was, though, no firm understanding of what form that learning environment should take. From his own political vantage point, John Carswell, saw the CATs as arising 'out of the womb of the educational system as it had been fertilised since 1944,[30] the pride and joy of the Ministry of Education. At first, everyone expected an entire raft of CATs to be re-designated from the existing pool of major providers and there was widespread disappointment that, in the end, only a handful were deemed suitable. Envy apart, the selection was hardly controversial, though a few eyebrows were raised over Cardiff. The general consensus is that this was a 'gesture to Wales'[31] and, certainly, the National Council were keen to appear even-handed. Three colleges in the North East of England, including Rutherford, entertained high hopes of being selected, fuelled to a certain extent by several high profile, official visits and the favourable intimations of Sir David Eccles, the Minister of Education. For their part, Newcastle upon Tyne Education Committee had every reason to expect that Rutherford College of Technology would be a strong contender for re-designation as a regional CAT; it had, after all, been the premier provider of technical education in the North East since the turn of the century. Initially, the Northern Advisory Council for Further Education was asked to make a recommendation but they sensibly demurred. The Newcastle LEA was not kept in the dark for long. In June 1957, with the proviso that certain conditions were met, Rutherford's selection was finally confirmed. The City Council was positively encouraged to increase its investment in order to bring Rutherford up to the official specification; conferment of CAT status, they were assured, would follow automatically 'in due course'.[32]

Rutherford College

In theory, upgrading Rutherford College should have posed few real problems for Newcastle Council had long taken a fairly progressive approach to the city's educational needs. As far back as the mid-1930s councillors had sought official approval for a radical building programme[33] but other priorities had assumed greater precedence. Inevitably, those plans were shelved not merely for the duration of the war but until the end of the 1940s, when more money became available, and the lack of facilities and resources at the College began to have a negative effect upon recruitment.

In the immediate aftermath of the war the College was operating from multiple sites in the city, a far from ideal arrangement. As the Head of the Department of Electrical Engineering later recalled, 'in 1947 I had over forty part-time staff, working in thirteen different locations, at different parts of the city'. The pressure on space was so great that even the Principal, Dr Scarborough, shared a table in his office with his secretary.[34] These *ad hoc* arrangements and the pressure on resources took their toll. That same year, London University withdrew recognition for its external degree in Mechanical Engineering because the laboratories failed to meet the required standard.[35] Later on, as the post-war population boom prompted an urgent reappraisal of education strategy, provisional plans were, once again, drafted to address the projected increase in demand. Unfortunately, the need for prudent financial management stymied radical progress at local as well as national level. These same plans were already in the process of being substantially overhauled as the National Council was reaching the end of its deliberations. In the event, they generated considerable debate and controversy: the more progressive members of the City Council favoured the creation of an 'education precinct', an ambitious project which envisaged the eventual location of all further education institutions together in the city centre, and in close proximity to Newcastle University; other councillors, though, expressed deep reservations about the costs involved and the enormous impact the scheme would have on the local community.

This contentious blueprint for educational reform dominated the landscape of Tyneside politics throughout the fifties and beyond, for the process of winning over the opposition proved torturously slow. In planning and architectural terms it was a period characterised by the new 'modernism' and, in political terms, by a resurgence of provincial municipal governance, assisted by a new technocratic elite. The idea of having a precinct was probably conceived by Wilfred Burns, the City's new Chief Planning Officer, who had worked on similar urban structures for war-torn Coventry. The site was planned and laid out by George Kenyon, the Newcastle city architect, as a series of linked spaces roughly quadrangular in shape, the traditional form of 'college' design since the Medieval period. The £4 million scheme dominated the headlines of the local press, fuelling fears (not altogether unfounded) that some significant buildings would be sacrificed. 'Education may demolish two churches' was *The Journal's* dramatic headline in June 1960.[36] A compulsory purchase order, under the terms of which 200 families and forty businesses in the city centre were to be forced to sell up and move on, galvanised the opposition into forming a Citizens' Defence Committee. As battle lines were drawn and tempers flared, Harold Macmillan was called upon to intervene and, briefly, it seemed that the plan might indeed flounder.

T. Dan Smith, Chairman of the Planning Committee and later leader of the City Council, recognised that if Newcastle was to regain the eminent position it had enjoyed in the late nineteenth century it would require a new urban infrastructure, especially at its geographical centre, to carry out economic and social functions. It was also important for the city to improve its image to accord with the way it was perceived by inward investors. As part of this concept, Smith saw further education as having a central role. As he later recalled 'people look on planning as something they don't like',[37] but this was a somewhat simplistic gloss on the situation. There was, in fact, rather more to it than that; compulsory purchase was then quite rare, viewed with suspicion and mistrust, and widely held to be an infringement of civil liberty. Equally, the education precinct itself was an inordinately ambitious development and not everyone accepted that this was the optimal way of delivering change.[38] Smith, who was a maverick character as well as being the scheme's most determined advocate, seemed energised rather than daunted by the strength of opposition. He pressed ahead with his plans on the grounds that it was a 'socially justified exercise'.[39] He was, amongst other things, a master of political rhetoric and, to be fair, he was alive to the real sacrifices that people were being called upon to make; he also genuinely believed that he had a mandate to decide what was, and was not, in the public interest. With his political reputation on the line, Smith proved remarkably adept at making the requisite placatory statements, refusing to entertain the possibility that he might be forced to modify his plans. In any event, the art of compromise was just not his style. Instead, he invested his considerable energies in talking up the schemes' socialist objectives by launching a major public consultation initiative, hosting countless meetings and personally addressing some 30,000 people. Aided and abetted by Gladys Robson and Jessie Scott-Batey, his stubbornness eventually paid dividends. Newcastle gained an inner city educational precinct that was to be the envy of many LEAs and, in the short-term, Smith's career as a local politician was assured. By the time it was approved the cost had soared to £5 million but, by then, the precinct was being hailed as 'the finest in Europe'. It would, Smith claimed, 'put Newcastle on the map'.[40] Even today, the ramifications of Smith's high-risk approach to city politics and subsequent imprisonment continues to excite strong views[41] but, on this count at least, as the driving force in promoting a cohesive and enterprising education policy, his contribution is incontrovertible. He left behind a lasting legacy of his vision and political flair.

Idealistic visions apart, the investment potential of securing CAT status for Rutherford was self-evident, and, as already noted, the City Council was not slow to seize upon what it saw as a window of opportunity. A comprehensive development programme was approved, beginning with the transfer of elementary studies from Rutherford College to the new College of Further Education when it was opened in September 1956. Located in Bath Lane on the site previously occupied by Rutherford

Grammar School, and with an enrolment of some 2,688 students following full-time, part-time and evening courses,[42] the new college (Rutherford College of Technology) went some way to addressing the existing accommodation and resourcing problems which had been acting as a drag on curriculum development. At long last, Rutherford College was able to expand its advanced work and be more innovative. When the HND courses in Mechanical and Electrical Engineering were launched in 1957 the College had an intake of over 4,000 students, the majority of whom were registered for part-time and evening study. But there were plans in place to expand the small numbers of daytime classes, and securing recognition as an approved centre for the London BSc (Engineering) Degree examinations was an essential part of the strategy to expand and concentrate upon advanced level work. Staff had also begun to develop courses in nuclear energy and this was assisted by the scheme to release two teaching staff to attend a 3 month course in nuclear energy at Harwell.[43] Nor were the benefits that flowed from all this confined to Rutherford alone; with the building schedule for a new College of Further Education by then at an advanced stage, and the final stage expected to be completed by 1959, there was sufficient spare capacity to absorb the overspill from the city's other main providers: the Municipal College of Commerce and the College of Art and Industrial Design. These institutions, too, were being primed to upgrade their intake, to drop most of their lower level work and extend their links with local industries. 'Ambition', proclaimed the *Newcastle Evening Chronicle*, 'drives city's 18,000 evening students' in an upbeat article which asserted that 'there is nothing you can name that evening classes cannot teach, provided sufficient numbers are interested'.[44]

In the mid-1960s, when the government of the day turned its mind to the task of managing the unprecedented expansion in further and higher education, that had steadily gathered pace since the end of the Second World War, it did so in a climate of relative economic optimism. Until then, fluctuations in the post-war economy had served only to complicate further the debate on educational provision driven by traditional utilitarian ideas. Once again, education reformers wrestled with the thorny problem of how to address the challenges posed by technological and economic change, without compromising the elitism of the universities. The Ministry of Education, which had no permanent representative in the Cabinet until 1945, had few budgetary responsibilities, especially for higher education; in short, it had little to do. Moreover, the Ministry had no real control over the universities because they were funded by the UGC which received its monies directly from the Treasury. Universities were thus regarded as autonomous organisations and accepted as such in order to protect their academic independence from government interference. Hitherto, the accelerated demand for degree courses in the technical and other colleges had been met largely by external providers. For some years London University had played a major role in servicing the needs of full- and part-time matriculated candidates and, by the time that the Robbins Committee assembled in February 1961 to overhaul higher educational provision, some 11,000 external students were registered as undergraduates.[45]

This was not a Royal Commission but a supradepartmental committee whose report was 'one of the great state papers of the century', alongside the 1909 Poor Law Report and the Beveridge Report of 1943.[46] Although much of what Robbins recommended was not acted upon by the incoming Labour government, much of the evidence, submitted to the committee, pointed to the kind of status that Northumbria University now enjoys. For example, the TUC looked forward to a comprehensive structure to higher education with the possibility of universities, teacher training colleges and technical institutions all embraced in university-type institutions, under the central control of an enhanced ministry of education. Others argued for a single funding body for the whole of higher education. The Vice-Chancellors of the existing universities supported few of these radical ideas and on balance they were against any further expansion.

The Labour Party set up its own committee under Lord Taylor in 1962 and Harold Wilson launched its report a year later. The Taylor Report began with a call for 'a rapid and continuing expansion of higher education, on a scale never before contemplated'.[47] It went on to embrace the human capital theory linking economic growth to the production of skilled scientists and engineers. To achieve this, Taylor proposed the creation of twice as many universities as then existed. They were to be developed from upgraded existing colleges including the CATs, regional technical colleges (such as Rutherford), teacher training colleges (such as those in Newcastle and at Northern Counties) and located in close proximity to the major centres of population, business and industry. As Wilson said in his now famous 'white heat' speech, what was required was 'a crash programme… a tremendous building programme of new universities' with nearly three quarters of a million students.[48] As before, industrialists, economists and politicians were greatly preoccupied by the need to match and outgun their foreign competitors.[49] But, by this point in time, the inculcation of craft skills was no longer the main priority. Technical knowledge had come to be preferred over practical expertise as the effects of an insidious 'brain drain' penetrated the complacency of even the least-troubled of management sectors. What informed government policymaking was the dawning realisation that widening access to higher education and competitive advantage were intrinsically linked.

Municipal College of Commerce

Like Rutherford College, the Municipal College of Commerce was flourishing in the 1950s and although 948 students were reallocated to the College of Further Education they still had just over 3,500 registered students. The White Paper on Technical Education (1956) had recommended a 5 year, £100 million investment in both colleges and universities, and insisted that 'accountancy, costing, salesmanship, commercial skills of all kinds, including foreign languages, are equally important to a trading nation'.[50] Such initiatives were instrumental in encouraging local authorities to strengthen existing provision and the College of Commerce was already offering advanced level work. Among other things, they had established considerable expertise in the provision of management and work study courses but, unfortunately, the further development of new programmes was hindered by perennial accommodation problems.

As the Education Committee admitted in their annual report, the demolition of 14 Ellison Place had been protracted and, consequently, throughout 1956–57 staff had been obliged to teach in temporary classrooms in St Mary's Place and in Carlton House. The LEA had addressed the problem by commissioning a new building but re-housing the College proved to be a more prolonged and destabilising process than they had envisaged. Throughout 1960 the College of Commerce was operating from eight separate centres, utilising various school premises in the evenings and Rutherford College during the daytime.[51] In the short-term, the organisational difficulties created by the pressure on accommodation was offset by the dynamism of the staff and the range of courses they provided. Communal food and library facilities, and the activities of the Student's Association, also militated against the decentralising effects of the multi-site delivery of teaching.

With the invaluable support of nine Advisory Committees the College of Commerce steadily expanded its remit, seizing the opportunity to provide business training to officers who had retired early from HM forces and offering degree level work in Economics. In 1959 the College's School of Law was finally able to launch a full-time course for the London external LLB and increasing numbers of university graduates took advantage of the secretarial courses available. Its main function was to provide a service to the local cadres of civil servants, local government officers, clerks and shop assistants. In 1964–65 amongst the largest groups were those studying part-time to be executive grade civil servants, 'A' Level classes, examination classes for the institutes of banking and insurance, shorthand and typing courses and introductory language classes taught in the evening. As day-release provision became increasingly common in the private sector and the Civil Service, their non-vocational courses were also in great demand,[52] while in 1962 it became the first college in the country to offer the new HND in Business Studies, following publication of the Crick Report.[53] Such courses helped to lay the foundation for the later degrees in business. At least some of this expansion is attributable to the rising numbers of married women who were returning to the job market in need of refresher courses and audio-typewriting skills.

By 1963, however, recruitment levels were beginning to falter, partly because of increasing competition from other local providers of technical education who were, by then, offering ONDs and Certificate courses. The actual downturn in recruitment numbers was fairly slight and with a total student population of 5,355 the College's viability was never at risk. The significance of the shortfall was that it ran counter to the national trend and, more importantly, to the commitment to widening participation which had for so long been the defining ethos of the College. The acute shortage of suitable accommodation had led to the withdrawal of some popular secretarial and retailing courses, and thus accommodation difficulties, more than any other factor, acted as a drag on the College's overall progress and development in the late 1950s and early 1960s.

College of Art and Industrial Design

As already noted, the influence of the Department of Science and Art at South Kensington had served to privilege and foster technical skills rather than encourage artistic talent.[54] Under its aegis the national schools of art and design had concentrated their efforts on training arts teachers for the Board Schools, and on providing a specialist education for those working or planning to work in the field of industrial design.[55] Self-evidently, the stress on 'useful education', even in the 1940s and 1950s remained a constant and constraining principle. In 1949 the Newcastle upon Tyne Education Committee agreed that the existing provision for students of commercial and industrial art was inadequate and began to put in place a plan to develop new facilities.[56] There were a number of dissenting voices at the time, some of whom claimed that the plan 'was unnecessary, crazy and a waste of money',[57] and yet by the time the building was in commission it had already outgrown the facilities. Alive to the commercial advantages of having locally trained designers, city firms were quick to offer assistance, with the promise of accommodation and equipment.[58] As there was little or no funding available from the government for new buildings at that time the Education Committee purchased two adjoining houses in Clayton Road, Jesmond, and commissioned F. J. Hepple Ltd to convert them into suitable premises at a cost of £6,018. 5s. 11d. Once the work was completed in September 1953, the four storey building was equipped with facilities for full- and part-time courses in Commercial Design and Dress and for part-time study in Industrial Art.[59]

Behind the scenes, there had been some careful negotiation with the Fine Arts Department of King's College which was keen to ensure that any new provision did not intrude on its field of expertise. The Northern Regional Advisory Council had played a key role in the development, not merely as peacemaker between King's and the new College of Art and Industrial Design but also in ensuring that there was no resultant friction between other colleges of art at Carlisle, Sunderland, Middlesbrough and West Hartlepool and the School of Art at Darlington.[60] The School of Printing, which had been inconveniently located in a cramped uncomfortable hut in Bath Lane since 1951, was transferred from Rutherford College to new premises in Clayton Road and into a more suitable partnership with art and design. From these fairly modest beginnings the College of Art and Industrial Design quickly expanded its curriculum and student numbers – so quickly in fact that in 1953 the Education Committee approved an additional investment of £3,000. 15s. to enable the grounds adjacent to the College to be developed into additional workshops.[61]

In 1953–54 the School of Printing was formally recognised as the regional centre for typography and related subjects, and increasingly the College offered more advanced level work, such as the National Diploma in Commercial Design and courses approved by the City and Guilds of London Institute. In order to meet the demand, the School of Printing acquired St John's School, Bath Lane, while the College in Clayton Road was extended once again to provide specialist facilities for metalwork and jewellery, model-making and plastics and upholstery. The 858 students who enrolled in the academic year 1955–56 were taught by sixteen full-time members of staff and benefited from the expertise of a further thirty-two visiting lecturers. The distribution of a glossy Prospectus reveals just how much progress had been made in the first 3 years. As well as the School of Printing, the College had four Departments (Art and Design, Commercial Design, Dress and Industrial Design) and it was a recognised centre for training arts and crafts teachers. The quality of the student's work was unquestionably high. In 1956 the College was asked to design a silver dish to present to HM Queen Elizabeth, the Queen Mother, on her visit to the city in October to open the new Rutherford Grammar School.[62] By then, too, the growing numbers of full-time students were able to apply to the Education Committee for an award to cover the cost of fees and materials. This was a great help for full-time courses could cost anything from £9 to £21, according to the level and period of study. It is notable that students who infringed the regulations, most notably by smoking or failing to behave in 'a quiet and orderly' fashion, might be excluded from the College without any rebate on the fees paid.[63]

The Principal, Cecil Smith, was a man of great drive and energy, who was determined that the College should establish a reputation for high quality teaching in art and design. In 1957, he published a small pamphlet on the future of art education in which he outlined the failure, as he saw it, of art education in the past.[64] He complained that the training of industrial designers and art teachers, he claimed, together served neither purpose well; art teachers, he claimed, were over qualified while industrial designers were insufficiently trained. Moreover, he deplored the practice of teaching vocational and recreational courses in the same class, 'for the compromise which must invariably result cannot possibly prove satisfactory to both'.[65] Ultimately, he predicted, unless significant changes were made art education would decline. This was no doubt tactical as well as prescient for his call for modernisation was well-received, and the Education Committee responded positively to his demand for further investment. In 1956–57, the painting and decorating classes were transferred from Rutherford College and incorporated into the Department of Interior Design. With the addition of classes at Blenheim Street School, the College was now operating from three separate sites. The non-vocational work was pruned back to enable the College to concentrate upon national examination classes and advanced study.

In 1957 the College became the first in the country to be approved to provide a new type of training course for handicraft teachers or industrial designers which was 'regarded as being the equivalent of a university degree'.[66] The publicity material which launched the new training courses made much of the fact that handicraft teachers had been disadvantaged, both 'in status and financially', compared with teachers of other subjects.[67] Then, as now, the highlight of the academic year was the annual exhibition and this was initially held on site at Clayton Road. By 1958 the scale of the exhibition determined that it should move to more prestigious and commodious premises in the Laing Art Gallery. The College by this stage had 1,108 students and was able to boast of its students' exceptional success in national competitions.[68] To a large extent the success of the College rested upon its close relationship with local industry, not least because the latter provided the funds for the various annual competitions.[69] In effect, the Advisory Committees for Industrial and Commercial Design, and Printing, constituted a working partnership between college staff and lay experts from local businesses and firms. There were obvious mutual benefits: a vocationally-relevant training for the students and a model workforce for local industries. By the end of the 1950s, the College was the seventh largest art college in Britain with the largest Painting and Decorating School in the North East of England.[70]

Gradually, the colleges of art and design became more independent until 1961 when they were allowed to develop their own advanced courses, subject, of course, to the satisfactory approval of the National Council for Diplomas in Art and Design.[71] Such approvals were tightly controlled as there was a strong view that talented artists were a rarity. Thus, while this undoubtedly drove up standards in existing colleges, it necessarily acted as a barrier to the sector's expansion and greater accessibility by the working classes to advanced level work.[72] Increasingly the work of the College was attracting high profile attention and, in June that same year, the Department of Dress held a fashion show attended by the Lord Mayor and Lady Mayoress.[73] The entire collection was sold before the show began, and as the *Newcastle Journal* commented, 'If the Fashion Department of the College of Art and Industrial Design School in Newcastle were to turn itself into a commercial concern, it would be minting money overnight.'[74] A successful visit by the National Council in March 1962 was followed in 1963 by the launch of a raft of new Diploma courses, in Advertising Design, and Industrial Design and Fashion. Newcastle College of Art and Design and Sunderland College of Art had been selected along with twenty-seven other colleges to offer the new graduate-level awards, but while the local press were quick to publicise the achievement it soon emerged that the 'Beeching' plan would leave 2,000 students in Britain without a place on a DipAD course.[75]

The College had much to be proud of, not least the honour of securing the first Leverhulme £500 Travelling Scholarship in Industrial Design.[76] Headlines of a different kind were made when two students carried off first and second prizes in the underwear category of *The Sunday Times* Man-Made Fibres Competition! The award-winning red and brown brushed bri-nylon lingerie provided the two students with a £300 travelling bursary and the College with some invaluable publicity.[77] Professor Tom Bromly recalled that Newcastle emerged as the 'regional' college for art and design because of its breadth of provision and its size. Sunderland, for example, had a good fine art department but little else, while the College could claim that it had 'textiles, we had book binding, we had illustration, graphic design... it made sense for us to be a regional college'.[78] But fine art was another matter. King's College had appointed its first professor in 1917 and dominated education in painting and sculpture by the 1950s with prestigious staff appointments such as Richard Hamilton and Victor Pasmore.[79]

The new Diploma courses attracted great interest, not least because of the small number of centres which had been approved by the National Council, and the College was only able to enrol half the number of students who applied. Fortunately, additional premises were secured in Ellison Place for fine art, fashion and general studies, and this must have helped to anchor the new programme of study. Meanwhile, the Education Committee approved the introduction of a School of Music which would offer both full-time and recreational study. Although the overall development of the College continued on an upward trajectory there were some problems along the way. The bid to secure approval for additional Diploma courses in Fine Art and Textiles/Fashion in 1964 was unsuccessful, and great concern was expressed at the low pass rate in the Department of Education and Science Art examinations. While the College and the Education Committee were able to console themselves that Newcastle candidates had exceeded the national average, there was a strong belief that such failures created additional hardship to students. Undaunted, the College began to contemplate engaging in postgraduate work and to that end an application was made to offer a Postgraduate Diploma in Industrial Design (Engineering). Most of all, the College had begun to look forward to the completion of the first instalment of the education precinct which would house the School of Printing and workshops for painting and decorating.[80] Proposals for additional dedicated accommodation, at an estimated cost of £567,454, had already been submitted for inclusion in the Further Education Major Building Programme for 1966–67.[81]

The Education Committee assumed a proactive role in establishing a partnership between regional businesses and the three colleges, and it is a measure of their commitment that they moved so quickly to set up governing bodies that included representatives from a broad spectrum of industries and professional institutions under the chairmanship of Sir Claude Gibb. This was an ideal conduit for securing the industrial placements which were so important to the success of sandwich courses at Rutherford College and, of course, helped their students to secure employment in the region. In 1957, the same rationale underpinned the creation of similarly constituted bodies to oversee the management of the College of Commerce and the School of Industrial Design. The governors had a wide remit and put their executive powers to immediate effect by setting up advisory committees which would offer advice and guidance about tailoring courses to industrial needs. They were able to provide a level of expertise and applied knowledge that endowed the colleges with certain key advantages. All three institutions were thus able to target their developmental work, secure more day release students and, in respect of the College of Commerce, begin to offer a range of research and consultancy services.

Bidding for CAT status

In the late 1950s, competition for CAT status across the region's college sector was fierce, precipitating intense lobbying by interested pressure groups, and this must raise the question of whether there was any undue partisanship in Rutherford's selection. Most historians would concede that measuring the extent of such influences is always tricky. What can be said here, however, is that since the chief criteria for re-designation were the ability to deliver advanced level courses and to engage in innovative technological research, Rutherford's claim for special recognition was certainly substantive. On that basis, it can be argued that the inevitable political manoeuvring was of marginal significance. Edward Short, a backbench MP for Newcastle Central at the time (and now Lord Glenamara) encouraged Quentin Hogg (later Lord Hailsham) to travel to Newcastle to see Rutherford College. Later the Minister reported to Short that he had sat next to the Principal at lunch and clearly had not thought much of him.[82] In 1958, when research into atomic energy was still at an experimental stage, major revisions were made to the building plans in order to dedicate space and resources to support specialist advanced courses in Nuclear and Reactor Physics, Radio Chemistry, Applied Chemistry and Mathematical Computers. With such state-of-the-art facilities in place, Rutherford was able to recruit greater numbers of postgraduate students and to engage in important collaborative work with King's College, Newcastle. The *Atom 58* exhibition, hosted jointly by the two institutions, set out to promote the positive uses of atomic power and was attended by over 10,000 visitors.[83] In the wake of the exhibition, plans to build a sub-critical water-moderated reactor were approved by the Ministry of Education, on the basis that the equipment would benefit not just one but several colleges in the region. The development of atomic power as a specialism had additional spin-offs too: Rutherford was called upon to provide courses in Reactor Technology and, to assuage growing public anxieties, Radiation Protection and Public Health. In a relatively short space of time, this led to a marked increase in the range of studies leading to the highly prized Diploma of Technology which many industrialists, with an eye to their own competitive advantages, then regarded as a more appropriate and valuable qualification than a degree.[84] Throughout the fifties, therefore, the Education Committee was at great pains to align developmental plans with the stated recommendations of the NCTA.

Given their elastic terms of reference the NCTA were not merely concerned with the delivery of courses. Creating the optimum educational, vocational and social environment in which students worked was recognised as essential to the pursuit of excellence, and so they strove to endow their new educational framework with an overall coherence. With this in mind, dedicated living accommodation for students was viewed as a high priority, in the belief that halls of residence conferred additional educative benefits, and all CATs were positively encouraged to make suitable provision. It has to be said, however, that their efforts were not entirely successful and most CATs outside London had great trouble securing the necessary finance. This was where Newcastle had a distinct advantage. One obvious outcome of the decision to consolidate educational resources on one major site was that incorporating living accommodation, libraries and leisure facilities was both physically feasible and cost-effective. Consequently, students at all three Newcastle colleges were unusually well resourced.[85] The first hostel for Rutherford College students, the Claude Gibb Hall of Residence, was opened in January 1965, at a cost of £202,547, with a commitment to build additional facilities into the city's long-term strategic plans. The one area of difficulty impeding this forward trajectory was the problem of recruiting suitably-qualified teaching staff. Notwithstanding the exemplary standard of course design and college facilities, in 1960 the NCTA withheld approval for the planned DipTech qualification in both Mechanical and Electrical Engineering and Applied Chemistry, insisting quite rightly that the appointment of quality staff was a non-negotiable prerequisite. At first, efforts were concentrated on releasing existing staff for specialist training but this process was much too protracted, and the college authorities soon realised that they would have to recruit more teachers with graduate and postgraduate qualifications.

The Annual Report of the Newcastle Education Committee for 1961–62 was deservedly upbeat: Rutherford College had met the guidelines on all fronts, even the graduate staff profile had improved dramatically, persuading the NCTA to reverse its earlier decision and validate the College's new raft of DipTech courses. Student successes in external and professional examinations also testified to the exacting standards that were being upheld. With so much effort expended in proving themselves worthy, and every reason to feel proud of what had been achieved in a few short years, the Committee were understandably dismayed when the Robbins Report (1963) decided against the creation of any further CATs. It seemed that all their hard work was to go unrewarded. Rutherford was not the only college in the region to lose out; Sunderland College of Technology had also been rebuffed and the governors of the two colleges had met to discuss the way forward in late 1962 and early 1963.[86] In the anxious weeks that followed, urgent representations were made to the Minister of Education, in a desperate bid to have Rutherford's CAT status ratified before the Robbins' proposals became official legislation, but to no avail. While Sir Edward Boyle readily acknowledged that remarkable progress had been made since 1957, and was not unsympathetic to the arguments presented by the Newcastle delegation, he was not prepared to deviate from the Report's recommendations. All he was prepared to concede was that there was a strong case for promoting a North East college to 'technological university status'.[87] That decision, however, was to rest with the UGC.

There was much to play for. Despite the apparent ambiguity of their ranking as an institutional hybrid which left them in an educational no-man's land – envied by the technical colleges and patronized by the universities – the Colleges of Advanced Technology were advantageously positioned by 1963. The perceived financial difficulties had been tackled in April 1962 when they became direct grant institutions and, as the Committee of Chancellors and Vice-Chancellors (CVCP) acknowledged, the quality of academic work, research activity, staff salaries and independent administrations were commensurate with that of the established universities. Recommendations by the national Taylor Committee that 'higher education should become synonymous with "universities"', and that selective colleges should be included in any future restructuring, proved highly influential.[88] The following year, when the Robbins Committee produced its own mandate for expanding higher education, it seemed to make perfect sense to begin by upgrading the CATs, not least because diversification was such a high priority. The Robbins Report specifically addressed the anomalous position of the CATs and the negative effect that this had, and would continue to have, on student numbers.[89] Fear of economic decline loomed large for, despite countless government initiatives, the percentage of students graduating in technology was still substantially lower than that of Britain's main competitors: West Germany, France, Sweden, Canada and the USA.[90] There is general agreement that radical measures had to be taken. The CATs, it was thought, might just be able to reverse the downward trend, though much would depend on whether their financial and professional status could be sufficiently improved. As Burgess and Pratt observed, the plan was little short of 'a revolution in academic thinking'.[91] With the approval of the CVCP, financial responsibility was transferred to the UGC in 1965 and by then re-designation procedures were well under way. The eleven existing CATs were expected to be awarded either university status in their own right or to amalgamate with an existing institution, and this is what happened: all but one of the CATs received their university charters in 1966, Chelsea became a constituent college of London University and Cardiff joined the federal University of Wales. The creation of six Special Institutions for Scientific and Technological Education and Research (SISTERS) was floated as an additional means of consolidating progress but the plan was later dropped. In their new guise as fully fledged members of the university fraternity, the CATs would have to bear the burden of responsibility.

To begin with, the majority of these newly created universities were deeply wedded to the idea of maintaining their existing strength in technological education, but only two of them, Bath and Loughborough, deliberately sought to distinguish themselves as universities *of technology*. In truth the pressure to conform proved an irresistible force and, as the popularity of the social sciences began to outstrip that of both pure and applied sciences, institutions had to compete with each other for their share of the UGC direct grant.[92] Expanding social sciences was the best bargaining counter for the technological universities but, naturally, this involved a significant shift away from the curriculum priorities envisaged by Robbins. Interestingly enough, the Robbins' Report had not ruled out further expansion of the university sector, intimating that there was 'scope' for elevating regional colleges with the capacity for advanced work.[93] But for those colleges, such as Rutherford, which had come so close to success, the future seemed bleak. The new hierarchy left them in an educational limbo and, as the pronouncements of the Labour government confirmed that plans to expand the university sector were to be abandoned, Rutherford's staff had every reason to feel cheated and demoralised.

Newcastle Education Committee had two alternatives: they could either continue to press for CAT/technological university status or to integrate Rutherford College with the University of Newcastle. The latter was recommended to the City Council and the Education Committee by the governors and, remarkably, it was accepted. The Committee remained concerned that Rutherford's part-time students, some 83 per cent of the student body, would be the losers if a merger took place. The University of Newcastle's principle objection to such a merger was that their staff might have to teach students at below degree level, and, worst of all, might have to teach in the evening if a full-blown merger took place. The city's main concern was that it would lose its brand new buildings, the latest equipment and its best, most highly qualified staff – all for a handful of full-time students. The work, staff and buildings that might be transferred were only in part complementary to what the university did – it had always had a strong practical and vocational bias towards the needs of regional industry. There surely could not be a case for two universities in the city at that time. Four further meetings were held, the last in October 1965 was adjourned following Secretary of State Anthony Crosland's Woolwich speech in the previous April that promulgated the binary idea for higher education.[94] The stalemate was eventually resolved in 1963 when King's College successfully separated itself from the University of Durham; from then on it had more pressing matters to attend to.[95] Councillor Abrahart was able to report to the Education Committee that 'we are becoming less disappointed that the negotiations failed... we are actually going to work out a scheme of a consortium of our own higher and further education colleges in the precinct... so that higher education will be possible not only in Rutherford but in other colleges as well'.[96] This was the beginning of the 'polytechnic idea' in Newcastle.

With all the wisdom that hindsight allows, it is possible to appraise the transitions of this period and be critical of the short-term thinking that constituted educational policy. Driven by economic objectives on the one hand and cultural snobbery on the other, it is hardly surprising that the progress of working class education should have run aground. Part-time courses, often the only programme of further study available to the working classes at that time, were neither needed nor favoured by the new universities; their overriding concern was to promote their shiny, new 'advantaged' credentials and gain acceptance as an equal partner. This is not to argue that improved working class provision had been a wholly cynical exercise, for what distinguished the post-war period was an attitudinal shift in favour of freeing up educational opportunities. Albeit briefly, the CATs had been in the vanguard of radical change, opening up new subject areas and creating access for an entirely new constituency of students. Their commitment to widening access is not at issue; what needs to be registered here is that the educational policy which created the CATs in the first place had an inbuilt aspirational rationale which made their evolution, and institutional conformity, inevitable. Beyond the question of access there is also some doubt as to their effectiveness as a mechanism for tackling the national deficit of qualified technologists. According to Burgess and Pratt they were not quite the success story they appeared to be: during the 10 year span of the 'experiment' the further education colleges had actually produced far more technologists than the CATs, despite the latter's advantaged position.[97] From their vantage point, writing in 1970, the authors were naturally prompted to draw comparisons with the creation of the polytechnics and to strike a warning note. In 1956 educational policy had been merely sketched out, with little thought for its consequences in the long-term, and they feared that the 1966 White Paper was similarly flawed. Education policy, they cautioned, was 'not so much a plan as a peroration... whatever comes, good or ill, will come by chance'.[98]

Prime Minister Harold Wilson arriving at the official opening of the Lipman Building with Derek Webster (then Chairman of the Education Committee) on 21 February 1975

Chapter Four

'Bullies at the centre, snobs at the periphery':[1]
the beginnings of the binary idea and
the Polytechnic, 1966–1979

The binary idea

The publication of the Robbins Report was unfortunate in its timing occurring as it did 12 months before the general election of October 1964. Both major parties gave considerable prominence to higher education in the build-up to the election and both made extravagant promises (see p.62) but only the victorious incoming Cabinet could translate these into practice. Labour's Taylor Report had advocated a massive expansion of the university system, Robbins had suggested 'only' six new universities but Wilson's new government was faced with a tiny majority and a Cabinet, with the exception of Wilson himself, with no experience of command, hardly appropriate for a party with radical ideas and fire in its belly. The Civil Service soon put a check on many of the overly ambitious schemes that ministers brought from their manifesto. In the case of higher education, Reg Prentice was given the task of drawing up a programme for the promised expansion of higher education.[2] His principal civil servant was Toby Weaver, the son-in-law of Sir Charles Trevelyan[3], Labour's first Education Minister in the 1920s, and a Department of Education and Science (DES) Deputy Secretary since 1962, who had been reared in local government with Essex County Council.[4] With local politicians clamouring for their share of any expansion[5] but at the same time not wishing to lose the 'investment' they had made in advanced further education, it may be that a local authority-controlled alternative to the autonomous university could be considered feasible. In Newcastle's case, its Education Committee had already turned towards some kind of comprehensive reorganisation of further education in the early 1960s, as we have shown. Is there a possibility that their ideas and those of similar cities aspiring to obtain university-like institutions could have influenced the DES and government thinking on the establishment of alternatives to the traditional university? With Wilson having such a slender majority and likely to have to face another general election in the near future, the support of the party machinery in the provincial cities was vital. There was a tension, of course, between those local authorities who wanted the prestige of having a university – perhaps mainly counties wishing to emulate the recent success of the 'Baedeker' county towns like York, Norwich and Lancaster – and the big cities like Manchester and Birmingham and some of the London Boroughs who had invested heavily in their further education infrastructure.

Hints that something other than the traditional university was in the offing came in 1964 and 1965. The Association of Teachers in Technical Institutions (ATTI), the further education lecturers' trade union, had produced an influential document supporting local authority control of a new sector. The Union's Edward Britton had drafted a paper for Prentice's group which 'broadly set out the policy eventually adopted, that is, a binary structure'[6]. In Newcastle, the council learned of what might be coming from its Westminster contacts. However, the key source was Tony Crosland's famous (infamous to some) Woolwich speech in which he announced what became known as the binary policy under which a series of new higher education institutions would be established as equal and parallel to the universities, controlled and funded through the local government system and not through the Treasury and the University Grants Committee (UGC). In the Woolwich speech and in the later Lancaster version Crosland set out Labour's thinking on these new colleges. In his view there were four key considerations: the increasing demand for vocational and professional courses which universities could not meet; universities should not have a monopoly of degree awarding powers; there was a need for a substantial part of higher education to be under social control responsive to social needs and lastly, there was a case for a parallel sector, equal but different. Clearly the government did not want the notion of autonomy to spread to the public sector even though there was already a blurring between the two parts. In addition, if the public sector was controlled more directly, it would be easier to grow than the largely independent universities. The relative expansion numbers from Robbins and the White Paper up to 1975 are shown in Table 1.

Table 1. Students in Higher Education ('000s)

	Universities	Colleges of Education	FE	Total
Robbins	346	146	66	558
White Paper	375	75	300	750

Sources: Robbins Report (1963); White Paper (1966).

At the time there was a strong suspicion that cost factors were important, an issue that has characterised higher education through to the present day.

This was not what Robbins had wanted. He advocated something of a 'seamless robe' of higher education in which it would be possible for technical and teacher training colleges to migrate over time to university status but 'the ladder from the technical college to paradise which Robbins had left leaning against the wall, still disturbed the educational world'.[7] Labour and the DES did not want drift towards the autonomous sector. In his Woolwich speech Crosland said, 'let us now move away from our snobbish caste-ridden hierarchical obsession with university status'.[8]

Lord Robbins' own response to the White Paper can be found *inter alia* in a speech to the House of Lords in 1965 where he reminded their lordships that he and his committee had wanted a flexible system but 'because the abracadabra of this precious binary system prevents transfer, all suggestions for union are ruled out'.[9] He believed that parity of esteem between the university and the public sector was impossible to achieve. The binary system would produce 'an educational caste system, more rigid and hierarchical than before... I am confident that the system as presently conceived, is not ultimately viable'.[10] It was a course of action 'which can bring no pleasure or benefit to any but a few snobs at the centre and bullies at the periphery'.

Soon after the publication of the White Paper, thirty of these '*polytechnics*'* were identified, twenty-nine in England and one in Wales, dependent in some cases upon neighbouring authorities working together to produce a common scheme. Newcastle had a number of immediate advantages: it was a single authority, it had three colleges capable of providing the broad, comprehensive curriculum the White Paper called for, and it had already begun to develop a central site to accommodate them. These new colleges, insisted Edward Short, 'should remain the tip of an educational pyramid within the FE system... any kind of progression from the LEA system into a university... would be completely alien to the concept'.[11] The Labour government expected the polytechnics to follow the lead set by the myriad of post-war reports that we have identified that advocated the need for trained manpower in order to improve economic performance. However, by the mid-1960s the national economic and social contexts were changing. Polytechnic development came at a time when the structure of the economy was rapidly shifting from manufacturing to service industries: Britain's manufacturing employment reached its historical peak in 1966.[12] At the same time the

* There is some debate about the origin of the term 'polytechnic' as used here. It is often ascribed to Toby Weaver (qv) but in a recent obituary of Ben Pimlott by Kenneth O Morgan (*The Guardian*, 12 April 2004) it is claimed that J. A. R. Pimlott, his father, a civil servant, invented the term. Eric Robinson (qv) also has a claim, some say. However, the term dates back to at least revolutionary France when the Ecole Polytechnique was established in 1795. It seems to have been first used in England by Quentin Hogg in connection with the college in Regent Street that he founded. Following the passing of the City of London Parochial Charities Act of 1883 various other polytechnics were established in London including those at Kilburn and Chiswick. After 1966 many of these were obliged to drop the title. In April 1840 Newcastle held a Polytechnic Exhibition of works of art and engineering. (See *Allan's Illustrated Edition of Tyneside Songs*, (Newcastle: T. & G. Allan, 1891) – *A glance at Polly Technic*, by Thomas Wilson, p.273.)

idea of higher education was moving from its 'classical' origins, including the small number of traditional vocational fields such as medicine, to embrace much newer areas such as the liberal arts and the social sciences on a much larger scale. After '*les evenements*' of 1968 students were less willing to accept what was offered by the academy but wanted increasingly to explore and express their own ideas. So that in addition to the conventional bourgeois emphasis on vocationalism, the professions and employability many students wanted to examine wider themes and ideas in the humanities, art and above all, the social sciences. This was not the government's preference, of course. The largely public school- and Oxbridge-educated front bench of Wilson's government that had set up the new colleges saw their future – if they saw one at all – in vocational education, taking a narrow view of what was necessary for preparing young people for the world of work. Over the next decade students and staff in polytechnics were to take a rather more liberal view of what they wanted to see in the colleges' shop windows. Similarly, the Crosland-Weaver idea of the polytechnics being 'equal but different' to the universities was not to last. In 20 years there would still be differences between the institutions but the gap would be closing from both ends. In the 14 years covered by this chapter, the seeds of this closure were being sown.

The key to any kind of course development likely to reflect the emerging curriculum of the polytechnics lay in their relation to the Council for National Academic Awards (CNAA). The Robbins report had said, 'in other colleges (other than CATs) a new system of degrees should be established, covering business studies, languages and other subjects as well as science and technology', giving a new impetus to vocational higher education in the UK.[13] Labour was able to accept this element of the report. The CNAA's immediate future was symbiotically bound up with the polytechnics because Crosland and the DES expected most of the growth of higher education to be in public sector colleges, which of course, had no degree awarding powers. At the same time the CNAA had to be aware of the sensitivities in dealing with local authority controlled colleges, that is, non-autonomous bodies often subject to political interference, a treatment that had to be 'somewhere between stringent paternalism and laissez-faire flexibility'[14], '…operating in the interstices of a status-ridden and status conscientious higher education system'.[15] At the time of the White Paper, CNAA was considering 136 proposals but approving only 40 per cent of them. Many colleges found their methods difficult to come to terms with and CNAA reciprocally often found colleges dominated by their Directors and senior management, with barely democratic academic boards, sometimes interfered with by local authorities, with poor facilities and buildings, operating on many sites. There was a clear need to raise standards which, it was thought, would be best achieved in an increasingly autonomous, self-managed organisation. This approach was perhaps not surprising given the fact that in its early years CNAA was characterised by a membership drawn largely from traditional universities where things were done differently. Even as early as 1971 the Council was beginning the long process of encouraging polytechnics to develop greater independence and freedom. The next chapter will show how this developed in Newcastle's case, eventually leading to accreditation – the next best thing to degree-awarding powers – being granted in the mid-1980s.

In addition to the conversion of the DipTechs and DipADs to honours degrees, some of Newcastle Polytechnic's earliest successful submissions to CNAA were Business Studies (1970), Law (1970), English and History (1973), Quantity and General Practice Surveying (1974) and parts of the Combined Studies programme and Geography (1977). By 1979 there were fifty-four CNAA degrees operating in the Polytechnic, the overwhelming majority at undergraduate level.

In the next chapter we will show that this was a period of remarkable curriculum development, an era of introducing a wider range of courses in the polytechnics, but it was also a period in which Newcastle Polytechnic was to show to many of its fellow institutions, that it was not necessary to be a dependent institution for the ownership and quality of awards. On reflection this was a very rapid move towards 'maturity'. Even though CNAA was only established in 1963, by 1975 Newcastle Polytechnic had pioneered 'partnership in validation' and by 1984 had acquired institutional accreditation, to all intents and purposes awarding its own first degrees and soon after, higher research degrees. This link between course and curriculum development, the degree awarding body and rising demands for increased autonomy and a greater parity of esteem with universities, forms a central theme in the evolution of British higher education in the second half of the twentieth century. On to this foundation was laid new leadership, acumen and foresight from the top of the Polytechnic, and innovation, vision and flexibility from nearer the bottom but, as Eric Robinson has pointed out, 'the growth of the public sector was a huge triumph not for the DES or the local authorities but for the teachers in what were the 'techs'… those in power played the role of sleepwalkers'.[16] But in Newcastle Polytechnic both management and staff were characterised by sheer hard work and often, dogged bloody-mindedness.

Newcastle's fledgling polytechnic

The newly appointed first Director of the Polytechnic was George Bosworth, a Cambridge trained engineer who had become head of personnel at English Electric, a major British electrical engineering company with its principal plants in Stafford and Rugby. He was a good example of the limited value of so-called vocational education. His early training was in engineering but he spent 22 years in the world of personnel management. He was a member of the Institute of Electrical Engineers and the Institute of Mechanical Engineering but had no professional qualification in personnel work. He was not an academic but had acquired an expertise in 'training', author of the Bosworth Report on engineer training.[17] Harold Wilson, the Chancellor of Bradford University – one of the CATs elevated to university status following Robbins and itself a college with a strong practical and vocational emphasis – awarded him an honorary doctorate to go with his Cambridge MA. He never discouraged the staff at Newcastle from calling him 'doctor' but it was not strictly necessary. On appointment his first task was to acquaint himself with the arcane practices of further education and local government; in this he had to rely on senior staff in the pre-polytechnic colleges.

In his first interim report from the Academic Board to the Polytechnic Council, Bosworth, in a paper on the forthcoming decade (1969–79) planned for a student population of 7,000 FTEs, on the city centre site (the Precinct) with a focus on education for the professions,[18] the latter something of a nineteenth century idea for the education of the middle classes. For the newly formed Polytechnic to accomplish these aims it would have to begin by overseeing the merger of the three colleges and setting up the necessary management structure. For this he would require the services of a first-rate administrator to assist him. While Rutherford College may have developed considerable 'advanced' work, and as we have seen, had aspirations to become a CAT and hence a university, the same could not be said for the other two colleges, Art and Industrial Design and the Municipal College of Commerce. They were much more rooted in the traditions of *further* education than higher education.

The art college had with some difficulty begun diploma courses in 1969[19] but just prior to the Polytechnic's formation still had household painting and decorating and elementary printing courses;[20] now, 'its preoccupation with craft gave way to a world of ideas'.[21] In this it was to echo what Rutherford College had begun in the 1950s, the teacher training colleges in the 1970s and nurse education in the 1990s, that is, moving from a training-based system to one characterised by more liberal educational values. The move of art and design education into the polytechnics did not meet with universal approval. A joint committee of Sir William Coldstream's National Advisory Committee on Art Education and Sir John Summerson's National Committee for Diplomas in Art and Design (NCDAD) had reported in 1970 to the new Secretary of State, Margaret Thatcher. They recommended that design technician and fine art foundation courses locate in the further education colleges, leaving the polytechnics and other advanced art colleges to pursue DipAD routes with their five 'O' Level entry requirement.[22] One implication of this new diploma was that it would attract student grants so that for the first time art and design in the Polytechnic could recruit nationally. Just over a year later the art education world was again split following a scathing attack on what he called the 'polytechnicisation' of art colleges by the distinguished painter, Patrick Heron. He and many members of the NCDAD fine art panel including amongst others, Professor Lawrence Gowing, Tom Hudson, Jonah Jones, Euan Uglow, Professor Claude Rogers and Professor Kenneth Rowntree, resigned. In a letter to *The Guardian* they pointed to 'the loss of art college autonomy and the departmental splintering resulting from the incorporation of colleges into polytechnics'. They were also concerned with the deleterious effects merger would have on the remaining free-standing art schools.[23] Over the next 2 weeks a stream of letters was published by *The Guardian*. Hubert Dalwood, one of the resigning members said of the polytechnics: 'they are too big, too static, too institutional, too degree orientated, and too stupid to ever be the natural habitat of practicing artists and designers…'.[24] In reply some others noted the errors in Heron's piece and many wrote in pointing to the autocratic rather than autonomous nature of many of the old style art schools. What really seemed to worry Heron and his colleagues was the danger that the use of practicing artists as visiting or part-time lecturers in the new polytechnics would be reduced. Many believed that it was their presence that had promoted British art education to a leading position in the world in the 1960s. The truth was that the merger experience was variable across the country. In Newcastle the evidence seems to point to the benefits of amalgamation. Professor Bromly thought it a 'logical' solution even though the division of the work meant that about 50 per cent of the old college's staff and students went to the city's further education college.[25] Certainly under Bromly the Faculty of Art and Design went on to be one of the most powerful and comprehensive of the polytechnic schools nationally.

The College of Commerce had begun a London University external general arts degree on a part-time basis in 1967 and similar courses in law and economics, but its strength lay in preparing people for professional examinations. Just prior to 1969 – indeed to pave the way for its higher level work – the College of Commerce too had shed many of its lower level courses. In 1968 the governors approved transferring evening courses for commercial travellers and technical representatives and for 'intermediate grocers'.[26] The college did have a good reputation for 'A' Level teaching by staff with more academic aspirations. Some of the more academic staff, however, had transferred within the authority to the city's training colleges when they expanded in the mid-60s and some had gone on to university posts. One area of the college that had a national reputation was the School of Librarianship founded in 1947, but even here part-time courses for local people made up a significant part of its effort.[27] At the time of the merger the College of Commerce was preparing submissions to CNAA in law, business studies, economics, information science and modern studies (humanities).

In Rutherford on the eve of the Polytechnic's formation the position was somewhat more advanced. In its striving for CAT status the local authority had not only invested heavily in new, modern buildings south of Northumberland Road but they had also poured money into first class laboratories and equipment. The college had developed DipTech courses at an early stage, although its various forays into external degree work were not always successful as we have seen. Engineering, physics, chemistry and surveying courses were complemented, rather curiously, by a specialism in sociology, Rutherford being one of the more successful colleges nationally preparing students for the London University external degree. This had grown out of its liberal studies work, a recently required aspect to the curriculum for all scientists and technologists following the reforms to NCAT led by Lord Hives.[28] The foresight for this development had come from Col. James Grant, a teacher with the city for many years in various schools and colleges but who eventually became head of Rutherford's Department of Social and Community Studies.[29] Between 1962 and 1972 over 400 students graduated in sociology but the course was not without its difficulties. On one occasion in 1965 the core of staff resigned and went elsewhere precipitating something of a crisis. One of the new staff hurriedly appointed in the summer of that year was Monica Shaw who had not yet even graduated from Sheffield University, such was the urgency to plug the gap.[30] Monica went on to spend her whole career at the Polytechnic and University retiring in 2003 as Dean of the Faculty of Social Sciences. One of the last graduates of the London University external course was Robin Smith who in 1972 obtained the highest marks in the country for this award in his year of graduation.[31] Robin, after service at Durham University Business School, returned to his alma mater as a professor and eventually, Head of the Carlisle Campus.

Filling academic posts generally, then, was to be a challenge for the Polytechnic management in its first few years. Robbins had estimated that if higher education was to grow at the rate he predicted then:

> '20% of all graduates of 1960 would be needed to staff the expansion of higher education. Inevitably less well qualified staff were taken on and… they were to remain in the system for 40 years.'[32]

Secretary of State Shirley Williams calculated in 1965 that 50 per cent of all 'good' graduates would be needed to teach the expanded HE provision being proposed, at a ratio of 8:1.[33] Robbins had predicted that student numbers would increase from 328,000 in 1967 to 392,000 in 1973 but with only 12.5 per cent of the increase to be in the local authority sector. This proved to be an underestimate. As higher education in *all* sectors was expanding so a hierarchy of staff recruitment began to develop with older universities recruiting from younger ones and younger ones from the non-autonomous sector.[34] The 1966 White Paper expected staff would have a background in professional experience rather than in the academy. This was largely true for some of the original core such as business and the professions but as the humanities, social sciences and fine art were added so staff with more traditional academic backgrounds and the attendant higher degrees were appointed.[35] In science and some parts of engineering, Rutherford staff were especially well qualified academically.

Despite the fact that Newcastle was somewhat ahead of the field in polytechnic formation in 1969–70, and despite its inheritance of relatively new buildings from Rutherford College and the College of Commerce, Bosworth reported that much of the Polytechnic's work was located in poor quality accommodation outside the precinct.[36] Carlton House in Jesmond Road remained an active centre for work in business and commerce, Clayton Road was the major locus for art and design and 1 Ellison Place (formerly the Mansion House), 54 Northumberland Road and various other outposts were leased by the city on behalf of the Polytechnic. Such buildings were to be used for a number of years and new short-term leases or purchases were added. One such was the Government Buildings within the proto-campus and Cambridge Hall in Northumberland Road. The former, Bosworth suggested, might be used for a students' union, the latter as an annexe for the recently completed library that was already too small. Government Buildings had been a centre for the fitting of artificial limbs and false eyes. Eventually it was to house sociology and it is said that the head of subject retained samples of the latter to keep an eye on his staff. Cambridge Hall had been a warehouse for British Road Services. This use of such rather bizarre buildings may seem strange now but it was not at all uncommon for institutions of higher education to be accommodated thus. Hull and Keele Universities used Nissen huts for some years after the Second World War. At least the embryo-polytechnic in Newcastle had the advantage of being developed by one authority – many others were managed by two or three, such as Middlesex which was scattered among many sites along the North Circular Road. Or Thames, which eventually, as the University of Greenwich, was to consist of twenty sites spread over 500 square miles of south east London.[37] For the Director of Newcastle Polytechnic and his chief administrative officer to deal with only one LEA was to give them an enormous advantage, especially as that authority was so supportive in the early years.

One of the key figures in this link with the local authority was Ron Hopkinson, the Polytechnic's first Chief Administrative Officer. Hopkinson had a first class honours degree from Birmingham University in geography and geology and after service in the RAF he had gone into local government. He came to Rutherford College in 1959 and he recalls[38] that bureaucratic services in the three colleges were rudimentary with only a few clerks in each one; the local authority had done little to assist. In 1963 he moved to become an assistant education officer with North Riding County Council, rising to be deputy chief education officer, then returning to Newcastle and the proto-polytechnic in 1969. He brought with him not only a memory of earlier days at Rutherford but by then considerable seniority and 'know how' in the mysterious ways of local government administration. His perception was that the LEA saw the merger of the three colleges as a means of saving on administrative staffing. He recognised that sophisticated administrative machinery would have to be created if Bosworth's vision was to be realised. In the early 1970s this entailed drawing up articles of governance, establishing the academic structure of the Polytechnic and making estimates of future expenditure.

Maintaining links with the city's education department needed to be done from a position of increasing autonomy. This tension between the two was to remain finely balanced. Crosland and Weaver, as architects of the binary policy for higher education, had decided that the so-called public sector was to remain under the control of local government, part of the 'national service, locally delivered' that was education. As we have seen there had been discussion in Wilson's first and second governments as to whether or not the 'autonomous' sector of higher education – the universities and a few directly funded institutions – should be the model for expansion. Once it was decided this should not be the case, then in future, all polytechnics were to depend to a greater or lesser degree, on relations with their local authority.

The further education colleges that had become the Polytechnic were funded by the Advanced Further Education (AFE) Pool set up in 1958; a lucrative source for those authorities that had a polytechnic, since all authorities contributed and fewer than forty took substantial sums out. A major task then, for Newcastle, was to learn how best to fish in this pool. The LEA had obviously developed some experience here in the development of the precinct, 33 per cent of the new College of Commerce building (Northumberland Building phase I) had been financed from this source.[39] The government's vision was that the councils of the polytechnics would be at arms length from the local (funding) authority, the assumption being that polytechnic estimates, once agreed, would be passed to the college. However, much of the revenue funding for higher education in a local authority was bundled up with all other expenditure for education, for example, for primary and secondary schools. It would be left to the LEA to decide how much its polytechnic was to receive each year. In many authorities up and down the country there was little certainty that they would receive their proper dues. In the case of Newcastle, this was rarely the case. The key to this success lay with the chairs of the Education Committee and of the Polytechnic Council, and the political pressure they could exercise on colleagues and officers in the authority.

Newcastle Polytechnic was fortunate in having Dr Cyril Lipman as Chairman of the city's Education Committee from 1968 to 1974, and Vice-Chairman of the Polytechnic Council from its inception; (the Right Hon. Viscount Ridley was appointed the first chairman). The City Council was Tory controlled for all of this period. Lipman had a background in higher education, a man with a PhD in chemistry and formerly a lecturer at Trinity College, Dublin. He was in power when the polytechnics were being promulgated and in presenting a report to the Education Committee in September 1967 he had said:

> '… I consider two things in that an institution that awards degrees should be master of its own destiny; purely and simply, they should decide what courses, how they are controlled and what degrees should be put forward… we must work as hard as possible to give every encouragement to the Polytechnic, so that it becomes a university, a technological university, an institution of university status as soon as possible'.[40]

Although his sentiments were not those of Short (quoted p.69), Labour members did not demur from them. Above all, it was clear that Lipman was going to give his support to the fledgling institution – and in such a way for it to be on a considerably long leash from its local authority. His influence was to be considerable. As Chairman of the Education Committee he had overseen the appointment of Bosworth and the establishment of the Polytechnic's governing body, its Council. Although he was out of office after 1974 his influence remained substantial so much so that he later became chairman of the governors under a Labour Council.

Lipman and the Tories were succeeded by a Labour Council in 1974 following the reorganisation of local government and the establishment of the new metropolitan boroughs. The new Chairman of the Education Committee was Derek Webster, not only the youngest member of the City Council but also at twenty-six, the youngest leader of an LEA nationally. Webster was Head of Humanities at a North Tyneside high school. He had already served as an opposition member on the Polytechnic Council under Lipman and his translation ensured a continuous commitment to Polytechnic as remaining politically neutral. He and his colleagues immediately set in train an ambitious plan for the city's education service, including a longer term aim of providing free and on-demand nursery places for everyone in Newcastle. For the Polytechnic Webster was adamant that funds should continue to flow across Sandyford Road to support the institution he passionately supported. In some LEAs there was a tension between them and their polytechnics which, of course, had a national role, drawing many of their students from all parts of the country and abroad. For 20 years chief education officers, chairmen of education committees and of polytechnic councils had to tread a politically careful path between their various constituents. In Newcastle, under Webster and Lipman, their commitment to Newcastle Polytechnic offered a more generous underpinning to its continuing success.[41] Many a polytechnic director elsewhere looked enviously northwards on Bosworth's and later Barden's experiences.

Webster did not automatically become Chairman of Polytechnic Council, that office was held by Lord Wynne-Jones, who had succeeded Viscount Ridley, but who spent much of his time away from Newcastle. Webster suggested to him the he should become the first Chancellor of the Polytechnic instead, to which he agreed. Webster was then able to occupy the more powerful position of Chairman, as well as being Chairman of the Education Committee.[42]

By 1972 Bosworth could report that student numbers had risen to nearly 3,500 FTEs (over 7,000 actual registered students) taught by 540 academic staff supported by 116 technicians and 148 administrative staff. Alex Bell who had been Principal of the College of Commerce and Cecil Smith formerly Principal of the College of Art and Industrial Design – both of whom had been appointed Assistant Directors to Bosworth in 1968–69 – announced their retirement. Bell was perhaps the last of the old school of college principals. He wore a bowler hat and stout boots and could often be found at lunch times in the Northumberland Arms lunching on a pork pie and pint of Exhibition bitter. Smith was rather a more remote figure, who seemed perhaps a little out of his depth as his college moved from craft-based courses into the world of fine art. Both men had given unstinted service and helped Bosworth lay a realistic foundation to the Polytechnic.

The new deputy

This presented the opportunity to create the post of Deputy Director; filling it was more problematic. Twenty-nine people applied including three internal heads of department but the shortlist of six did not include any of them. A Dr J. Banfield of Sheffield was appointed as from 1 September 1973 but a Polytechnic Council minute noted:

> '...the circumstances resulting in the chairman, Alderman Dr C. Lipman, on behalf of the council, withdrawing the appointment... confirmed the action taken and agreed that the post of deputy director be re-advertised'.[43]

There is no record of why this action was taken. In its papers for October 1973 the Polytechnic Council gives a shortlist of five persons (no women) from fifty-two applications for the re-advertised post, including two internal candidates. This time the job was offered to Dr Terence Burlin of Central London Polytechnic who initially accepted but then declined the post. Eventually Professor Laing Barden of Strathclyde University accepted the post.[44] Derek Webster recalled, however, that the appointment committee was not convinced at the time the new deputy would ever become the Director.[45]

Barden's own recollection of these events accords with the record. He admits that he knew 'not a bean' (about polytechnics), 'I didn't know what the word (polytechnic) meant' but he was 'very, very happy to have a much broader job than running an engineering department or faculty' as he had at Strathclyde. He was also pleased to return to his native North East. He had been at grammar school in Washington, County Durham and had taken his first degrees at Newcastle University, then King's College, Durham. Essentially he was a researcher rather than a teacher with considerable university experience at Liverpool and Manchester as well as Strathclyde. For some years he was the only member of staff to have a higher doctorate (DSc) given for published work. Over the next 25 years or so Barden was to have a dramatic effect on the Polytechnic and subsequently the early University. In his first few years he was a flamboyant character, often restless and impatient, not an administrator nor someone who delved into the niceties of financial matters. He was sometimes rather careless with the spoken word and less concerned with administrative detail than he might have been. Sitting still was often something he found difficult. But he did know what made people tick and recognised early on that he should harness the energy and expertise of others. Although trained as a 'rational' engineer, when it came later to management of the Polytechnic he relied strongly on his powerful academic instinct and what he would often call 'a feeling in his waters'. He came with little knowledge of the wider political processes but soon learnt the necessity of cultivating contacts in 'high places', something that probably took considerable courage given his acknowledged social awkwardness. He wrote few papers on his particular philosophy for the Polytechnic but, as we shall see, he was to lead Newcastle Polytechnic to a position of national eminence in its field, a man to be judged by his achievements rather than his style. All of these were symptoms of his restless energy, his deep-felt desire to 'get things done' and his total commitment to the institution. Nearly everyone he worked with at Newcastle showed him considerable loyalty, was prepared to support him and follow his vigorous lead.

Building the precinct

One of the more daunting tasks facing the Polytechnic in the early 1970s was expanding its real estate. Because the city had been prescient in establishing the further education precinct under T. Dan Smith and Wilfred Burns, it seemed so much easier to persuade the DES of the Polytechnic's future building requirements in February 1972. The 26 acres of land were available and adaptable buildings were nearby. Among the new buildings proposed in 1972 were Northumberland Building phases 3 and 4 (the latter to be known as the Radnor Building) – a replacement for Northumberland Road School (known as the Northumberland Annexe and still being used at the time of writing), the acquisition of the Sandyford Building of the college of further education (and also still being used by them today!), an extension to Ellison Building and Stage 4 of the halls of residence complex. Meanwhile, the Students' Union and the Sports Hall were opened in February. Phase 2 of Northumberland Building, although well underway, was to be delayed until 1974 largely thanks to a builders' strike. The library 'tower' was put into the starts programme for completion in 1975. To accommodate the rapid growth in student numbers the city had acquired Pandon Building from the North East Electricity Board in 1972 and Cambridge Hall from British Road Services. In addition, St George's Drill Hall was taken over but would not be available for use until 1974–75 when new facilities for the Territorial Army were opened on the east side of the motorway. Negotiations were underway with the University of Newcastle for the purchase of the Dental School (now Sutherland Building) in 1976 on the corner of College Street and Northumberland Road.

The Faculty of Art and Design, rather like the College of Commerce, had been scattered over many buildings in Chillingham Road, Ellison Place and Bath Lane as well as its base in Clayton Road. By 1972 it was able to move into the precinct to the brand new and purpose built Squires Building.[46] Clayton Road was, in turn, soon occupied by the expanding Department of Management Studies which moved out from Rutherford. Other stop-gap buildings included St Dominic's school in Sandyford (for education and sports studies) and 2 Ellison Place.[47]

New courses

On the academic front a new BA (Hons) in English and History was approved by CNAA to begin in September 1973. This was the Polytechnic's first degree-level venture in the humanities, a move that 30 years later was to culminate in many more students reading for degrees in arts and social sciences than the 'founding fathers' had envisaged for such institutions. On more traditional technological grounds a new MSc in Materials Engineering was also approved. A truly pioneering venture was the approval of a 4 year BA degree in nursing at a time when very few universities or polytechnics had such a course and when the thought of graduate nurses was looked on with some reservation, especially by doctors. Within 20 years most universities – and most doctors – had followed where Newcastle helped lead.

1972–76: enter the teacher training colleges

The great national event in higher education in 1972 was the publication of the James Report on teacher education[48] and the White Paper that followed it. Because of the impact of the subsequent reform of the training of teachers on the Polytechnic they are worthy of detailed treatment, particularly from a national perspective.

As we have seen in an earlier chapter teacher training came rather late on the scene of higher education. From its beginnings in the early nineteenth century, through the expansion of church-based colleges in the 1840s to 1860s and up to the McNair Report of 1944,[49] teacher training had been just that, 'training' based on apprenticeship notions. In the post-Second World War period there arose an increasing demand for a broader and more liberal 'educational' foundation to the courses. Numbers being trained in colleges in the late 1950s and early '60s rose rapidly and colleges expanded considerably to accommodate demand. This demand was largely in response to a rising school population following the 1944 Education Act, the raising of the school leaving age to fifteen in 1947 and a rising birth-rate. The ready 'supply' to complement this demand came from increasing numbers staying on in sixth forms and a growing desire amongst young people, especially women, for access to higher education. A shortage of teachers in the late '50s resulted from a second post-war bulge in school populations. The Robbins Report, which it should be remembered was concerned with higher education as a whole, and not just universities, recognised that the 3 year teacher training certificate introduced in 1960 was already bringing the colleges more into line with degree courses in universities. His report recommended that teacher training colleges should be absorbed into the higher education system properly as part of Schools of Education, based on universities so that students could receive a degree in education. We have seen that Wilson's incoming Labour government in 1964 was more than hesitant about accepting Robbins' ideas for university expansion; so it was also with teacher training colleges. Michael Stewart, the first Labour minister for education would not permit the reform of financing and administration of the colleges, but he did accept the idea of the BEd degree. Stewart was not to last long in this post and was replaced by the Oxford intellectual Anthony Crosland. Another Oxford man, Richard Crossman, records in his diary Wilson as saying about the replacement of Stewart, 'If we can't have Jenkins (who had already turned down the job), let's have Crosland', and later 'You'll laugh, Dick, but when I talked to him (Stewart) he said he felt like crying at having to leave education'.[50] Crosland, like many in that first Labour Cabinet was ambitious for success: he was 'adventurous, enthusiastic and confident like a man who feels a strong horse between his knees'.[51] The training colleges immediately gave him a problem he could get his teeth into. In April 1965 he introduced a fourteen-point plan to try to solve the teacher shortage, a problem which was about to be aggravated because the Newsome Report[52] was about to recommend that the school leaving age be raised again, to sixteen, in 1970. The post-war bulge was continuing but about one third of the teachers recruited left the service; the colleges had to expand. Crosland proposed doubling the numbers of places in the 8 years from 1965, to be accomplished largely by increasing throughput and output from the existing colleges, a crash programme that also involved setting up new day colleges, including the City College in Newcastle. By 1967–68 the colleges had expanded to a massive total of nearly 95,000 students, nearly 20,000 more than Robbins' estimate. By 1969 over 43,000 students entered training colleges and university postgraduate courses in education, 16,000 above Crosland's 1965 recommendations.

By the mid-1960s the teacher training sector was dominated by local authority colleges – 108 out of a total of 161 in England and Wales.[53] The LEAs' concern for higher education was considerably boosted by Crosland and Weaver's White Paper of 1966 setting up polytechnics. It is worth noting that in their proposals that five new departments of education were to be established in polytechnics, though not one in Newcastle. David Henke[54] saw all this as an opportunity for the no-man's land between universities and training colleges to be occupied by a rapidly expanding local authority sector of higher education. Universities which oversaw the schools of education set up in 1964 never really regarded their BEd degrees, awarded only in local colleges, as their own. Many universities thought such courses lacked academic rigour but in contradistinction to the degrees now awarded under the aegis of a university – and thereby having greater cachet – the colleges began to attract a new generation of staff, often with masters degrees and doctorates. These new men and women saw themselves, not as elevated school teachers passing on their skills to 'apprentices', but more like university lecturers. In social terms many of them came from their own schooling in public and grammar schools but with little experience of the secondary moderns and comprehensives for which they were preparing their charges.

Against this background Edward Short, appointed Secretary of State for Education in April 1968 in succession to the ill-fated Patrick Gordon Walker, launched an inquiry into the training college curriculum in 1970. A parliamentary select committee also began to examine teacher education. Although the civil service at the DES saw little need for change, pressure elsewhere was mounting and the Tory opposition gave a pledge for an inquiry into teacher education should they come to power in the 1970 general election. When to most people's surprise they did, they honoured that pledge and set up a committee under Lord James of Rusholme, the Vice-Chancellor of York University, formerly High Master of Manchester Grammar School and one of the most ardent defenders of the grammar school in the 1940s.

It is not possible in a local university history such as this to go into James' Report in great detail but its salient points are worth noting. In the end many of his recommendations were ignored by Edward Heath's Conservative government and the Secretary of State for Education, Margaret Thatcher. His committee was given a fairly wide remit and therein lay its weakness. Commentators at the time, and later, have suggested that James went too far in his examination of the need for the reform of higher education as a whole, at a time when the civil servants had other ideas, as probably did the Secretary of State. James proposed a three cycle system: a new award – a Diploma in Higher Education (DipHE) – and/or a 3 year degree in Education with the possibility of an Honours degree in 4 years; from a college's original cohort those intending to be teachers would take professional training both in college and in school, leading to licensed teacher status. The probationary year was to be replaced by 'induction' in a school. Thirdly, there was to be an in-service award leading to a master's degree in education. Although James suggested a new National Council to award these diplomas and degrees, he was not opposed to universities and the CNAA offering them too.

His proposals were not exactly greeted with unalloyed joy. Indeed, Hencke says they were 'almost condemned out of hand, the radical and fundamental reform was blocked from the beginning'[55] for a variety of reasons, first amongst which was James' attempt to reform too much of higher education – new DipHEs, 2 year degrees, a National Council – alongside the reform of the colleges. More significantly his scheme would have isolated teacher education from the rest of higher education, creating a third, inferior, tier to the universities and polytechnics. However, there is some evidence to suggest that James' ideas were doomed before they were broadcast. Hencke[56] notes that

James' proposals were predicated on the expansion of teacher education that began in the 1960s continuing, but what if school rolls started to fall, particularly if they were to fall dramatically? Harding and Weaver, the two senior civil servants in the DES, may have been aware of this from population projections they had access to but few members of James' Committee were as well informed; the final report does not hint of this possibility. If the numbers qualifying as teachers were to fall and the colleges had more and more of their students taking non-education courses then there was a case for 'ending the distinction between teacher education and further education'.[57] Teacher training colleges would simply not be able to compete with their more prestigious neighbours in universities and polytechnics. The previous expansion of teacher training had given the colleges, or was in the process of giving the colleges, considerably more 'plant' in the form of teaching accommodation, libraries and halls of residence; this could not be allowed to be left idle. It did not take a great deal of imagination to suggest that a rationalisation of higher education might be achieved by merging this sector with one or possibly two of the other sectors. This brings us nicely to the 1972 White Paper on education.

Margaret Thatcher was appointed Secretary of State for Education in June 1970. Prior to becoming leader of her party and Prime Minister she had two claims to fame: one was as 'milk snatcher' who was said to have abolished free milk in schools (not actually true); the second was for the reforms set out in the White Paper of 1972, the first major policy statement on education of Edward Heath's government. When the Paper was published it revealed that numbers in higher education were to rise to 750,000 (full-time and sandwich students) by 1981, an increase in the participation rate of 18-year-olds from 7 per cent in 1961 to 15 per cent in 1971 to 22 per cent in 1981. The policy was to deal with the scale, organisation and cost of higher education rather than its content, topics close to Tories' and Thatcher's hearts. It soon became clear that as far as the colleges of education were concerned the DES and the James Committee had somewhat different views as to their future role. Instead of implementing James' proposals for a third sector, the Paper did indeed announce a merger of the colleges with polytechnics and further education colleges and an increase in higher education numbers largely outwith the universities. The polytechnics, including the numbers from the merged colleges, were to expand from 66,000 students in 1971 to 180,000 in 1981.[58] Numbers undergoing teacher training were to fall from 114,000 in 1971–72 to 60–70,000 in 1981.[59] By 1981 the universities would contain half of all higher education students, the remainder in the public sector. To achieve this reduction in the colleges of education rationalisation was required. The White Paper said that many of the 160 colleges were too small or in the wrong place. There was a need for some to close, especially the more isolated rural ones. In urban areas mergers between colleges of all types, including a small minority with universities, were outlined. Circular 7/73 showed thirty-seven merging with their local polytechnic and twenty-four with further education colleges to form new colleges of higher education. There were to be twenty-six mergers between two or more colleges of education, twelve amalgamated with universities, leaving only twenty-seven as free-standing colleges. Twenty-five were to close. David Hencke has written that 'the *problem* of the colleges was to be solved by almost abolishing them as a significant sector'; this was 'a plan to reorganise higher education into a *firm binary system*'.[60] In the debate in the House of Commons Roy Hattersley said that the polytechnics were to grow more quickly than the universities for cost reasons – a university place cost £1,625, a polytechnic one only £1,120.[61] In the related debate on teacher supply[62] (at which, incidentally, only one Tory backbencher bothered to attend) Roland Moyle (Labour) focussed on the effect of this rationalisation on women. He said that the reduction in college of education numbers would result in:

> '...a decline in opportunities for young women in higher education. Only 40% of young women appropriately qualified go to university compared to 60% of young men. The balance of young women goes to colleges of education. That is the route which has been selected for them. This is not a happy situation'.[63]

We shall see later how 'young women' were radically to alter the make-up of higher education in the 1980s and '90s, accounting for a major source of growth.

The DES then asked LEAs to plan their numbers against their regional circumstances so the North had to accommodate a reduction from 8,600 to 5,900 in the coming decade but little advice was forthcoming as to how to do this, allowing the central government department to dictate terms. By 1975 30,000 training college places were transferred to the polytechnics, only half of them for teacher training. Fifty thousand were allocated to the new Colleges of Higher Education (only 60 per cent for teacher training). Four thousand went to universities and 15,000 to the few old style colleges that remained. Fourteen thousand places were to be lost by closures. To quote Hencke again, 'The DES had succeeded in reorganising a large slice of higher education in England and Wales, all done with a marked degree of secrecy and little public discussion'.[64] But it was not over yet. In March 1975 further cuts in numbers and more reorganisation were announced. By July eight more closures were notified and with the birth-rate still falling and the national economy worsening more reductions were expected. The final decision announced by the then Secretary of State, Shirley Williams, on 27 June 1977 was for a total of only 46,000 teacher training places although five colleges were reprieved from closure, the result of special pleading, often on grounds of religious affiliation.

More college mergers

What did all this mean for Newcastle? It will be recalled that the city originally had two colleges it controlled – Kenton Lodge and the City Day College – with a considerable interest in a third, Northern Counties College in the eastern suburbs. With some foresight the city Education Committee had set in motion as early as September 1968 a scheme to merge its two colleges under the title of the City of Newcastle College of Education, a move that was approved in December 1969. The two respective Principals chose to leave at about this time and Miss Vera Gibbon, one of the Vice-Principals, produced a memorandum on the advantages and disadvantages of this new college amalgamating with the fledgling Polytechnic.[65] On 1 January 1971 Gerald Dearden from Lady Spencer Churchill College of Education in Oxford was appointed to be its new Principal. At the same time the plan for the city's education precinct had already included a site for a new education college, alongside the Polytechnic. Also, in the late '60s the city had expressed the view that one authority would be preferable to the three that were responsible for Northern Counties College.[66] Again, Newcastle was ahead of the field at least in terms of structures and building plans.

However, as far as the teaching staff was concerned the future looked uncertain. The city Education Committee and the Polytechnic had little choice but to merge the colleges. It was agreed that Dearden become an Assistant Director of the Polytechnic and that a new fifth faculty be formed to accommodate both teacher training and the diversified work that it was hoped could be developed to offset the fall in teacher training numbers. This was to be the Faculty of Education and Humanities with Joe Collerton, from the Polytechnic, as its head and Gibbon to be in charge of teacher education. There were to be two departments created from the college, Creative and Recreational Arts and Teaching Studies including a division of intercurricular studies, the whole shooting match to be housed in the Lipman Building named after the former chair of the Polytechnic Council and of the College's governing body and opened by Prime Minister Harold Wilson in 1975.

When the reduced numbers for teacher training were introduced in 1975 other colleges had to reconsider their futures. Among them was Northern Counties College located in Coach Lane. This College had begun life as one specialising in training domestic science teachers (known locally as the 'pudding school') and originally located in Northumberland Road, Newcastle. However, by the early 1970s it had become one of the largest teacher training colleges in England with over 1,700 students. Following the call for expansion in the late '60s new halls of residence and a new resource centre had recently been opened and many new, well qualified staff appointed. Although its Principal, Dr Peter Underdown, knew the College would have to take its share of the reduction in training places, surely its very size would make it immune from closure or merger as might the fact that it was close to receiving CNAA approval for its BEd degree.[67] He suggested to his colleagues at a staff meeting that if a merger were necessary, it would be better to join with threatened colleges in neighbouring Ponteland and Alnwick.[68] Perhaps because it was largely overlooked in the first round of cuts it seems to have been exposed to the possibility of disproportionate reductions post-1975 with proposals to reduce staff levels from 102 to sixty-five and student numbers to 640. By this time the Newcastle City Education Committee had taken over as the sole authority for the College so that merger with its Polytechnic was inevitable. By 1976 this was complete and again, the Polytechnic was faced with the problem of redundancies, early retirements and diversification. The 'solution' was to absorb staff where possible into a Combined Studies degree scheme (see below), to develop additional new degree schemes and, where practicable, to transfer staff to other departments in the Polytechnic.

For staff that could not be 'fitted in' there was the Crombie compensation scheme originally introduced to cushion the effects of local government reform on staff in 1974.[69] With some ingenuity from Whitehall its very generous terms were allowed to be applied to college of education staff who wished to leave 'in the interests of the efficiency of the service'. It may not have been the goose that laid the golden egg but its terms were sufficiently attractive to permit many staff from the colleges of education to leave the service. Many a retirement home and many golf club fees were paid for by its generous settlements. Of course, many who left under it would much rather have stayed and finished the careers they had entered so hopefully some years before.

For those remaining on the establishment of the now expanded Polytechnic in Newcastle, a new and unpredictable future lay ahead. Lynch has written that the amalgamation of the colleges:

> '... into institutions where the dissemination of rationality as a highly valued goal in a modern industrial society is now daily endorsed', brought about 'a clash of cultures... between the values of social and literary romanticism and those of economic efficiency and rationalism'.[70]

It was a rude entry for them into a somewhat different and rather crude world. An early meeting of Polytechnic geography staff at Kenton Lodge was greeted by a serving lady dressed in bombazine black serving delicate cucumber sandwiches on silver platters, a very far cry from the canteen at the 'tech'.

Diversification

While some enterprising staff from the colleges of education had already begun to take advantage of the merger by applying successfully to move into areas like the humanities and librarianship, the majority were attracted to a totally new scheme of degree work initially developed by Dr John Clark, technically Head of Physics in the Polytechnic but spending most of his time as chair of the course coordination committee. The James Report had suggested that in order to provide a stronger academic foundation to teacher training a 2 year DipHE be introduced. To this could then be added either a 1 or 2 year BEd/BEd (Hons) route. Clark's scheme was to develop a unit-based or modular combined studies programme that embraced teacher training at degree level, diversified degree work for college of education staff and created new opportunities for Polytechnic staff to expand their activities. Together these would help retain some posts from the colleges and produce an increase in student numbers for the 'new' Polytechnic. A modular scheme of this kind would produce economies of scale and increased choice for students. Subject-based course units could be available for BEd students as well as the new DipHE and new named awards in Combined Studies in Environmental Studies, Industrial Studies, Creative and Performing Arts and European Studies. It was 'the most ambitious academic programme undertaken by the Polytechnic with seventeen departments contributing'.[71] Perhaps it was over ambitious, or before its time, because little of the structure was to last for long. The degrees in education, environmental studies and creative arts survived but as separate degrees;

industrial studies struggled from the beginning and European Studies was never submitted to CNAA for validation. James' DipHE was never a success; 'it appeared as a failed degree'.[72]

Another area that sought to take advantage of this decline in teacher education and that also helped mitigate some of the worst excesses of possible redundancy was geography. This was a subject that could trace its origins to the teaching of commercial geography in the old College of Commerce, had developed as part of the London External degrees in arts and economics and contributed to professional courses in surveying. There had been considerable debate at the time of the Polytechnic's formation as to whether or not the subject should survive. It nearly went the way of courses for commercial travellers and transferred to the local further education college but thanks to the determination of staff, and despite the fact that at one point Polytechnic geography staff were reduced to two in number, it progressed after 1969. Geography was a very popular subject in schools at this time – 7th in the 'O' Level list and 3rd in the 'A' Levels – creating a strong demand for degrees in the subject. With the encouragement of the Deputy Director, Laing Barden, the small nucleus of geography staff in the Polytechnic worked hard with their colleagues in the former colleges of education to devise a BA (Hons) degree in the subject. Although not successful with its first submission to CNAA – so often the fate of new proposals – it was approved to begin in 1977 with an intake of thirty students. Thus, with Environmental Studies beginning in the same year – a subject in which geographers played a major part – all except one of the staff in the geography/ environment area in the former colleges were found new employment – and he retired! Many received study leave to gain higher degrees.

The majority of education staff remained at or were transferred to Coach Lane. However, the Faculty they joined in 1976 was a new one, of humanities, education and librarianship, unfortunately spread over the two campuses. One of the reasons for this was the reluctance of staff already well ensconced in the city centre campus to move out to the less accessible Coach Lane. The city centre site was always perceived to have high value in terms of psychic income with Fenwick's, Bainbridges, the Portland, the University, and the Tyneside cinema all in close proximity. The eastern campus was perceived as being in some kind of urban fringe-belt, marginal in every sense. There were other difficulties too in attempting to integrate staff from the colleges of education. They saw themselves as being as part of a university ethos having been part of first an Institute of Education and later a School. Although they had taught students for a University of Newcastle BEd, other university staff were reluctant to see them and their students as full members of that university. Many observers, including Robbins, had argued strongly for such colleges to have closer relations with local universities; in practice they had been determinedly kept at arms length. Staff from Kenton Lodge and Northern Counties, in turn, saw the Polytechnic as a rather rough and ready outfit, thrown together from three different colleges each with its own take on higher education, none of them close to the university 'model'. It will be recalled that when there was a possibility of the University of Newcastle taking over part of Rutherford

College in the early 1960s one of the things that put them off was the prospect of evening classes and part-time students. Something similar seemed to go through the minds of some college of education staff 15 years later. Even amongst Polytechnic staff, or at least among the many cynics, there was a sense that the Polytechnic was seen as 'night school during the day'.*

Coach Lane: the beginning of a two-campus Polytechnic

When the college of education came into the polytechnic the LEA had to decide what to do with the sites of the colleges of education. There were three: the home of the former City Day College, initially set up to provide 2 year emergency training for teachers in Northumberland Road; Kenton Lodge which had numerous buildings in Gosforth and Kenton, including the former home of local paint manufacturer Max Holzapfel (the Lodge itself), large houses in close proximity and small halls of residence set among the high status suburban housing of Gosforth. Thirdly, there was Northern Counties College at Coach Lane. The core of its site was a manor house but with ample land available for development on the borders of Newcastle and present-day North Tyneside**. Numerous teaching and residential buildings had been built there in the heyday of teacher education in the 1960s.

The Newcastle LEA took over the site in 1975. But the merger of all the colleges of education with the Polytechnic resulted in too much space that the LEA could not afford to service unless the use of land was intensified. The solution was twofold: a plan to house the newly created but short-lived Newcastle College of Education and its staff in the new Lipman Building on the city precinct, and to find further uses for Coach Lane. But what was to become of Coach Lane? It was decided that this complex would house the surviving Northern Counties BEd work, teacher education and in-service activity. What was being lost on the teacher training swings could be compensated for by the roundabouts of other areas of Polytechnic work with greater potential. Such areas presented some opportunities for diversification and retraining for education staff such as the development of food science out of the older domestic science tradition. Some subjects were considered for transfer from the city centre such as social work. The newly acquired courses from the health service were also to be housed there. Lastly, Coach Lane provided a land resource that could later be developed for student accommodation and new teaching buildings, though much of that had to wait until the better times of the 1990s.

The merger of the Polytechnic with the colleges of education had been a traumatic event. Simply on the question of size Bosworth estimated that 'this represents between

---

* This cant phrase is usually attributed to the late Herbert Sutherland, a former lecturer in English and a well known local novelist.

**The manor house was originally the family home of the Haggies, a well-known local rope manufacturing company. Later it was taken over by the National Coal Board.

three and four years normal growth at one stroke'.[73] Not only did new courses have to be developed to accommodate the surplus staff resulting from the run-down of teacher training but, of course, additional staff were added to the original Polytechnic's complement, seventy-five from the City College and about 100 from Northern Counties. The merger presented an opportunity for restructuring at the level of the faculty and amongst senior management. It was decided to create a proper focus for all the education and teacher training work in a new Faculty of Education and Librarianship, headed by Reg Snowden, the former Vice-Principal of Northern Counties. For some years the work of this Faculty was to be split between the city and Coach Lane sites leading to a certain degree of commuting. In addition a new Faculty of Humanities was created under Joe Collerton, an English and communications specialist formerly part of Col. Grant's team in Rutherford. Added to Collerton's outfit was a new department of Modern Languages under Peter Hubsch, a Germanist.

Change at the top: a new Directorate

At the most senior level of management – what became known as the Directorate (shades of the French revolution) – and known facetiously to the teaching staff as Moscow Centre (shades of le Carré) – the city's chief executive Kenneth Galley commissioned Peat, Marwick, Mitchell and Co. to provide a report on structure.[74] Besides recommending the new faculties, they suggested keeping the Deputy Director post (Barden) and the Assistant Director posts (Dearden and Talbot). The Northern Regional Management Centre at Washington New Town had collapsed – it did not generate sufficient business to justify its existence – and its director, D. E. Crowe, had to be made a rather supernumerary member of the Directorate. The consultants also examined in some detail the role of the chair of the course coordination committee, noting that John Clark who occupied this post spent most of his time on its activities and not on his substantive duties as head of the Department of Physics and Physical Electronics. This was a post:

> '...which could cause a great friction for a head of department to occupy an executive position of such potential power... and it should be performed by someone with an academic background within the central management of the Polytechnic'.[75]

The outcome was Clark being made an Associate Director.

Once the merger with Northern Counties College was complete and most of the transition arrangements in place George Bosworth decided to retire in 1976, as did Dr Peter Underdown. Of the Director, the governors recorded that 'members will miss his presence and the atmosphere and calmness and good order, even when the most contentious issues were being discussed, which his style of chairmanship conveyed'.[76] Bosworth had overseen the birth and early developments at Newcastle in a difficult period. Most will remember him as an entirely affable man, not very interested in the world of academe. He was a good communicator of the rather dated 'gin and tonic' school.

The process to replace him as Director was one of the more curious events in the Polytechnic's early history. It appears to have been a somewhat drawn out and contentious issue about parts of which the records are not clear. Initially Laing Barden, the Deputy Director, *acted* as Director but the Polytechnic council does not appear to have been in any hurry to advertise the post although their papers record a verbal report on the appointment procedures to be adopted. At a meeting of the teaching staff on 24 May 1978 a motion was passed calling for the post to be 'readvertised'. It was presented to the council by its teaching staff members but withdrawn following a statement from the chairman. By June 1978 he reported that the appointment committee had continued to meet and consider a variety of candidates but 'without yet feeling able to make an appointment'. However, they did formally confirm Barden's appointment as Acting Director from September 1977. A year later, the chairman reported that Laing Barden had been made Director, a unanimous decision.[77]

All of these changes in the organisation demanded considerable effort and flexibility from academic staff who were not particularly well valued outside their institution. Nor in an age of rapidly rising inflation were they well paid. When Labour returned to government in 1974 Prime Minister Wilson commissioned Lord Houghton, a former back-bencher and an accountant, to examine lecturers' pay. Much to their joy he recommended an average increase of 20 per cent. His Report also suggested an increase in the proportion of senior posts at principal lecturer level so that some got a double benefit: promotion and more pay. Many were the new houses bought and the foreign holidays taken in 1974. But staff were going to have to earn their money as the staff-student ratio rose inexorably through the decade.

The burdens on staff were considerable. On top of the traumatic mergers and their consequences, many new courses were started and class sizes rose. Full-time equivalent student numbers rose from 2,836 (6,989 registered students) in 1969 to 4,348 (7,702 registered students) in 1975. Staff numbers rose from 377 teaching staff, seventy-eight technical staff and 180 administrative staff to 640, 133 and 169 respectively, in the same period. And all this time the City Centre campus, at least, was a building site. When new buildings, such as Lipman and Northumberland phase 2, were completed they were immediately occupied and soon found to be overcrowded. As we have seen the Polytechnic was having to use temporary buildings too. To make matters worse, though eventually better, the central motorway east and the Metro were being constructed all around the campus at the same time. The working environment could hardly be described as pleasant, a long way away from the Oxford quadrangle or the parklands of Essex or York universities. There was very little social space for staff though a staff bar was opened in Ellison Building in 1978; at least the students had their Union. The only eating place was the canteen in Ellison Building. When staff complained about the quality, George Bosworth had told them, 'We're not in the food business'.

The last years of the decade: reorganisation and change

If this were not enough, another constant was internal structural reorganisation. No history of any higher educational establishment, especially in the public sector, would be complete without some account of this process. Where did these notions of changing divisions, departments, schools and faculties come from and why were they necessary? One explanation, of course, is bound up with the fact that polytechnics were constantly growing, and rapidly. They were merging with other colleges, as well as being products of merger themselves. They were taking on new activities from outside areas such as the health service. New degree courses in completely new and additional subjects were started; each one of these would have a course team with a growing body of students attached to it. Each new unit represented a new element of political power, representing income and expenditure. So political cadres grew and wanted proper representation in the structure and the hierarchy. Some of the explanation, then, derives from the process of growth and differentiation. Another part is surely the product of managerial ambition. Many observers have noted that reorganising a 'business' is a way of making a mark, something specific to demonstrate to a promotion panel. Pressure for restructuring came from above as well as from below. It was not a simple management tool to improve productivity or save costs although it was often presented as such. It was a complex social and political process.

For the lecture-room foot soldiers the price was often high: new reporting relations had to be learned, new management styles experienced. It was rarely a matter of simply changing the label on the door. Usually, it meant relocating your office, teaching in different classrooms, lecture theatres and laboratories, even moving lock, stock and filing cabinet from one campus to another. Staff patience often wore thin; morale often plummeted.

In the last 5 years of the 1970s a slow movement for a major reorganisation at Newcastle Polytechnic began to take off. The post-1972 faculties – eventually five in number – were subdivided into departments of which some were further divided into subject groupings, a fairly traditional university model. Whereas the faculty and the department were nationally recognised entities and their heads paid on a national scale*, any other division was *ad hoc*. Most of the innovativeness for the development of new areas of academic activity came from the teaching staff, not from 'management' and it was usually these subject-based groups and their leaders who wanted proper recognition and reward for their efforts.

From management's point of view what the Director wanted was a span of control and a set of reporting relationships that worked efficiently, at the same time recognising

*All academic staff from the Director downwards were paid on the Burnham scale, the national pay bargaining system. It gave little room for local flexibility.

the claims of emergent groups. The small Directorate rarely included the heads of faculty who were elected from amongst the heads of department at this time. A newly appointed faculty head recalled that at 'executive' meetings there was often no agenda and only rudimentary minutes taken; few position papers were prepared.*

It was proposed, first, that heads of faculty become permanent appointments and called deans and second, that a series of 'schools' be formed to represent the proliferation of subject groups now demanding recognition. In true academic style many working parties were set up, reports written, debated at academic board and finally an agreed structure emerged in early 1979, 4 years after the process started under George Bosworth and completed by Laing Barden. The new Director argued that the traditional university model with which the Polytechnic had begun gave strong departmental leadership but weak central direction, perhaps acceptable in a university where the Vice-Chancellor was largely at the mercy of his senate but unacceptable to a polytechnic without a royal charter where the Director was the Chief Executive answerable only to his board of governors, a state of affairs written into the instruments and articles of government of all polytechnics in the legislation that followed the 1966 White Paper. Departments were far too concerned with their own interests, not those of the institution. On its quinquennial visit to the Polytechnic in 1975 the CNAA had been particularly critical of this aspect of the structure at Newcastle.

One of Barden's first acts after his appointment was to visit California in 1978 which he considered something of a model for the organisation of higher education in Britain. One influential figure he met there was Martin Trow who was to remain a friend for many years, later receiving an honorary degree from Northumbria University. Besides advocating the use of the heads of faculty as a part of a formal executive, Barden noted the need to sponsor devolution, the principal source of academic innovation. It was a matter of getting the balance right between 'centre' and 'periphery'. It took a remarkable 4 years of discussion at Academic Board before the final scheme was presented for approval. This proposed setting up eight faculties** and more than twenty 'schools' to represent the emerging subject groups. The latter would have permanent heads paid as grade IV heads of department on the Burnham scale, a level that was to prove contentious and irregular. They were to be responsible for staff and subject development and research. For management purposes they would be part of a faculty executive, led by a permanent dean who would control all non-staffing budget heads. To enhance the position of the 'course', course leaders – usually principal lecturers – would report directly to the dean of faculty. This new devolved faculty system would be supported by a more devolved system of faculty offices but Hopkinson was keen to retain a strong central control over all aspects of the administration. Students only ever seemed to identify with their course; in most cases this was largely related to the school. Creating all these new management posts involved competitive interviews that did not always leave historic relations between subjects and faculties undisturbed, often leading to the kind of disjunctions described earlier.

*R.J. Buswell, interview with Professor John Rear, 24 August 2004.
**In the event only seven were finally set up.

One of the new faculties created was Professional Studies to include the schools of law, accountancy, economics and government. It was the only one whose dean was recruited from outside the Polytechnic. In this case Professor John Rear was appointed from Brunel University. Rear was an Oxford law graduate with academic experience in universities in Hong Kong and Kent. He is someone who will figure strongly in the next chapter as he emerges as the Deputy Director of the Polytechnic and later Pro Vice-Chancellor of the University of Northumbria but he joined at a time when the Polytechnic's national and regional success was about to be severely tested.

Somewhat hectically, then, in this first decade (1969–79) Newcastle Polytechnic had drawn together many of the elements thought necessary to this new type of institution of higher learning. It had successfully merged five colleges, it had taken in some work from the health service, founded an academic board, appointed its first two Directors (one rather mysteriously), structured and restructured itself into faculties, departments and schools, taken student numbers to over 10,000, developed a unique relationship with the national degree awarding body, built a magnificent library, expanded student accommodation and appointed a whole raft of support staff in student services. To many it had the appearance of a university. While staff and students often looked enviously across the Great North Road to their rival institution it was clear that apart from the relative wealth of the University of Newcastle and its greater emphasis on research, there was not a great deal of difference between them. One ingredient that was missing was a professoriate, and even this was now beginning. As early as 1973 Bosworth had been persuaded to add this titled set to the establishment. He said it was important to distinguish between a head of department and a professor, 'the former being a person selected for his (*sic*) ability to administer affairs, the latter being honoured for his academic eminence. It is, of course, reasonable to expect that in many cases the two categories may coincide'.[78] In fact, the majority of the early appointed professors also held senior management posts, though there was no doubting their 'academic eminence'.

As the decade drew to a close Laing Barden presented a paper to the governors reviewing the first 10 years of Newcastle Polytechnic.[79] The main thrust of his report was, ironically, the distinctiveness of the Polytechnic from a university. He drew attention to, among other things, the fact that only 10 per cent of students were on arts and humanities courses. That of the 10,000 students only 3,500 were on degree courses. Five thousand students were registered as part-time, taking twelve of the college's fifty-four degree courses. Two thirds of the students were over twenty-one. Nearly all the research was of an applied nature often related to local business and industry. He recorded a strong commitment of service to the community in many areas of the Polytechnic's work. Undoubtedly this was a proper reflection of what had been achieved but as we shall see, within a decade, Barden would be one of the leaders of the movement to convert polytechnics to universities.

Early in the same year Derek Webster, who had been such an important link between the college and the local authority, resigned as Chairman of the city's Education

Committee (and as a member of the Polytechnic Council) as a matter of principle over cuts in the city's education budget of £1.2 million in 1978 and a proposed further cut of £1.4 million in 1979. The Polytechnic would have to take its share of these reductions, which, combined with reductions in the AFE Pool imposed by the Secretary of State, Shirley Williams, as part of the Labour government's anti-inflation 'no growth' policy, would have placed the Polytechnic in a difficult position.[80] He was replaced initially by Cyril Lipman, a Tory, showing again, the neutrality with which the Polytechnic was treated politically. But it was not long before Webster returned to the Polytechnic Council, this time as a co-opted member. Soon he and his colleagues were to be faced with a radical reforming Conservative government under Margaret Thatcher. At a special meeting of the governors in January 1980 the Polytechnic was confronted by the capping of the AFE Pool, cuts of between £1 and £2 million and the raising of overseas' students fees by 22 per cent. A new era was dawning for British higher education and Newcastle Polytechnic would need all the friends she could muster to face new and different challenges.

There's a whole scene being made at Newcastle, where the Polytechnic is turning out the sort of people who will make the world a better place to live in, thoughtful people with an intelligent and mature outlook on life.

The large new Students' Union with its 40 clubs and societies, together with a wide range of sporting and recreational facilities of which skin diving is one, helps make for a full and satisfying student life.

The Newcastle upon Tyne Polytechnic offers a wide range of courses, of nationally recognised standards, through Degrees awarded by the Council for National Academic Awards, by London University, and Diplomas of various bodies.

Newcastle upon Tyne Polytechnic

Degree Courses
CNAA
BA (Ord) Applied Modern Languages
BA (Hons) Business Studies
BSc (Hons & Ord) Chemical Technology
BSc (Hons & Ord) Electrical
    and Electronic Engineering
BSc (Ord) Information Science
BA (Hons) Law
BSc (Hons) Mathematics
BSc (Hons & Ord) Mechanical Engineering
BSc (Hons & Ord) Physical Electronics
BSc (Ord) Quantity Surveying
BSc (Hons) Sociology
MSc Advanced Experimental Physics
University of London
BSc Economics
BA General
NC DipAD
DipAD Graphic Design
DipAD Painting
DipAD Sculpture
DipAD Furniture
DipAD Industrial Design (Engineering)

Professional and Other Courses
Professional
Accountancy
CEI Part 2
Environmental Engineering
Environmental Technology
General Surveying
Hospital and Community Nursing
Law
Librarianship
Management Studies
Municipal Administration
Private Secretarial for Graduates
Social Work Training
Higher National Diplomas
Business Studies (Accountancy,
    Distribution, Languages, Marke
    Retailing, Secretarial, Transpo
Business Studies with Design
Chemistry
Electrical and Electronic Engineerin
Institutional Management
Mechanical Engineering
For details of these and other cours
write to: The Registrar, Department
Ellison Building, Ellison Place,
Newcastle upon Tyne, NE1 8ST.

It's a great scene

'It's a great scene', Newcastle upon Tyne Polytechnic advertisement.
Source: The Journal, *Tuesday 17 August 1971*

Chapter Five

The yellow-brick road:[1]
from local authority to
higher education corporation, 1979–1988

THE SECOND period of Newcastle Polytechnic's history is from the general election of 1979 up to and including the White Paper of 1987 and the Act of 1988 that followed, a time dominated by stronger central government control of higher education and financial stringency. A significant theme running through the whole of this period was the growing pressure from the polytechnics for more autonomy, for more independence to run their own affairs. An important ally in this process was the CNAA which had argued from fairly early days for more independence for the colleges that took its degrees. As they matured so they looked increasingly over their shoulders to their rival institutions, the universities, and wondered why they could not be more like them. Robbins' prediction, that the two sectors could not be kept separate, seemed to becoming true. However, the Polytechnic found itself devoting much of its energy to fighting the government for a better share of available resources. It was often only the generosity of Newcastle City Council that prevented enforced redundancies and reductions in the academic programme. What was ironic was that these battles were taking place when other agencies were describing Newcastle as the best Polytechnic in the country! Internally, the Polytechnic naturally could not stand still despite the severity of these measures. New degree programmes were added, the numbers of students increased quite dramatically and a long haul towards yet more restructuring took place to cope with changing circumstances. It also had to deal with the loss of influential figures such as John Clark, Joe Collerton, Gordon Rendall, Peter Torode and Ron Hopkinson and to set in place a larger and more professional bureaucracy in support of its ever growing academic endeavours. At the same time at the national level the government was engaged in the Falklands War and the miners' strike and the large scale reform of public services. It is not inappropriate to wonder aloud on the extent to which higher education really did engage the imagination of Thatcher's various governments.

Barden, Clark, Torode and the CNAA

If welding together the various colleges into one polytechnic was the major challenge of George Bosworth's period of office, then two events were to help propel Newcastle to the forefront of this new and burgeoning sector of British higher education. One was the improving relations between Newcastle Polytechnic and the CNAA. The second was the appointment of Laing Barden to the post of Director, having been Bosworth's Deputy since 1972, together with the promotion of John Clark, who we have already come across, to an Assistant Director post with responsibility for academic development. It would be wrong, of course, to ascribe Newcastle's advancing position to these two men alone. Peter Torode had been appointed from Leeds Polytechnic as Academic Registrar. As Ron Hopkinson took on more administrative responsibilities, so Torode was to become a key figure in developing relations with CNAA. It is an unfolding story of interaction between CNAA, the local authority and central government that saw gradual increases in the Polytechnic's autonomy, a process over the next 10 to 15 years eventually involving most of the teaching and administrative staff. Later, John Rear, from the academic side, also played a prominent part.

In those first few years after their establishment, polytechnics grew at a slow pace despite the mergers with the colleges of education and a rapidly rising demand for higher education.[2] Out of 377,000 students in higher education in 1967 in Britain, 200,000 were in universities, 105,000 in teacher education and only 72,000 in the public sector (polytechnics and colleges). A decade later the respective figures were 281,000, 60,000 and 150,000 out of a total of 491,000. While polytechnics had more than doubled in size universities increased by less than 50 per cent but still polytechnics contained less than half of all higher education students. In these early years the emphasis remained on part-time students taking sub-degree level courses. In 1967–88 about 123,000 polytechnic students were taking advanced courses and 70,000 non-advanced ones but only 22,000 were taking degrees in polytechnics; 'advanced' did not mean graduate level. Ten years later there were 71,000 taking degrees and fewer than 30,000 taking non-advanced programmes.[3] The catalytic agent for this reversal was a combination of the CNAA and the innovative powers of the staff in the polytechnics, added to the fact that more and more young people were obtaining the minimum two 'A' Levels necessary to obtain a place on a degree course and a student grant.

The CNAA was established immediately post-Robbins: 'it was to be different (from NCTA) in many ways but it was to take over principles and practices that NCTA had pioneered'.[4] Unlike its predecessor the CNAA could validate degrees in areas such as business studies, languages, humanities, social sciences and education. By 1965–66 there were 4,000 students enrolled on eighty-nine courses including twenty-nine on courses leading to a degree in business studies. A year later it considered 136 proposals for a variety of first degrees but approved only about 40 per cent of them. From the beginning colleges found it puzzling when proposals from different departments in the same institution elicited different responses. Validating panels, at this time dominated by university members, had to reconcile course proposals with conditions obtaining in a department or indeed, a whole college. Once the polytechnics were established these fledgling organisations needed to develop a close symbiosis with the CNAA if they were to prosper. In the early days each course was largely devised by a team of subject-based academics and put up to CNAA with little or no internal scrutiny by an academic board. Thus, there was little consistency in the proposals coming from a particular polytechnic, leading to a high failure rate and a growing undercurrent of discontent. Many directors began to feel they would have more success if they had a higher level of autonomy. However, Silver in his detailed history of the CNAA, points out in defence of CNAA that the management of colleges was often too authoritarian, dominated by strong principals or directors. In some cases the local authority interfered too directly in a polytechnic's affairs so that academic boards were often unable to safeguard their own standards. Many polytechnics often took too long to merge their founding colleges into one whole with a common set of values. On top of all this, the Labour government, having set them up, passed the buck to the local authorities who were often starved of resources so that poor physical environments, libraries and buildings, often operating on a multitude of sites, were simply not up to the standards required by CNAA.

Notwithstanding, the CNAA was to prove a liberalising force for the polytechnics, having no fixed agenda as to what subjects a college should have in its curriculum nor how students should be taught and examined. What colleges had to be able to show was that their courses had a defensible rationale, that students should progress academically over the course of a degree and that the processes were open and accountable. Nonetheless, it would be foolish to suggest that academic convention played no part at all. After all, the subject panels set up to validate the courses would expect them to conform to current paradigms. But slowly, as Silver recognises, the general innovation that CNAA encouraged would be best served if it emanated from colleges with a large degree of self-management rather than them dancing to the some tune of central prescription.[5] As early as 1971 the Committee of Directors of Polytechnics (CDP) had begun to call for charters for their colleges to secure their independence and thereby the ability to award their own degrees. From the beginning of the binary movement, however, the government of the day was to resist any drift towards the university model of autonomy. By making course approval more dependent on internal procedures, by reducing paperwork and above all, by developing a partnership, the CNAA helped to encourage a greater degree of independence. In the same year the CNAA was already beginning the process of partnership by differentiating between colleges and courses: where experience and quality were evident, then 'control' could be more relaxed.[6]

Newcastle Polytechnic was to respond positively to this encouragement under the guidance of John Clark who was by then the chair of the Polytechnic's Course Coordination Committee. In an extensive interview with Silver, Clark set out the stages of the evolution of the new processes.[7] Because of the variability of the success of submissions from Newcastle, Clark realised that the 'strike rate' would improve if some kind of centrally managed review of courses was established by the Polytechnic with courses having to be approved internally before being submitted. After all, Clark argued, Newcastle saw itself as a mature institution, quite capable of managing its own affairs, a notion supported by the fact that, as we saw in the previous chapter, it was given a long leash by its local authority to do just that in most other aspects of its development. Over time Newcastle Polytechnic saw that there was a reasonable correlation between its own processes of course review and success with CNAA; if this were true, the Polytechnic argued, then why duplicate procedures? For its part the new Chief Officer of CNAA, Edwin Kerr, published a milestone paper in 1975 entitled 'Partnership in Validation' in which many of Newcastle's internal procedures were adopted.

The polytechnics soon learned to play the 'game' of validation. Of crucial importance was the largely unofficial exchange of ideas between subject board members and course proposers. The 'invisible college' of a discipline knew few boundaries; what kind of an institution an academic came from was of little importance so, for example, a physicist on a CNAA panel from a university was often more than happy to discuss course proposals with a physicist from a polytechnic on the basis of them both being from the same subject area.

In 1979 CNAA published a second document that gave colleges an expectation of even more delegated responsibility for their courses.[8] Newcastle sought to take advantage of 'those clauses in the document which offered to institutions individually, the opportunity to put forward for consideration their own variations on the basic CNAA model' so that a more mature college like Newcastle could rely on its own procedures and progress at its own pace. At the same time it would offer the possibility of courses being in indefinite approval, subject to progress reviews. Increasingly, approval of academic developments would be linked to reviews of institutions rather than individual courses. Newcastle was poised to take full advantage of this. Indeed, following its quinquennial review visit to the Polytechnic in 1981 CNAA wrote that its report was 'undoubtedly one of the most favourable produced… on any institution'. It went on to say that the Polytechnic had developed:

'…a process of institutional planning and resource management which was perhaps unique in terms of its comprehensiveness. What was particularly striking was that this would go hand-in-hand with an internal process of course validation and review, which

would ensure that quality was safeguarded or enhanced while costs were reduced or maintained at a fixed level'.

And, incidentally, the library was described as 'one of the outstanding libraries in British higher education'.[9] No wonder Laing Barden was able to tell an *Evening Chronicle* reporter, 'It is always dangerous to say you are the best, but I think it would be difficult for any other polytechnic to say they were better than we are'.[10]

The CNAA was proposing to build on Newcastle's experience in the mid-1970s of having detailed quinquennial visits to faculties as well as to the institution. Peter Torode, the Academic Registrar, thought that the Polytechnic's advanced position nationally in this emerging process was the result of his close working relationship with CNAA officers and frequent visits to CNAA headquarters.[11] Many colleges were somewhat suspicious of what Newcastle Polytechnic was doing, perhaps breaking rank from the CDP position:

'…it contained the implication that some polytechnics were stronger than others… we were arguing a case that we had taken a number of initiatives in validation and course review that represented a strength that could be built upon… there was an implication that we were different in that respect and more deserving of a relationship… it wasn't necessary that the full panoply of CNAA validations and revalidations to continue to apply to us'.[12]

Torode's second point was that the 'Newcastle way' was perhaps a better way: '…if you bring together the group of people internally… and the group of subject specialists which the CNAA would put together… you could actually create something that was qualitatively better than two quite separate processes of validation'.[13]

From this he helped Newcastle Polytechnic develop its interpretation of 'joint validation' in which CNAA subject specialists only participated in the final stages of course approval, and then only as equal members of a panel that might be largely composed of Polytechnic members and their external advisers.[14] It was not only other colleges who looked on developments at Newcastle with some suspicion. Amongst academics internally there was a concern that non-subject specialists from the Polytechnic could not make proper judgements about the intricacies of, say, English literature or chemistry; in the long run these fears proved unfounded.

After 2 years of this joint process in which twenty-two courses at Newcastle were approved in this way the Polytechnic began to look towards even greater responsibility for its own academic affairs. This came with moves towards some kind of licensing system, a move towards *accrediting* the institution rather than validating every course separately. Newcastle was a pioneer in the development of this new method. Peter Torode recalled that he and John Clark were regularly consulted on various approaches that might be adopted. Some polytechnics found the Newcastle system too bureaucratic and cumbersome and sought complete delegation of powers from CNAA but its view was that its Royal Charter could not be altered in this way; central government would certainly have been against it. Its case was reinforced by events at

North London Polytechnic where serious complaints were made about some course content and teaching methods and concerns for freedom of expression which led in turn to Sir Keith Joseph setting up the Lindop Committee, chaired by Sir Norman Lindop, Director of Hatfield Polytechnic. Its Report[15] was rather critical of CNAA's rather heavy handed approach to validation and favoured:

> '...the growth of a teaching institution as a self-critical academic community' and recommended to the secretary of state that 'any institution that so wished, to apply... to award its own degrees and thus become self-validating... with a broad range of powers for those who failed this or did not wish it, including accreditation'.[16]

Joseph was a notorious vacillator, slow to make his mind up on almost anything – Patrick Cosgrave described this as 'his temperamental inability to take big decisions'[17] – and it was March 1986 before he replied to the Report. His view was that CNAA should continue in existence but with a more limited function. Colleges should explore ways towards self-validation, with the result that CNAA's establishment would be reduced by between 30 and 50 per cent.[18] In the meantime under Torode's guidance Newcastle and CNAA had already moved forward to something approaching that position with 'joint validation' and a new institutional agreement was signed, 'the most far reaching that could be achieved under the existing Charter'.[19] Much to Peter Torode's chagrin he read in the *Times Higher Educational Supplement* that Sheffield Polytechnic had reached a similar agreement with CNAA in June 1985. Despite good relations with Sheffield he felt 'slightly hurt that that they seemed to have overtaken us...'.[20] In 1987 CNAA published its proposals for accreditation[21] under which a college could be licensed to mount and modify courses providing it could show that its academic board had effective arrangements in place. If so, review of the institution would only take place every five years with courses reviewed every 5 to 7 years. In return colleges could appoint their own external examiners and award the CNAA's degrees in their own name. Peter Torode drafted Newcastle's proposals for accreditation to be approved by the Academic Board, his last act before taking up a post at Hong Kong Polytechnic where John Clark had already been appointed Director, a curious conclusion to one of the most significant episodes in Newcastle Polytechnic's history.

Newcastle had proved itself a leader in this movement towards the self-management of academic affairs. Its pioneering work set the pace for others to follow. It was part of a sequence of processes that was to place Newcastle at the top of the polytechnic tree. This included strong and certain leadership from above, an articulate and expressive Academic Board, a structure that gave a considerable degree of delegation to the subjects and their courses, good relations with its local authority that was happy to leave development to the college and its Council without undue interference, a terrific library and, above all, a hard working, innovative staff dedicated to high academic standards and to attracting able students. However, these achievements had to be ground out against a dismal background of financial hardship that was not of its making.

Financial crises

The election of the new Tory government in May 1979 was to herald a long period of change for higher education, culminating in the Education Reform Act of 1988. It is difficult to see if a more distinct policy for higher education emerged under Mrs Thatcher and her education ministers than those under Wilson and Callaghan. Certainly, continued expansion was the order of the day, and as under Labour, there was a strong belief among Conservatives that university level work ought to be increasingly characterised by vocational usefulness. However, one striking change of this period, especially under one Secretary of State, Sir Keith Joseph*,[22] was a concern to drive down the costs of higher education. This was born out of the fear of the rising inflation experienced under Callaghan and Labour – it had reached 27 per cent for a period in 1978 – and from a deeper ideological belief that where possible public services should be paid for by the consumer. Both would result in a reduction in public expenditure, reduce inflationary pressures, and increase the discretionary spending powers of everyone. The disastrous effects of this version of monetarism on British manufacturing industry are well-known, especially to North-Easterners. Its impact on universities and polytechnics was nearly as severe. The result was not wholesale closure – although three or four universities came close to that in the early 1980s – but a massive increase in the staff/student ratio. The government sought to portray this as an admirable increase in efficiency – more students taught by fewer and fewer staff, that is, for a more or less constant supply of public funds – but its long-term effect was to severely undermine the relationship between teacher and taught and to alter the learning experience of all students. Eventually it was to contribute the evolution of mass higher education.

One of the first acts of the incoming government was to 'cap' the Advanced Further Education (AFE) Pool with Whitehall now determining how much money should be available for public sector higher education. This was the first direct involvement of central government in this process since the Pool was established in 1958, although the origins of the idea of 'capping' can be found in the Oakes Committee set up by Labour's Shirley Williams in 1977.[23] In 1980–81 the sum to be made available to the polytechnics and colleges was £375 million, a considerable reduction in real terms, although part of a continuing series of reductions dating from the early 1970s. In

---

*Joseph was a remarkable man. The son of a baronet, educated at Harrow and Oxford, he was a long serving member under Macmillan and Heath but made his mark under Mrs Thatcher. He came to Education from the Department of Industry in September 1981. He said he did not discover what conservatism meant until late in his ministerial career; at Trade and Industry he was concerned to remove the hand of government from industry and advocated a tight money policy. By the time he reached Education he had shifted his focus to reducing the Public Sector Borrowing Requirement which would have massive consequences for higher education. In many ways Joseph was a 'poly' man though he probably would not have realised it. As a young man after the war he joined the family firm – Bovis, the construction company – and 'set himself out to qualify as a licentiate of the Institute of Building (probably at the Brixton School of Building which became part of the South Bank Polytechnic)… which meant digging holes and laying bricks by day and reading up the theory at night'. At about the same time he also successfully read for the Bar and sat for a Fellowship at All Souls, Oxford.

addition a new bureaucracy was required to allocate these sums but it had to be one that reflected the reality of the plural system of Town Hall and Whitehall. Existing legislation had to be used thereby restricting the extent to which national policies could influence the distribution of funds. This *ad hoc* system operated until 1982 when the government realised it needed a method over which it might hope to have more direct control. In that year the National Advisory Body for Local Authority Higher Education (NAB) was established to advise the secretary of state. It was a cumbersome but fairly representative organisation in which Tory and Labour local authorities often fought alongside one another against the DES. Salter and Tapper report that in the early years the DES 'lost on points'.[24] The Body was chaired by a politician but the Board was run by an academic, Christopher Ball, Warden of Keble College, Oxford and a member of CNAA. What Ball came up with was a complex set of formulae based on different kinds of institution, the level of work, student enrolment targets and the classification of subjects into a limited number of programme areas, that is, 'broadly on the basis of subject-weighted student numbers'.[25] Some hoped that the overall effect on budgets might be neutral largely because school populations were predicted to fall from 10 million in 1978–79 to 9.1 million in 1982–83 and therefore fewer would move into higher education. In practice NAB had to manage vicious cuts in public expenditure amounting to a reduction of 10 per cent in the AFE Pool by 1984–85.[26] Ball hoped to protect the most valuable work in the polytechnics and colleges, by persuading the colleges themselves to propose cuts. With only about half of all students in polytechnics being on degree level courses or above and about 35 per cent still part-time, there was a danger that the courses likely to be afforded the greatest degree of protection would be the more prestigious full-time and sandwich degree courses, helping to undermine the local authority sector's historic role as providers of a diversity of levels of awards and modes of attendance. Initially, polytechnics felt able to manage these reductions in the unit of resource by the fairly simple expedient of raising the staff/student ratio (SSR) or by taking more students but retaining fewer members of staff.

In Newcastle the impact of the new regime was felt almost immediately. At a special meeting of its Council at the end of January 1980 the Polytechnic was warned of a grave financial situation in which cuts of £1 million would have to be considered. It replied that it was not an expensive institution in comparison to other polytechnics. It had the sixth highest SSR in the country and the third highest teaching loads; nineteen other polytechnics had higher costs per student and eighteen others had higher administration costs. Nonetheless, it had to prepare budgets showing reductions in all parts of the organisation from field courses and visits, to hospitality, to building works. All staff appointments would be frozen.[27] In a later paper the Director sought to protect the generous financial support the city voluntarily gave to its polytechnic in addition to its contribution to the AFE Pool; this amounted to at least £700,000 a year.[28] By December 1980 the Chairman of the city's Education Committee had warned the Polytechnic Council of even more savage cuts of up to £2 million for the next financial year, 1981–82, which Laing Barden said would be impossible to sustain other than through large scale redundancies.[29] He produced more evidence to show the low cost profile of Newcastle Polytechnic: seventeenth cheapest out of twenty-three making returns to a survey by the CDP. Each Newcastle student cost £1,679 but by comparison a Portsmouth Polytechnic student cost £2,909. Clearly, this argument was one to try to force even larger reductions on some high cost polytechnics and away from lower cost ones like Newcastle. The complementary strategy was to raise the SSR to 10:1 over the next 3 years. By February 1981 there were reports in the local press that to help solve its financial crisis the Polytechnic would have to sell off its Coach Lane Campus. The Academic Board predicted that cuts on this scale 'would have disastrous consequences… with the inevitable withdrawal of approval of the institution by CNAA, thus placing the future of the Polytechnic in serious jeopardy'.[30] Reluctantly, the governing body approved a schedule of cuts amounting to £735,000 but proposed that delegations be sent to the City Council and to the Secretary of State. However, the City Council became the Polytechnic's 'white knight', offering £900,000 to assist the Polytechnic to meet its budget – £400,000 for non-advanced further education courses and half a million pounds as a direct subsidy. This left cuts of £145,000 to be found in addition to the £735,000 already agreed. This meant there would be no compulsory redundancies.

By the summer of this the first of many 'crisis' years, Gerald Dearden, the Assistant Director (Academic), had to demonstrate the effects of the new financial regime on the academic programme. Staffing was no longer to be driven by curriculum requirements but by the cash available to pay salaries. This would particularly affect teacher education where the SSR was low at 7:1 and would need to be raised to the new average of 10:1 but in this case, it was in an area where numbers were still controlled by the DES. While the LEA agreed that the 'surplus' posts (seventeen) could be 'Crombied' (see pp.84–85) the knock-on effect was to make the Faculty of Education too small, necessitating its merger with Humanities; home economics (food and consumer sciences) would join the Department of Chemistry. The Head of the Faculty and his Head of the School of Teaching Studies generously volunteered for Crombie.[31]

The tactic of raising the SSR was working, thanks in part to the fact that the country's universities refused to play this game of 'unit-of resource-reduction' and by not increasing their student intakes. For 1981–82 this meant that Newcastle Polytechnic was able to increase its first year intake by 14 per cent; there were now nearly 7,000 FTE students. However, the almost anarchic, hand-to-mouth, *ad hoc* funding system could not go on and in 1981 the DES produced a discussion paper on the future management and distribution of the AFE Pool to set relations between central and local government funding of public sector higher education on a better footing. This was perhaps in response to a House of Commons Education, Science and the Arts Committee report on the 'Funding and organisation of courses in higher education', under Christopher Price MP, the future Director of Leeds Polytechnic. This recommended, amongst other things, that polytechnics should become corporate bodies independent of local government, something which the Tories wished to avoid at this time. For 1982–83 £539 million would be available to the Pool but the fees paid by the LEAs for students in higher education would be reduced from £900 to £480 with the balance saved available to the Pool. The size of the Pool was reduced in effect by 6.5 per cent but inflation was running at 4 per cent on salaries and 9 per cent on other heads. Polytechnics were to take cuts ranging from 2 to 11 per cent. New SSRs were set as follows: 8.1:1 for laboratory-based subjects, 11.5:1 for classroom subjects and 7.5:1 for art and design. For Newcastle this would result in a cut of 3.2 per cent but Gordon Campbell (the Assistant Director, finance) was able to report that the Polytechnic, thanks to the £1 million from the City Council, would be able to live within its budget.[32] By March 1982 the government had produced its White Paper on expenditure[33] in which higher education was to contract by 10 per cent between 1980 and 1985. More disturbing was the differentiating by sector so that capital expenditure in universities was to *increase* by 5.5 per cent but in public sector higher education was to *decrease* by 20 per cent. Student numbers in the public sector were to rise faster than in universities to reach an SSR of 11.3:1 by 1984. To translate these targets into practice, the NAB was given a more formal status.

Newcastle's participation in its first planning exercise under NAB was on the basis of a 10 per cent reduction in funding, using 1982–83 figures as the base line. The Polytechnic, which by this time had emerged as the 'best' polytechnic in the country, understandably took a strong line against such a proposal, asking NAB to focus its attention on the smaller, less cost-effective colleges. The Director met with all the academic leaders in the Polytechnic together with trade union and student union representatives in order to ensure understanding of the position. A 10 per cent reduction would involve the loss of 500 students and about fifty staff, necessitating the total closure of the whole of the Combined Studies programme including Creative Arts, Industrial Studies and Environmental Studies. This was all of the diversified degree programmes that John Clark had developed following amalgamation with the colleges of education in the 1970s.[34] The HND in Business Studies and Languages was also to close, plus a large number of part-time day and evening courses at all levels. No explanation can be found as why any of these particular courses were selected for closure rather than others. If carried through it was said that savings of £700,000 on staff and course costs and £600,000 on non-teaching heads could be made.

Despite Barden's attempts at 'explanation' for the funding crisis, there was very considerable opposition from the areas to be most affected, indeed, from all parts of the Polytechnic, from the local authority and many sections of the community including trade unions. Flyers were circulated by the unions and the Students' Union. Numerous meetings were held between members of the Directorate and staff and students of the courses most affected. For example, Dr John Clark met with students and staff from Environmental Studies. It was quite clear that he expected his arguments for the course's closure to prevail but he met with an extremely articulate and well organised body of students, the majority of whom were mature and who had worked for some years in business and industry. Many were former trade union members and were well versed in conflict. For every argument Clark put forward, they had an equally strong counter. Clark, a large physical man, was used to getting his own way. The tough but well reasoned students were not to be intimidated and Clark left the room with a strong note of rational opposition ringing in his ears.

Staff and students in Creative Arts mounted a campaign based on support from outside bodies who worked with students from the course. Staff produced a detailed and well-argued paper for the retention of the course which was circulated to all members of the Polytechnic Council.

Under pressure the Secretary to the Council agreed to allow the four main campus trade unions to be observers at the meeting where a final recommendation to the local authority on budget cuts would be made. In the event the meeting had to be cancelled because of the grass roots pressure being brought on the Directorate who were rapidly seeking ways to ameliorate the position. It must be remembered that it was the local authority who would submit the proposals for cuts, not the Polytechnic itself. Thus, the City Council was subject to intense lobbying, especially from the trade unions, and a rally was held in the city. The Education Committee gave individuals and groups the opportunity to make representations to it, all to be reported to the Committee's March meeting.

At the national level, Lord Glenamara, who had recently succeeded Lord Wynne-Jones as Chancellor of the Polytechnic, addressed the House of Lords on 19 January[35] asking if the government was now abandoning the Robbins principle, noting 'the ludicrous attempts of the secretary of state… to apply the theories of a market economy… to the organisation of an educational system. I often think that Adam Smith must be rotating in his grave'.[36] Matters were not to improve. Joseph obviously thought NAB's mechanisms could deliver his policy objectives especially in relation to cost reductions. It is often said of Joseph that he was the only minister to offer up cuts willingly to the Treasury.

In July 1984 NAB was given formal establishment with a brief to continue the downward pressure on resources. For Newcastle Polytechnic student numbers had increased by 15 per cent from 1981-82 to 1984–85 but funding was 6.5 per cent less than inflation. The SSR had risen from 9.3:1 in 1980–81 to 12:1 in 1984–85. The effects were perhaps greatest on non-staffing heads where spending on equipment fell by 91 per cent and adaptations to buildings by 79 per cent.[37] In its revised modus operandum NAB asked that polytechnics produce development plans. This was a move that Newcastle approved of as it would give it the opportunity to demonstrate its obvious strengths and maturity and its cost-effectiveness. For the 1987–88 bid to NAB Newcastle's development strategy had, according to NAB's guidance, reduced its numbers to the 1984–85 base-line by decreasing first year intakes to the social sciences and humanities and planning any expansion in more vocational areas such as construction, health and design. However, the main objective would be to sustain overall numbers irrespective of programme area and therefore much would depend on recruitment to fragile areas such as engineering.[38] At this time the Students' Union was of a radical bent and at this same meeting of the Polytechnic Council, it tabled its own paper, a highly articulate, well argued opposition to dealings with NAB. Its language and logic appear superior to that produced in the Directorate's paper even if much less pragmatic. It saw NAB and Joseph's Green Paper of 1985 as part of a Tory government's attack on education and other welfare services; the government's stance to be one of economics, not educational policy. 'The Students' Union therefore demands that the Polytechnic does not face up to financial realities', it wrote, 'as these are not realities at all, but a statement of the government's political priorities. An acceptance of 'financial realities' is an acceptance of the political position of reduced access, and governmental control of educational establishments'.[39] In his Report to the Polytechnic Council Barden described the 1984–85 NAB exercise as 'a very difficult, needlessly painful and in the end, entirely fruitless exercise which should not be repeated'. He was at pains to point out that what mattered was the Polytechnic's own development strategy and plan, not the imposition of an outside agenda on courses and costs. This seemed to be part of the Polytechnic's growing confidence in its own authority, parallel to its mature and more autonomous relations with CNAA.

When NAB produced its draft proposals for Newcastle's funding for 1987–88 they contained, yet again, some wholly unacceptable measures aimed at, as before, reducing provision in humanities, languages, and social and administrative studies. On this occasion the proposal was even more draconian. This time all the humanities degrees were identified for closure. Student numbers were to be reduced from 7,570 FTES in 1985–86 to 7,246 in 1986–87. The Polytechnic reacted angrily and with venom,[40] protesting that 'the proposals do not come about through any rational ,considered approach to this particular Polytechnic but are in part a 'random' effect of a relatively mechanistic approach to planning...' The proposal for the humanities courses was received with 'shocked incredulity'. Barden went on to say that 'it is not possible to call to mind any issue in the history of this Polytechnic which has so united staff and student opinion, and generated such strong external support, as opposition to these NAB cuts'. He, the Chancellor and the Chairman of the Polytechnic Council planned to meet with senior NAB officials; meanwhile, MPs, senior DES officials, major employers and parents were to be lobbied. HMIs were asked to prepare reports on the threatened courses. The Polytechnic pointed to its above (national) average SSR of 12:1 and the very high demand for its courses with over 20,000 applications for about 1,700 places each year, nearly twelve applicants for each place; in some popular areas it was over thirty. NAB was clearly shaken by the strength of the opposition to its plans and in September 1986 it sent revised target numbers to the Polytechnic which were more acceptable, including withdrawing the threats to close the humanities degree courses. As in 1986–87 this volte-face came about by government increasing the size of the AFE Pool at the last moment and by the Polytechnic agreeing to maintaining student numbers but at a lower unit cost – the so-called 'efficiency option'. As Pratt notes:

> '...the polytechnics conformed to the current government ideology, though not necessarily out of sycophancy... the new "rules of the game" meant that this was the only way to maintain their overall funding levels. The alternative was even greater cuts, particularly of staff'.[41]

NAB was a means of bringing together course approvals and funding thus making it a planning body as well as a funding body. This enabled government to control the structure of at least one sector of higher education, assisted by selective, competitive measures for priority areas. Understandably, Whitehall did not like Town and County Hall's 'topping up' of funds, especially important in Newcastle and assisted by the fact that Derek Webster had become Chairman of the city's Finance Committee from 1985.[42] Such actions appeared to breach the fiscal significance of NAB's decisions for the Treasury. Slowly the role and function of the local authority in managing its polytechnic was weakened. By the time the White Paper on Education was published in 1987 polytechnics had, to all intents and purposes, been put some distance from their local councils and were on their way to becoming the national institutions they had always meant to be.

Kenneth Baker's 1987 White Paper, the 1988 Education Reform Act and the Polytechnic's reaction

By 1986 the Tory government's policies for education at all levels were in tatters. School teachers were threatening strike action over pay and conditions, many local authorities resented the growing centralisation of the education service and, as we have shown, in higher education there was a constant battle with NAB and all its works. Nearly all observers put this chaotic position down to the rule of Sir Keith Joseph at the DES. Perhaps because Mrs Thatcher saw him as something of a 'guru' for her political philosophy, and especially for her early economic policies, he was treated too kindly by her. After the disastrous local government and by-election results of May 1986 when much of the government's poor performance was attributed to education, Joseph finally resigned on 16 May. He was replaced by Kenneth Baker, previously at the Department for the Environment. He soon recognised that fiscal policies had ensured low levels of expenditure by the local authority education service and he was soon able to announce an increase in education spending from £10.5 billion to nearly £12 billion by the end of 1987. In the schools' sector he promised a national curriculum, the devolution of financial control to schools and their governors and the opportunity for some schools to opt out of LEA control altogether. In the general election of June 1987 the government was returned with a majority of over 100, heralding the opportunity for Baker to announce an Education Reform Bill in the Queen's Speech. For higher education this had been foreshadowed by the 1987 White Paper.[43]

When the Bill was published its main thrust was seen to be the apparent centralising of power in the hands of the Secretary of State. For higher education it foresaw the abolition of NAB and its replacement by the Polytechnic and Colleges Funding Council (PCFC) for the public sector and the UGC replaced by the Universities Funding Council (UFC). Yet again, increased emphasis was to be put on matching the curriculum in universities and polytechnics to the needs of the economy. If higher education did not respond positively to this then steps would be taken via the new funding bodies, dominated as they were to be not by academics but by businessmen, to correct the position. As Stevens put it: 'British Telecom and British Rail were to be privatised; the universities were to be nationalised…' They were now 'clearly part of the state apparatus of education… part of the public services'.[44] Fortunately, most of these more extreme positions were modified by the Bill's passage through the House of Lords. For the polytechnics the principle change proposed by the Bill was that they be taken away from local government control and set up as independent corporations, with new boards of governors but containing few if any locally elected representatives: 'the break with the pluralistic past was complete'.[45]

But it was a Bill that would have a rough passage, particularly in the Lords. Eighty-five lords spoke in the 2 day debate in the upper chamber, surely a record. There were seven former secretaries of state for education in the house, five of them made a contribution including Lord Glenamara who called the Bill, 'the biggest peacetime grabbing of power by a British government in modern times'.[46] There was little concern amongst their lordships for polytechnics; most of their attention was directed towards the threat to universities' academic freedom. However, Lord Monkswell (Labour) ejaculated, 'You may think you had it hard over the last few years under LEA control; you do not know what is coming to you, because it is going to get that much worse under central government control'.[47] In the Commons, the Bill's promoter said that, 'Honourable members are proud of our polytechnics. They provide a splendid education',[48] but he only offered the paltry sum of an average of £85,000 each to pay for the transition to corporate status.[49] Baker liked to trumpet this Bill and the subsequent act as a 'great reform bill' but it was hardly in the same league as those of 1870, 1902 and 1944.

At Newcastle Polytechnic this Bill came soon after the appointment of John Rear as Deputy Director. Having a lawyer like Rear in such a powerful position gave Newcastle someone with the necessary skills and acumen to translate government policy into local practice. It would be vital for the Academic Board and the newly constituted Board of Governors (the former Polytechnic Council) to understand the new and considerable responsibilities they were now being given. With Hopkinson and Torode both gone from the senior administrative posts it was also something of a baptism of fire for Richard Bott who had recently been appointed from North Staffordshire Polytechnic as the new Registrar and Secretary to the Governors. Inevitably there was a longish period of transition between Newcastle City Council's control of the governing body/council and the eventual establishment of a new and quite different board. One of the major stumbling blocks was the transfer of local government property (the Polytechnic's lands and buildings) to the care of the new corporation. Many cities and counties that were about to lose their polytechnic saw this transfer as 'nationalisation without compensation' and did all they could to retain as many of their assets as possible. In Newcastle there was not too much dispute, the principal bone of contention being the site of the old St George's Drill Hall which was used as a car park by the city. To resolve issues such as these the government had established the Polytechnic and Colleges Assets Board to negotiate and agree any transfers, but all this took time.

In May 1989 Derek Webster was to resign from local politics at the end of his period of office as the city's youngest Lord Mayor after 21 years of distinguished serviced. The question then arose as to who would become the Chairman of the Board of Governors that was then being constituted for the newly formed higher education corporation. Although Baker's Bill had made it clear that it was unlikely that local politicians would be acceptable as members of the new governing bodies, the office of Lord Mayor was politically neutral and many expected Webster to be appointed as Chairman. However, his resignation meant a search had to be made for an alternative for which there was no precedence.[50] In the past Chairmen had simply been appointed by the local authority, but who was now responsible? Approaches were made to various likely candidates but clearly it was important for the Director to have someone he could work closely with although, of course, under the new regulations there was no guarantee that even the Director would be an ex officio member. A key figure in the search appears to have been Sir Horace Heyman, a relatively new member of the old Polytechnic Council and a local industrialist who had also originally worked under Sir Sadler Foster on the post-war development of the northern region. Heyman introduced Barden to Reay Atkinson, at that time Chairman of the Northern Development Company. He, Atkinson – a graduate of Durham University – had previously been under-secretary at the Department of Trade and Industry under Sir Keith Joseph and Kenneth Baker (note: both of these politicians went on to be secretaries of state for education) and later, northern regional director of the same department. These posts gave him an insight into the value of the Polytechnic to the local economy and the help it might give with inward investment. In addition, his wife had been a student at Rutherford College.[51] The Board, once agreed by the secretary of state, was large, too large many thought. Besides its majority of private sector people, it did have representation from the staff and students and the Academic Board, and could number amongst its members, a prominent trade unionist, a representative from the University of Newcastle and, surprisingly, given the original opposition, three local authority members including Derek Webster!* Baker's original plans had clearly been thwarted.

---

* The members of the new board were: Independent Governors – Reay Atkinson (Northern Development Corporation), Margaret Barbour (J. Barbour and Sons Ltd), Dorothy Blenkinsop (Northern Regional Health Authority), John Frost (Communications Media Consultant), Lord Glenamara (formerly Deputy Leader of the Labour Party), Bent Henriksen (Marketing Consultant), Charles Herzberg (Industrial Consultant), Peter McKendrick (Sanderson, Townend and Gilbert), Christopher Smart (Northern Rock Building Society), Graham C. Stanton (Evening Chronicle), David Stephenson (Newcastle Breweries Ltd), John S. Ward (Barclay's Bank) and Sue Wilson (Vickers Defence Systems). Local authority members – Derek Webster (Newcastle City Council), Joan M. Lamb (Newcastle City Council) and Alan Brazendale (Gateshead Metropolitan Borough Council). Academic Board members – Dr David Booth (Department of Chemistry and Life Sciences) and Malcolm Macourt (Department of Applied Social Sciences). Teaching staff member – Jacqui Barry (Department of Modern Languages). Non-teaching staff member – Mike Clarke (Department of Physics). Student member – Sigrid Fisher (President, Students' Union). Director –Professor Laing Barden. Co-opted members – Joe Mills (Transport and General Workers' Union), Jenny Robson (Northumbria Tourist Board) and Professor John B. Goddard (University of Newcastle).

To brief the new Governors Barden and others produced a set of background papers which drew their attention to such things as the diverse nature of the Polytechnic's programme, the new responsibilities for property and the estate and the current financial position.[52] Barden took this opportunity to remind Governors of the growing need for a change in institutional title. '…the binary line is bound to break in the next five years', he wrote in July 1988 and that '…the binary line has outlived its usefulness and is now an arbitrary division'. However, little seems to have been said about the new funding mechanism that the government was about to set up which would continue the possibility of the Polytechnic remaining in a precarious financial position. It has to be remembered that with the exception of Webster and one or two others the composition of the board was quite different from its predecessor. Unless the new members were avid readers of the educational press they would have had little idea of the crises through which the Polytechnic had been living.

The 1988 Act established the Polytechnic and Colleges Funding Council (PCFC) to replace NAB and Baker wrote to Sir Ron Dearing, its first Chairman, to remind him of the many, more radical Conservative beliefs that were enshrined in its constitution. Sir Keith Joseph would have approved of them. They included, *inter alia*, the need for greater cost-effectiveness and improved quality, that the block grant was no longer sacrosanct, continuing the shift towards vocational areas, widening access but at the same time noting a projected fall in student numbers. There were to be many changes to procedures that were brought about by the 1988 Act in addition to incorporation amongst which might be numbered the need for polytechnics to produce 5-year institutional plans, a new system of quality assessment since HMIs would no longer have any remit in the newly independent polytechnics and the introduction of a variety of alternative, additional funds that were subject to intense competition. Baker was clearly a keen advocate of the corporate business model.

We have seen how Newcastle Polytechnic had had to make a significant retrenchment in the period leading up to the 1987 White Paper, making about £2.3 million savings from a combination of methods including freezing posts, raising the SSR and restructuring the organisation. Before the PCFC system could be introduced the Polytechnic had to deal with the last flings of the NAB method. It was already the fourth cheapest polytechnic in the country and it was able to demonstrate via some rather hurriedly arranged and perhaps suspect HMI inspections and reports that it had 'outstanding quality' (the highest category and therefore attracting the highest prices) in six out of the nine programme areas. This covered about 75 per cent of all of the Polytechnic's students, the highest in the country.

The new system introduced the idea of competitive bidding for a proportion of the number of students in a college. Initially, 95 per cent of funds would come from a block grant based on the previous year's numbers but the remaining 5 per cent would have to be bid for on the basis of a number of criteria including growth with quality, demand, and price with a premium for high quality, all to be set in the context of the institutional plans that were now required.[53] Here was the reforming Tory philosophy of 'markets' hard at work. Newcastle did well out of this new system. Its bid for the 5 per cent marginal funding came to £3.75 million with PCFC eventually awarding nearly £2.75 million, an increase of 138 per cent over what the Polytechnic would have received by strict application of the formula. With core funding of over £23 million, a total of £25,758,000 was finally allocated. This appeared to be an 11 per cent increase over the previous year but when adjusted for inflation it amounted to only 3 per cent.[54] Inflation was something over which the college had no control; that was the more the fiscal responsibility of the government. Although Newcastle was the second largest gainer of the English polytechnics, the enormously complex, bureaucratic and time consuming system had brought forth only a marginal improvement, even though a very welcome one.

Future rounds of PCFC funding were to be equally complex with frequent changes of the rules. For 1991–92 only 90 per cent was to be core funding and the remainder subject to bidding. Again, Newcastle was relatively successful with 88 per cent of its bid being accepted. Fully funded student numbers increased by 15 per cent. It needed to have only 2 per cent of its students funded by fees only. Some polytechnics had as many as 20 per cent.

Despite Newcastle's success the PCFC remained, like NAB its predecessor, a rigid body. It was '…clearly a colony of the DES, statutorily dependent upon the department for its membership, exclusive in its decision-making and unrepentantly executive in its style'.[55] Like its parallel for the universities (the UFC) it was inexorably moving higher education away from the traditional form of autonomy and bringing both sectors closer together.

Another reorganisation

If this period was dominated by changing relations with CNAA in the Polytechnic's search for increased autonomy and with a series of financial crises brought about by the government's macroeconomic policies, they were by no means the only matters that engaged staff's attention.

With the pressing need to operate within restricted budgets, and having no reserves to fall back on, the Polytechnic sought to raise its efficiency where it could. We have shown how the raising of the SSR was a constant ratchet; we shall return to its effects on teaching and learning and on staff morale later. Two other areas where savings could be made, it was said, were in the management of the organisation and in the accommodation of the Polytechnic's activities.

The reorganisation of the structure of the Polytechnic that had been completed by September 1980 produced over 30 academic sub-divisions – Schools – usually based on one or two disciplines, and Faculties – groupings of cognate subjects. This was a fairly traditional structure modelled on the quasi-independent university type of 'department', known here as the School. This was said to be to be an inefficient form of organisation with the Heads of School interested only in pursuing the interests of their subject. The Heads of Faculty, although now permanent appointments, were not really part of the senior management, only meeting with the Directorate on an *ad hoc* basis.[56] The Polytechnic was forced to become more 'managerial' in its style by the way in which funds were now generated and distributed by NAB and PCFC and by the rigours of the joint validation procedures described above. Heads of Faculty were now given considerable budgetary responsibilities and Heads of School could no longer bury themselves in their teaching, research and their subject allegiances. It became increasingly important for the Director and his assistants responsible for finance and academic development to have a shorter span of control over the institution. Heads of School and Faculty had to become managers as well as academics but within a structure that was leaner and therefore more cost effective. One other factor tipped the balance towards restructuring. It will be recalled that all 'heads' in polytechnics were paid on the national Burnham scale in which 'points' were allotted for such things as number and type of students and other responsibilities. At Newcastle most of the thirty-odd Heads of School, however, were paid at Scale 4, little more than that of a principal lecturer. It was not long before one of these Heads – Professor David Booth of Chemistry – calculated that he had enough 'points' to warrant being paid at Scale 6, the highest level. Clearly, the Polytechnic was in breach of nationally negotiated levels of pay, and after advice was sought and pressure brought by the trade union on behalf of its members, rapid adjustments had to made at some considerable expense. So, for a variety of reasons the Polytechnic needed to rationalise its structure by reducing the numbers of 'middle managers' so as to live within its budget. It was noted that 'the executive recognises that such exercises should only be undertaken in the most pressing circumstances… to meet financial rather than academic requirements'.[57] As it was only 5 years since the last shake up, the circumstances must have been pressing indeed.

It was against this background, then, that the Polytechnic embarked on yet another reorganisation in 1985. The last such exercise had taken about 5 years to complete. Although Laing Barden was always committed to the principles of consultation and participation in anything as complex as reordering people's jobs, this time the economic pressures advised a speedier conclusion. The Academic Board working party reported just a year later, recommending three options: leave things as they are, produce ten to twelve super departments or have fewer units like those established in the last reorganisation. If the latter option were to be followed savings of between £281,000 and £375,000 could be made.[58] Advantage could be taken of impending retirements. Following Gerald Dearden's departure Joe Collerton was asked to assist the Directorate in this restructuring process as an 'acting' Assistant Director before himself retiring. His Faculty of Humanities could then disappear. Gordon Rendall would retire after 27 years of service which made it possible to merge his Faculty (Construction) with Applied Science and Engineering. Ron Hopkinson's post as Chief Administrative Officer could also be declared redundant if his work were divided into a new Registrar's post (the former academic registrar, Peter Torode, was about to depart for Hong Kong), with some of the work transferred to Gordon Campbell, the Assistant Director (Finance). This enabled these men to take advantage of the redundancy scheme. Despite two rounds of interviews John Rear was still acting as Assistant Director (Academic)[59] and his substantive post as Head of the Faculty of Professional Studies was taken by the Head of the School of Economics, Brian Roper. This meant that it might be possible to remove that Faculty and divide into two of the new type Departments.

Following all this legerdemain four new Faculties were now proposed: Art, Design and Cultural Studies; Business; Community and Social Studies and Technology, Engineering and Science. At the next level would be twenty-four Departments, all eventually to be paid at Scale 6. The Business Faculty was to be different, having a unified structure and run on matrix lines. It was to be known as the Newcastle Business School, scooping any ambitions the University of Newcastle might have had for such a title. Only Professor Tom Bromly survived as one of the new Heads of Faculty, now to be know as Deans; the other three were to have new men in post shortly. Having been in an 'acting' capacity for about 6 months John Rear was eventually made Deputy Director, without interview, a post that Barden had apparently earmarked for John Clark but who proved unacceptable to the new Governors and had left to become Director of Hong Kong Polytechnic.

As far as the creation of these new larger Departments was concerned the reorganisation was even more dramatic. As an example the new Social Sciences Faculty contained economics and government and law from Professional Studies; geography and environmental management from Humanities plus sport studies from Education and estate management from Construction; sociology and psychology and social work and social policy from Social and Community Studies, and Education. Squeezing subjects from thirty-four Schools and seven Faculties into twenty Departments and four Faculties was going to be painful and not without bloodshed.

With Hopkinson gone it was also possible to decentralise a lot of the administration down to the Faculty and Departmental levels, all under the managerial control of a Dean. This made for closer working relations and decision-making within a Faculty and was appreciated by staff. Whether this produced financial savings is debatable particularly as two Faculties were scattered over a variety of buildings, even over two sites. All the senior posts both academic and administrative had to be filled by competitive interview. In the case of administrative posts the relevant trade union – NALGO – which incidentally was led nationally by a Rutherford College sociology graduate, Rodney Bickerstaff – insisted on close scrutiny of all gradings. This process took a considerable time and effort and led to the indirect shedding of some posts. It was not until 1987–88 that the process was complete. As we shall see the new set-up was not to last long.

Coach Lane crisis

Even while this reorganisation was going on and while the Polytechnic continued its struggles with NAB and PCFC, it became increasingly clear that the rapid increase in student numbers would need accommodating. In its first year of incorporation

(1989–90) the Polytechnic would face a deficit over £1 million with no local authority life belt any longer available to cling to. There would be no capital available for building in the city centre. The SSR had risen to 13.3:1; there were now over 13,000 students in the Polytechnic and nearly 1,800 staff, more than 800 of them academic. The great building programme on the City Centre Campus took place in the 1960s and 1970s – the Rutherford complex, Northumberland Building, Squires, Lipman, the Students' Union and the library – and since then, virtually nothing. Working conditions, especially in the Northumberland and Lipman Buildings were becoming intolerable. Meanwhile, at the Coach Lane Campus, where most of the buildings had been put up under the auspices of Northern Counties College in the 1960s, there was under-use as teacher education numbers had not grown significantly. Compounding difficulties was the fact that because SSRs had risen, so more efficient means had to be found to teach more and more students. One way of doing this was to increase lecture class sizes but at this time the Polytechnic only had one lecture theatre that could hold more than 100 students.

The solution seemed obvious: move some of the activity of the Polytechnic to its suburban site in Benton. If academic staff did not like being 'reorganised', they and their students liked relocation even less. For the next 2 or 3 years there were to be bitter battles over 'who goes where' in which weapons as diverse as rational argument and sit-ins were to be wielded.

It would have been easiest to move one faculty to Coach Lane Campus in its entirety. And the obvious one was the newly established Business School. It was about the right size, it was coherent and fairly self-contained and its image would benefit from a new location. Its selection immediately sparked off student protests including an occupation of Ellison Building from 1–4 December 1987. This prevented members of the Directorate from reaching their offices but more importantly threatened to disrupt a crucial CNAA visit to the Polytechnic that was to confirm accredited status. In the end the police were called and the president of the Students' Union removed under the Local Government Act of 1980.[60]

This forced the Executive to consider other options, what became know as Models A to H.[61] These were to be costed but other consideration were to be borne in mind including the quality of the accommodation and library facilities at Coach Lane Campus, transport between the two campuses, refectory and Student' Union facilities and womens' issues. This proved to be an enormous exercise. Given responsibility for all this was Brian Roper, newly promoted to be an Assistant Director to replace Bob Schofield who had retired through ill-health. Roper was an economist and a Fellow of the Royal Statistical Society. Perhaps it was his rationalist leanings that encouraged him to tackle this problem in an objective way with data and measurements, hoping this would lead to academics and students accepting a 'logical' solution. Naturally staff replied in an equally rationalist manner. Mike Cornish, Head of the Department of Education prepared twenty-eight pages of closely argued text setting out why his Department should stay exactly where it was! The psychologists, scientists to a man and woman, even calculated the length of shelf-runs in the main library used by their students – 92 metres for psychology, 52 metres for social psychology, etc! – that would have to be replicated if they were forced to the *ultima thule* of Coach Lane. Every conceivable reason was dredged up as to why a particular subject should not move to Coach Lane.

But it was really a political problem that needed a more robust approach. Roper was equally capable of that as his subsequent career was to demonstrate. He went on to be Deputy Director at Oxford Polytechnic and the Vice-Chancellor of London Metropolitan University. After much deliberation the Task Force concluded that Social Work and Social Policy and Health and Behavioural Science, and the Handicapped Persons Research Unit should be relocated to Coach Lane Campus and that Education Studies should stay where it was. By a combination of strenuous lobbying, direct student action and the presentation of 'rational' facts, the Business School and most of the Faculty of Social Sciences had avoided being transferred to Coach Lane's gulag.

But this wasn't the end of the matter. Some of those, like psychology, continued to argue their case, now more and more on cost grounds, something that Roper, an economist, might understand. Their point was that converting the consumer science laboratories at Coach Lane Campus into psychology laboratories and then building new consumer science laboratories somewhere in the Chemistry Department's space was a costly nonsense. So, as was so often the case in the Polytechnic's history, the mountain had roared and brought forth a mouse.[62]

The negative side of this was that it eventually led to a split in the psychology staff. Dr Don Watson the Head of the Department of Health and Behavioural Sciences and a small number of his of colleagues decided that a brighter future lay with health sciences and the rapidly growing professions allied to medicine including an area that was about to boom, nursing. A new degree in nursing was scheduled to begin in September 1988. The remaining psychology staff saw their futures in their degree course in psychology and its recognition by British Psychological Society. Moving applied consumer science in the opposite to the Chemistry Department was not fraught with the same difficulties, creating new opportunities for the development of food science.

It is difficult now, 16 years later, to appreciate why there was such antagonism towards Coach Lane Campus from staff at the city centre site. It seems to have been a combination of the benefits that staff thought they derived from being near the heart of the Polytechnic and the city centre with its cultural facilities, and the fear of being exiled to what was perceived to be an inferior place. In the short run, the cost to those who stayed and those who went were considerable. We shall see the longer run effects later. What dismayed many was being identified by management for dispersal, somehow marginal to the Polytechnic's central thrust. In the longer run neither group – stayers and movers – were unduly affected; indeed, both were to prosper considerably, but perhaps for reasons that had little to do with geography.

Nevertheless, a very significant set of decisions had been made that was to lead to two important changes. One was that Coach Lane was here to stay and that Newcastle was to become a two campus polytechnic. Once such a decision was taken then it became increasingly clear it could perhaps operate on many sites. We shall see how, soon, the Polytechnic was to develop satellites in Carlisle and Northumberland. The second change was associated with the growing political significance of higher education for the health services, adding a fifth vocational string to the Polytechnic's bow alongside the main ones of engineering, business, design and teacher education.

Some other effects of the 1988 Act

The highly centralising nature of Baker's reforms was largely about controlling expenditure and making higher education accountable for the public funds it received. It was also expected that polytechnics and universities to become more market orientated. To do this they were obliged to put in place new policies and new systems to carry them out.

The PCFC demanded that polytechnics explain what they were about; this meant 'mission statements' from academic boards and agreed by the new governing bodies. John Rear drafted Newcastle's in January 1988.

Funds were to be allocated against plans. This was not entirely new for Newcastle who had argued for them in its clashes with NAB but it meant more detailed planning had to be entered into. This would need a planning support office; Newcastle Polytechnic's was set up under Val Wilson, an English graduate, in July 1990.

Staff had to be shown to be proficient teachers. This meant establishing a staff development strategy, implementing a training programme for new staff and then having an appraisal system to make sure all this was working. Newcastle was one of the first of the polytechnics to insist on properly trained lecturers and most young staff for whom a post at the Polytechnic was their first, really welcomed the opportunity to be trained – mostly on the job – and to receive a certificate that had currency elsewhere. Appraisal was another matter. The training for this descended into farce at a series of disastrous 'away-days'. Some Departments never really implemented the programme and it was a scheme largely honoured in the breach. Nonetheless, the infrastructure for training and appraisal had to be set up largely *ab initio*, and new staff appointed to carry it out.

The Act also insisted on some kind of quality assurance so a mechanism for this had to be devised. This was a topic that was to loom much larger following the passing of the 1992 Act and it will be dealt with in more detail there.

With the Polytechnic, and its Governors, now responsible for its own real estate it would need to develop strategies and plans for its upkeep and maintenance, as well as looking forward to raising capital to expand it.

Finally, new funding initiatives were introduced whose income would come not come from the 'core plus marginal funding' described earlier. In effect this would be top-sliced and often linked to the demands of other government departments. This led to PICKUP, for example, which was to generate over £1 million per annum and Enterprise in Higher Education which brought over £5 million into the Polytechnic's coffers but both of these initiatives pitted polytechnic against polytechnic in competitive bidding. Similarly, polytechnics from now on were expected to generate an increasing proportion of their income from marketing their own skills and the outputs of their research.

There were two general outcomes from these changes. One was that everyone had to learn a new vocabulary based on a bastardised business language, including using many new acronyms. The second, and this was equally new, was that polytechnics had to develop a technocratic bureaucracy to carry out these initiatives. In some areas such as estate management and academic planning this meant recruiting a new breed of professional, often computer literate. In other areas academic staff could be transfered into this new workforce. This new cadre was crucial to the future success of the Polytechnic and resources were soon found – often from teaching and research programmes – to support them, at least until they could be self-funding. The 'core business' of the Polytechnic was being redefined.

Quite rapidly a new, *parallel* Polytechnic developed that had its own offices, secretaries and 'means of production'. New nameplates sprang up on doors throughout the institution: 'Planning Support Office'; 'Enterprise Initiative'; 'PICKUP Co-ordinator', later to be joined by 'Audit', 'Quality Assurance' and 'Research Administration'. All this was a long way from the library, the careers office and the chaplaincy of the 1970s. Naturally, this parallel universe soon had a life of its own; its political significance in the decision making processes soon became obvious. It was a long way too from the classroom, the studio and the research laboratory which had traditionally been the route to promotion and upward mobility for staff. No one would deny that without these 'support' activities Newcastle Polytechnic would not have been as able to cope with the demands now being made by the central direction of higher education from Whitehall and Westminster. And at Newcastle nearly all of these challenges were met with advantage. But it was no surprise to find this new cadre much in demand in the senior ranks of management to whom they directly reported. Few directors and their assistants dared appear without these 'experts' at their side. Soon these 'New Men' and women (*à la* C. P. Snow) would be joining their ranks. Even at the very top future directors no longer had necessarily to be first-rate academics but rather top-notch administrators. The production system for mass higher education that was about to be launched needed a new breed of leader. Industrialised higher education had set out on the yellow-brick road.

Procession of University dignitaries led by Lord Glenamara and Professor Laing Barden at the inauguration of the University of Northumbria at Newcastle, September 1992

Chapter Six

The ladder to paradise:[1]
from Polytechnic to University, 1988–1996

BEFORE LONG the Conservative government introduced yet another Act that would have far reaching implications for Newcastle Polytechnic including transforming it into a university. Meanwhile the effects of the 1988 Act were continuing to be felt through the early 1990s. With the institution now an independent corporation and free from local government control, only national politics had to be contended with. After Baker, John MacGregor became Secretary of State for Education but soon (November 1990) Margaret Thatcher and her zealous reformers were deposed and many of her acolytes were to go to the House of Lords. John Major had rather surprisingly become Prime Minister and he, like his predecessor, appointed a succession of chief ministers to the education portfolio; after MacGregor came Kenneth Clarke, who was then succeeded by John Patten and Gillian Shephard. Perhaps there was something about being in charge of the nation's schools, colleges and universities that was unattractive, certainly no one stayed long and most found it hard to make their mark from their Whitehall centre in Elizabeth House.

Baker had seen his own Act as a 'great' reform act but whereas most reform acts brought forward new opportunities and benefits, many commentators saw mostly the opposite with this one. It was an almost seismic move towards the State direction of education, loved by very few. One of its features was the large amount of small print that Baker's successors used to usher in many radical changes to higher education practice. The ladder to paradise was to have many rungs.

Enterprise in higher education

One of the technical memoranda accompanying the 1988 Act said, in effect, that financial allocations made by the government to higher education would be on the basis of services rendered, with the Secretary of State determining, in part, what those 'services' should be. At the same time higher education was encouraged to increase its income from other sources, including from other government departments but preferably from the private sector. This was, if not the beginning, then the formal recognition that higher education was to be subject to market forces. Some have seen this really as 'government stinginess' in disguise.[2] Others thought 'the State saw in enterprise in higher education a vehicle for assisting its wider plans for re-shaping the UK economy and its human capital'.[3]

The Enterprise in Higher Education initiative (EHE) began life in the Manpower Services Commission (MSC) in late 1987 but was the product of discussions with the funding bodies for higher education. In a wider context the whole business of 'transferable skills' became part of the language of enterprise and 'useful' education and its ability to raise Gross Domestic Product. Polytechnics and universities could submit plans to MSC for 5 years of £1 million p.a. of funding to enable students to develop competencies and skills relevant to the world of work, to be jointly assessed by employers and colleges. Many academics condemned the initiative as subordinating academic values to those of the labour market. Newcastle Polytechnic, like many higher education establishments, saw it as a means of raising revenue. Once it had decided to pursue the initiative, Laing Barden was heard to say to the Dean of the Faculty of Arts and Design, Professor Tom Bromly, who was initially put in charge of the project, "Tom, I want you to go to London and get us top whack". The Director's motives were not entirely cynical. One of his background papers for the new governors was about 'competencies', something of a buzz word at the time but the acquisition of enabling skills as part of the curriculum was something Barden was passionate about.[4]

Freda Tallentyre[5] became project director for enterprise. She wrote a persuasive submission to the MSC and was one of the first to secure maximum funding. Colleges could write their own proposals. Tallentyre found that any narrow definition that appeared too vocational would be met by intransigence and slow cooperation from staff. At first they viewed this initiative in the usual cynical way, seeing it as another example of Thatcherite ideology aimed at improving staff and students' approach to such things as profit maximisation, entrepreneurship, etc. If these perceptions had remained it would have been a programme that gained little support. However, Tallentyre cleverly revamped the concept of 'enterprise' with its capitalist overtones to

THE LADDER TO PARADISE

one of 'being enterprising'. This semantic twist opened all sorts of doors – after all, what member of staff didn't want to appear enterprising, teaching enterprising students? What it became, to all intents and purposes, was an adjunct to the staff development policy, sometimes involving cooperation with local firms. The most successful activity that sprang from this was integrating notions of 'enterprise' into the curriculum, usually focussing on student-centred learning and the development of 'generic competencies and transferable personal skills'. This led to a marked increase in skills acquisition, not so much of the skills associated with a particular discipline but rather personal skills in writing, presentation, use of IT, team-work and building self-confidence. Naturally, students soon saw the benefits of this aspect of their learning.

For the MSC it was important that 'enterprising' aspects should be integrated into the curriculum.[6] From now on all courses would include a 'skills' content. The enterprising polytechnic now became one characterised by even closer links with business and industry, the professions, continuing professional development and eventually with 'life-long learning'. But enterprise was also part of the new wider culture of mass higher education and some thought it compromised older values associated with teaching, learning, research and scholarly activity. The question for Newcastle was: whether to embrace these changes or try to resist them. Given its embeddedness in local and regional business culture and its continuing precarious financial position, it had little choice. In any case, it had no long-standing tradition of scholarly activity to fall back on. Ironically, one area that took to the information technology opportunities that the scheme offered was humanities, historians especially. Strong direction from the top coupled with subtle interpretation and perceived likely benefits ensured its adoption, so much so that when MSC funding ceased in September 1993, the scheme's main principles entered the University's curriculum on a permanent basis.[7]

Quality assessment

Another field that the 1987 White Paper and the eventual Act focussed on was quality. Perhaps even more than with enterprise Baker and his advisors were perhaps not as aware as they might have been that this was something higher education had always prided itself in, surely a *sine qua non*. The problem for the Secretary of State was that there were no open, accessible statements of how this characteristic was achieved so it became yet another area of accountability. Over the next 17 years it was to spawn a whole new industry with its own headquarters in Bristol, and all higher education was to become subject to intense scrutiny.

For the polytechnics that had grown up under the tutelage of the CNAA, the idea of testing their quality assertions was not new. They and their courses had been subject to robust challenges internally and externally through course and subject review, faculty and institutional review, in Newcastle's case from the early 1980s. All polytechnics, but not the universities, had always been open to scrutiny by Her Majesty's Inspectors. As we saw in the previous chapter, Newcastle Polytechnic had always benefited positively from their visits, particularly when their assessments were linked to funding. Universities on the other hand, had few if any such checks on quality. Their assertions were simply that, assertions. They had their external examiners (as did polytechnics, of course) but their role was primarily that of moderators. Although the UFC set up its academic audit unit in 1990 and PCFC had agreed to advise Baker on quality, it was clear that government did not trust self-regulation through voluntary action in higher education. It may have seemed perfectly acceptable for the private sector of business and industry but government generally did not trust the public sector.

The 1987 White Paper had indicated that polytechnics were to be responsible for the quality of their activities but the emphasis was to be on staff training and appraisal and the evaluation of results. Baker wrote to Sir Ron Dearing, the new chair of PCFC, saying he wanted 'high quality, cost effective higher education' and that there was 'further scope for improvements in efficiency and quality'.[8] Her Majesty's Inspectorate (HMI) had already reassured Baker that the English polytechnics had increased numbers of students and staff/student ratios without reducing quality.[9] We have shown that Newcastle Polytechnic came first in the national quality ratings for 1989–90, and it came fourth the following year. This method under PCFC rules attracted a price premium of 10 to 20 per cent.[10] However, it was about to come to an end. As far as quality was concerned two new developments were proposed. A new body, the Higher Education Quality Council (HEQC) would be established to assess quality by 'direct observation',[11] while the new funding organisation for the whole of higher education, the Higher Education Funding Council for England (HEFCE) would be responsible for institutional audits.

The mechanism under HEQC became known as teaching quality assessment (TQA). This required a department or subject area to submit a self-assessment document, followed by a 3 or 4 day visit of external assessors who would make judgements based on observation of teaching, scrutiny of documents and student work and discussions with staff and students. Subjects or departments that claimed that their provision was 'excellent' would automatically receive one of these visits; those that merely claimed to be 'satisfactory' would probably not.[12] At Newcastle everyone was encouraged to claim 'excellence'. Under this scheme the Polytechnic was to receive three 'excellent' and eight 'satisfactory' classifications. When the system moved in 1996 to a points score (maximum 24) Newcastle Polytechnic maintained its high level of performance by scoring an average of 22 points across twenty subject areas with two maximum scores in nursing and education. Its modern languages department came second only to Cambridge University.

With the advent of a unified higher education system it was possible, for the first time, to compare the relative performance of former polytechnics and universities in terms of quality. Over the period 1992–95 former polytechnics and colleges scored 11 per cent 'excellents', 85 per cent 'satisfactories' and 4 per cent 'unsatisfactory', compared to 46 per cent, 54 per cent and 0 per cent respectively for the university sector. Universities also claimed more 'excellents' (88 per cent) against the polytechnics' more modest (and probably realistic) 43 per cent.[13] These data seem to undermine the myth that universities with their mission more orientated towards research, would not be as good teaching institutions as the old polytechnics. There seemed to be some superficial evidence that quality was concentrated in the better funded institutions.

The merit of the TQA was that it was based on peer review but there were some visits to 'old' universities by assessors from former polytechnics that were resented. Perhaps the greatest drawback was that it became more of a paper driven exercise. The self-assessment document itself was a relatively modest affair but departments were expected to have available to the assessors practically every document they had ever produced. And if they did not have them, they would be especially written, sometimes just hours before the visiting party arrived. A whole room – the base-room – would be set aside for the assessors to work in. It was usually floor-to-ceiling with box files and filing cabinets. In time these exercises became too onerous for individual departments to manage so a quality assessment unit was set up, overseen by yet another committee, the Quality Improvement and Academic Standards Committee (QIAS). This unit helped train and prepare staff for TQA visits – 'have a word with the cleaner or porter if there is anything shabby about the rooms you use… in lectures make sure that you ask questions and elicit questions… prepare nice (*sic*) OHPs and handouts'[14] – but less facetiously, the University established an internal review procedure that vetted a department's or subject's submission to HEQC. This was typical of Northumbria's thoroughness so that eventual submissions were an 'institutional judgement of quality', QIAS noting that '…the reputation of the University rides on it',[15] a sort of moral imperative.

The HEFCE's concern was for the mechanisms and structures used by a college to manage quality assurance against its own aims and objectives. It required them to submit annual reports and to be open to visits. Its basic technique on such a visit was to sample documentation, follow audit trails and interview staff and students as necessary, and then to publish a report on its findings. Although it was 'audit' and not a comprehensive review, it did require, like TQA, enormous quantities of paperwork and preparation. Internally, this increased considerably when 'central', that is, non-teaching departments (such as, for example, personnel and the library) were also included by the University in the assessment and management of its quality. In its report in 1994, the HEQC found few flaws in Northumbria's systems and many complimentary points, noting that staff showed a 'deep awareness of quality issues and concerns'.[16]

Later that year the new Secretary of State, John Patten, a former Oxford University geography don, shifted the emphasis somewhat from 'quality' *per se* to 'standards', something that had worried at least one of his predecessors, Sir Keith Joseph. This was a field even more difficult to define than quality. As a result of pressure being brought by vice-chancellors and others on the cost-effectiveness of the HEFCE/HEQC systems, the two bodies being merged into a single agency, the Quality Assurance Agency (QAA) in 1997.

This concern for quality, arising as it did out of the 'proper accountability for the substantial public funds invested in higher education',[17] is difficult to dismiss. However, the need for an assurance that 'money was being well spent' was in part, of the government's own making. It arose from the tensions between resources and a changing intake both quantitatively and qualitatively, driven by the ratchet effect on student numbers that successive funding methods had imposed. The question was: How could 'efficiency' and 'quality' be maintained against a constantly declining resource base? This is essentially a business-based idea, as is the language, and it is questionable whether it was applicable to higher education. Once the concept of competition was introduced by Joseph, Baker *et al.* there seemed to be an inevitability about the infusion of the whole culture of the market place.[18] Vice-Chancellors readily adopted the trappings: the image of the university and its promotion, the concern for reputation, share of applications, promo-videos, recruitment fairs, etc., all of which Northumbria vigorously adopted. In 1992 Derek Webster, the former Chairman of the city's Education Committee, the Chairman of the Polytechnic Council and a Governor, post-1988 incorporation, was appointed as Director of External Relations for the University after holding a similar post at Sunderland. Around him was built a new non-academic department including marketing, press and publicity, the alumni office, public relations, regional, European and international offices, transport and the University's commercial arm. The main base for this was to be accommodated in newly acquired and converted houses in 21 and 22 Ellison Place.[19] The Vice-Chancellor clearly believed that this and the high 'quality' scores Northumbria was achieving would improve its competitive position.

Unitisation of the curriculum; semesterisation of the academic year

These American terms heralded yet more work for academic staff that at first sight seemed a long way from what they considered to be their primary task. Their adoption introduced a 'cultural revolution' in teaching and learning with a fault-like shift for students, moving from 'being taught' to 'learning'. Initially many staff found these profound changes all the more unwelcome because they felt their direction came from the top downwards; some of the more naive members even believing they originated in the Vice-Chancellor's office. As with 'enterprise' and 'quality' they had their origins in the 1988 Act and its call for greater efficiency in British higher education.

A number of polytechnics, notably City of London, Middlesex, Oxford and Brighton, had already adopted a modular- or unit-based form of curriculum for some or all of their courses. Compared to the traditional English single honours degree that had been the model for most polytechnics under CNAA, the modular degree was said to offer a number of educational advantages including the pursuit of interdisciplinarity, combined subject degrees or multidisciplinarity, delayed choice of specialism, 'majoring' in one discipline, credit accumulation and transfer and economy of course delivery. Few universities had adopted modular schemes partly because of their belief in the traditional honours programme, and probably because their more generous funding did not force their consideration. There were many sarcastic descriptions of modular degrees at the time: 'pick and mix', 'cafeteria' degrees, 'rag bag' courses, 'soft centred', and especially, 'Mickey Mouse' degrees. Their detractors were clearly not aware of the popularity of such programmes with students, and in the new world of 'the market place' and 'competition', popularity and choice were important. Pratt quotes the example of Oxford Polytechnic that in 1988 received over 20,000 applications for 923 admissions.[20] Such courses were clearly different from most university schemes and many polytechnic ones. Newcastle Polytechnic was deeply committed to the predominance of single or joint honours degrees in its curriculum, pointing to the prestige it had derived for them in its dealings with CNAA in the 1970s and 1980s (see Chapter 5). In addition, some professional bodies remained sceptical of modular programmes. For example, at the Polytechnic the law degree schemes were to remain largely outside the unitised system thanks to opposition, it was said, from the Law Society.

The proposed changes were widely debated throughout the Polytechnic and no one could claim that the adoption was imposed by the Directorate. During a dispute with the trade union much later (October 1995; see below), Professor John Rear, whose job it was to oversee any major changes in academic activity, took the opportunity to write at length to the branch chairman about the history of unitisation and its 'democratic' adoption;[21] it is worth summarising it here. It began in early 1988 with a concern for making the Polytechnic's part-time courses more flexible and accessible but only a minimal response was forthcoming. A year later a new working party consulted widely in the Polytechnic and recommended that the institution adopt 'a flexible, modular, mixed mode' curriculum. By November 1989 the Academic Board established yet another working party, to 'bring forward recommendations on a unit-based structure policy for the Polytechnic'. Its report, incorporating the views of all the faculties, was accepted in principle by Academic Board in February 1991. A unitised system was described as having benefits for the student, the course and the Polytechnic. A year later another working party, this time chaired by an Assistant Dean, Professor John Wilson of Engineering, Science and Technology, recommended that unitisation be undertaken of a 'substantial number of courses in each faculty' within an institutional framework by July 1994. Faculty comments varied. Engineering, Science and Technology saw it as an 'inevitable development within the institution, though one accepted without great enthusiasm'. Social Sciences wanted local control of it, saw it as a costly exercise and was concerned about the reaction of validating professional bodies. The Business School welcomed it, saying it vindicated developments it already had in hand. Finally, Arts and Design was prepared to consider unitisation openly and on its merits in educational terms. None of these gave what might be called resounding support for the massive changes it entailed but the Polytechnic went ahead with a budget of £300,000 to support implementation.

In answer to the union's later concerns Rear recognised that not all staff were reconciled to unitisation even after it had started: 'they have their counterparts in every university which has modularised'. He pointed out that a unitised curriculum moved the locus of power from the staff (the 'teacher') to the student (the 'learner') and warned of the dangers of trying to retain the values of former programmes within a unitised scheme; that would give the worst of both worlds. He concluded: 'But after taking seven years (1988 to 1994) to reach this point... it would be foolish to move back instead of forward – particularly as nearly every UK university is moving in our current direction'.[22]

Although it certainly became a national movement, to begin with each polytechnic devised its own system. However, another aspect of this search for efficiency as demanded by the 1988 Act was the inclusion of a credit-based system with credits being transferable between institutions. In principle this appeared a sound idea – students could take their time in getting a degree or diploma, a mixture perhaps of full- and part-time study; they could move from place to place to study in order to take advantage of their changing circumstances, even studying abroad. Unfortunately, the culture in Britain was for degree courses to be short and intense by world standards (3 years) and for students to be residential (the college or hall system), all quite different from many continental countries and the USA from whence this system was borrowed. Eventually, the outcome was a standardised product: a 30-week year with 360 credit-points required to gain a degree level award, each year consisting of 120 points with four units each worth 15 points in each semester. This could be modified to include 4-year courses, sandwich courses and a variety of placements at home and overseas.

One factor that worried the government and its civil servants in their search for greater efficiencies from higher education was the shortness of the academic year from October to July. For the three or four summer months much of the 'plant' was said to be idle, or at least, could have been used more intensively by universities and colleges. This concern was coupled with a feeling that if the year were to be structured differently, then perhaps it might be possible for a student to obtain a degree in 2 years not three or four. To examine various options Lord Flowers was commissioned to look into some alternatives and to present a report.[23]

It was said that the usual three-term year was a reflection of either the ecclesiastical calendar (hence the prayer book language – Trinity, Hilary, etc.) or the farming seasons so that young men could be released from their studies in time to get in the harvest. This omits the fact that in the nineteenth century and before, many public schools had a year of two halves. What Flowers initially favoured was dividing the year into four with staff guaranteed one session in four free from duties; students would be able to start their courses at a number of points during the year so that buildings would be in use all year round. Flowers knew he was likely to be opposed and, in any case, he could not be prescriptive. Those universities with charters believed that such interference in their affairs by government was legally difficult. Under pressure, what most universities opted for was a two-semester year.

The problem faced by Northumbria in changing to a semester system was twofold: most of Britain worked on a three-term basis with a long break in July and August so that fitting two semesters into this would not mesh with most people's domestic arrangements, especially those with children at school. In addition, most former polytechnics, worked longer teaching years than universities. Oxford and Cambridge have 8-week terms, Durham nine and most others ten whereas polytechnics typically had 35- or 36-week years. Naturally the question was asked: Why did it take 36 weeks of attendance to get a degree at a polytechnic but only thirty at a university? Over the years that particular problem had been partially solved by the introduction of so called 'reading weeks'. Fitting a two-semester year into a year divided by Christmas and Easter proved much more difficult. The protagonists of the American semester had forgotten that the USA is officially a secular society and religious holidays are short and of less significance. The third problem was with English and Welsh 'A' Levels taken by 17 to 18-year-olds in June with the results not available until mid August which did not give enough time for an early September start for a degree course.

The solution was to have two 15-week semesters, to start the year as early as possible in September (a decreasing proportion of 'new' university entrants came with 'A' Level qualifications gained in the same year anyway) and to have a 10-week teaching term before a later and shorter Christmas vacation, with assessments afterwards. The movable feast of Easter created much more of a headache. One side-effect of this new kind of year was to reduce the number of unseen examinations and replace them with coursework assessments. Whether this was a more efficient way of delivering the academic programme it is difficult to say as no one has calculated the costs and benefits. As with 'modularisation' the front-end costs were certainly high.

These radical changes were introduced at about the same time as many of the other changes brought about by the 1988 Act which we have described. The burdens on the teaching staff were very considerable. It should also be remembered there was a significant degree of lecturer resistance to changing a curriculum that had served Newcastle very well and upon which it had built its considerable reputation. Despite Rear's plea, in fact, a number of honours degrees at Northumbria although superficially unitised did retain much of their fairly traditional form to begin with. Nonetheless, for many staff, and especially course leaders, all this meant large amounts of additional work which in turn cut into time for research and the preparation of new teaching material. Students, on the other hand, despite their sometimes being described as 'customers' at about this time, had little say in the diet to which they would be exposed. The effect of the introduction of the unitised, semesterised curriculum was to reduce the number of courses (units) a student took so that average class size notably increased. This meant that small group teaching now largely disappeared. So called seminars – another American import – replaced tutorials in almost every course at Northumbria. Eventually these could have as many as thirty students in them. Students no longer received as much personal attention as they once had. Staff conceptions of 'teaching' had to change and in their turn, students had to accept that their 'learning' was increasingly in their own hands.

Because teaching and learning were now open to outside scrutiny via TQA it meant the 'what, how and why' of the process had to be fully documented. Gone were the days of a lecturer issuing a reading list or a set of laboratory exercises, and of the extempore lecture. Now, course handbooks and unit descriptors had to be produced, much more detailed and compendious handouts written, aims and objectives had to be set, the content and purpose of each lecture explained. While all this may have been thought of as best practice, it was highly systematised and convergent. There was a belief amongst many staff at the time that most students saw each unit they took as being self-contained, and that little needed to be carried forward or across from one unit to another, from one year to the next. Success was measured by assembling the right units in the right order and collecting the requisite number of points.

The unitisation of the curriculum and the semesterisation of the year were not without their problems. It was as if the 'hand-crafted' degrees that had evolved over many years that were largely self-contained in a particular department had to be converted to a much more regular and standard product, one made up of standardised components. For success these components had to fit together easily and smoothly. Timetabling was one of the major challenges. At the beginning of the 1995–96 academic year it was proposed that the dates of semesters be altered. Staff were angry too that the IT support for timetabling and the 'production' of units simply could not deliver what was required. At a branch meeting of the union (NATFHE) a motion was passed that 'this branch believes the present unitised system is fundamentally flawed' and a vote of no confidence in the senior management was passed.[24] The University had committed itself to this radical change in its teaching and problems like these had to be resolved.

In the same year the government pressed for British universities to improve the usefulness of their output to industry. This resulted from a growing concern amongst employers that while graduates might be well versed in their respective disciplines they were often short on many everyday skills; there was talk of weakness in simple mathematical abilities, report writing and team working, for example. Too few had sufficient IT skills particularly those with arts and social science backgrounds. We have already drawn attention to the 'enterprise 'initiative'; it now became incumbent upon universities to build on that by integrating a package of skills into the curriculum (see pp.120–121). At Northumbria, perhaps because of the relative success of adopting 'enterprise' this did not meet with too much resistance, but, of course, the curriculum in each degree or diploma course had to be altered to accommodate it. To have a free-standing programme of skills units available to all students would not have been practicable at a large and diverse university like Northumbria, rather each course team devised its own approach, putting on units such as 'IT skills for historians' or 'presentations in business' or 'report writing for engineers', much of which was not new anyway. Students took to these new aspects of the curriculum with some enthusiasm, believing that the acquisition of many of these skills would give them an advantage in the labour market. Some of their more conservative tutors, dedicated as they were to the intricacies of their disciplines, remained sceptical. For them, it all seemed a long way from Newmanian ideas of what a university should be about.

Research

The 1988 Act had already hinted that funding for the two principal activities – teaching and research – could and should be separated. It would not be long before a new method for assessing what was done in the name of research would be introduced and how it might be paid for.

A university without some kind of research base was considered by most to be a contradiction in terms. As a polytechnic Newcastle had always been research active despite the shortage of funds to support it. Indeed, the output by staff by the end of the 1980s was very commendable. The Polytechnic had prided itself on being the first polytechnic in the country to be granted full delegation of powers for all its research awards which meant that it could register and examine all higher degrees including MPhil, PhD and DSc degrees of CNAA. When university title was granted and CNAA wound up, these powers naturally passed to the Academic Board. As with the undergraduate programmes the architect of this achievement was Professor John Clark, a mission he achieved prior to leaving for Hong Kong.[25] To attain such a high status the Polytechnic had been able to demonstrate that a significant proportion of its staff were actively engaged in research and that its research degrees committee was capable of managing research students and their supervisors. Where supervision was lacking outside academics could be registered but the Polytechnic had early on instituted a training scheme for inexperienced staff. By the late 1980s research activity was increasingly becoming a criterion for appointment and all departments had to have a research policy.

This had not always been the case. In the early years of Rutherford College and the College of Commerce research was not as highly regarded as it might have been although in science and technology there was usually an expectation of a higher degree and publications among staff. Indeed, as we have shown, as more and more of the work of the Polytechnic moved out of further education into the higher branch, research became increasingly a defining activity. Despite staff having to receive approval to undertake research from the governors in the early days,[26] many were assisted financially by the local authority to obtain research degrees through the payment of fees and expenses. By the 1980s it was rare to appoint staff without a higher degree, usually a doctorate, but of course that varied from subject to subject. In some areas professional or business experience was equally highly regarded. In accountancy and law, for example, there was no real expectation of staff having doctorates. Art and design, and especially fine art, had something of a problem here too; to painters and sculptors the concept of 'research' was quite different. The inclusion of some of these professional- and practice-based subjects into a university type of academy increasingly called for their conformity.

The Polytechnic's research policy in the late 1980s was still largely based on the ideas found in the national Rochester Report[27] with its emphasis on applied research and the needs of the local economy. Funding, if any, came from robbing Peter's teaching budget to pay for Paul's research and from the more conventional sources of the Research Councils and industrial or business sponsorship. Research rarely accounted for more than 5 per cent of the Polytechnic's turnover; in universities it often approached 50 per cent via the dual support system. When NAB was replaced by the PCFC more funds for research found their way into polytechnics. When HEFCE took over then for the first time polytechnics were included in the research assessment exercise (RAE) that applied to the whole of British higher education, a highly competitive arena.

The University was now able to access more public funds for research in ways that were denied it as a polytechnic and began to reassess the role of research in its range of activities. The original Mission Statement had described research as supporting teaching. Many now began to argue that it should now be a freestanding activity in its own right and that describing it as 'supporting' was to lower its importance.[28] The reform movement to raise the status of research was led by Professor Derek Gardiner. He was supported in his ideas by all Heads of Department except Professor Kenny of Law.[29]

The Executive was divided. Professor Rear was 'wholly opposed to any such change' to the Mission as approved in February 1989. Teaching funds, he said, should not be diverted to research:

> 'By changing on this key issue we will be signalling that like every other traditional university we are now pursuing twin, equal goals – teaching and research – except that everyone will know that, really, when it comes to where staff priorities are actually placed, when the chips are down, research is the most important goal: the place where staff want to make their mark with their peers – a more prestigious thing to do than teach.'

Dr John McGinnety, a Pro Vice-Chancellor, supported the case for change, reminding Academic Board that through the new arrangements with HEFCE the former polytechnics now had an opportunity to compete for research funding. His view and that of the Heads of Department prevailed and the Mission was changed from 'teaching and supporting research' to 'teaching and research'. Losing one word was supposed to mean so much. Perhaps Board members should have recalled that the 1992 Act said that polytechnics were not expected to change their broad research missions when they came to be called universities. For the government and the DES the decoupling of research funding from student numbers meant that they could now monitor research as well as teaching, income and expenditure, all part of the centralising process.

Nonetheless, the decision to change gave an important boost to staff morale with the result that Northumbria entered into the first RAE with a reasonable expectation of success. Although the funds received were modest by the standards of traditional universities – a mere £1.35 million – they made a significant difference to those Departments that were successful, aided by the fact that central overheads were kept small and monies were returned to Departments that had earned them. With submissions in twenty-two subject areas by 155 active researchers (about 15–16 per cent of all staff), Northumbria came eighth in the list of 'new' universities.[30]

In time RAEs became political weapons whereby 'old' universities had to become more successful at winning research funds at the expense of the ex- polytechnics. Under the previous system 30 to 50 per cent of their income came from research and they simply could not afford to lose any of it. Although Northumbria resolved to double its income from the next RAE in 1996, and indeed almost succeeded, the proportion of total income that came from such exercises remained small. The early euphoria gradually gave way to new realities.

Becoming a university

We have seen, as this story of Northumbria unfolds, that from at least the late 1950s that there was always an aspiration to achieve a higher status than the current one. It was thought that this would be achieved if only the institution could be in control of its own affairs. Thus, there were early moves to obtain College of Advanced Technology status and to break free from local authority control – or if not free, to act as independently as possible. In terms of powers to confirm awards the college similarly sought to act at arms length from its degree and diploma awarding bodies, especially from CNAA. But where was real autonomy to come from? Most believed the only source of such status was to come from a change of title. And the title to which all aspired was *university*. Why was this? Primarily because in Britain 'university' was a title that could be conferred by a Royal Charter with all the legal paraphernalia of Letters Patent, etc. or, more rarely, by private Act of Parliament. Such a charter conferred on a corporate body certain powers enshrined in law that could not easily be interfered with by government, national or local.

The other source of autonomy was believed to be the college or *collegium*, a self-managing body of scholars whose membership and its head was elected but with the latter's powers restricted to being *primus inter pares*, so that decisions were reached collectively by agreement or by majority voting. Checks and balance would be in place to prevent the concentration of power in one person's hands. Thus, a *university* with its Royal Charter could be run and organised on *collegiate* lines. The reason why this was said to be important for academic institutions was so that freedom of expression could be protected – the freedom to write and say, within reasonable bounds, what research, scholarship and teaching 'discovered' and needed to disseminate in the search for 'truth'. These characteristics became increasingly important for universities in the twentieth century as a rising proportion of their income came from the public purse and it was essential, it was said, to ensure that the paymaster did not directly control what was researched and taught, that academic freedom was not compromised. Much of this kind of thinking lay behind the opposition to the 1988 Act in the acrimonious debate in the House of Lords.[31]

Now, this is not a history of the older type of university in Britain where some of the characteristics of such an institution as described above may or may not have been followed. In the case of Northumbria, and similar universities that were to grow from local authority colleges, a quite different pattern of governance emerged, as we have seen. Firstly, the original colleges were the product of local government's idea of further education. Secondly, the Polytechnic, when formed, was one of thirty created by central government dictat. Thirdly, they had no independent degree or diploma awarding powers but were dependent upon a central body which itself had the Royal Charter. Fourthly, they were funded (before 1988) by local government and after directly by Westminster, with little or no funds of their own, and forced to manage on annual budgeting systems so that 'reserves' were difficult to accumulate. Fifthly, the polytechnics were given quite specific (vocational) roles, though as we have demonstrated, they soon branched out from that position. They were to be managed by a chief executive answerable only to a board of governors and not a person first among equals in an academic board or senate. Kenneth Baker's 1988 Education Reform Act, while appearing to give a much higher degree of autonomy to polytechnics like Newcastle's, in fact consolidated the *in statu quo*, only more so.

Amongst polytechnic Directors, then, in the late 1980s there was considerable frustration that the institutions they had patiently, and very successfully, built up since 1969 were not accorded the status that the Vice-Chancellors in the universities enjoyed. This was especially galling because the polytechnics had done practically everything that had been asked of them: they had pushed up national targets and participation rates for the number of students in higher education; they had, by and large, maintained a strong vocational focus in their courses; they had helped rationalise higher education by taking in colleges of education and some health service training. And, by adopting what has been called the 'efficiency option' achieved all this at relatively low unit cost, including keeping the salaries and wages of staff at lower levels than in universities, despite doing similar work. Indeed, 'similarity' is a key word to understanding the polytechnics' desire for university title and status. When Laing Barden drew up his list of achievements for Newcastle Polytechnic's first decade (see p.92) he was keen to emphasise the differences between his polytechnic and a university. A decade later he was to become one of the national leaders of the movement to obtain university title for polytechnics, based largely on the notion that 'similarities' now outweighed differences. However, it was 'title' that was wanted more than status or autonomy. One reason for this was said to be that the word polytechnic was not understood abroad, a growing market for students.

In a paper Barden wrote with Clive Booth, the Director of Oxford Polytechnic, for the Committee of Directors of Polytechnics in December 1989, he was able to point to the achievements of the polytechnics that had made them similar to universities,[32] especially to those created just pre- or post-Robbins. The authors highlighted the apprenticeship of polytechnics. For example, the CATs were only in existence for 7 years before being made universities whereas the polytechnics had been in business for 19 years. However, at least as evidenced by this paper and its proposals, polytechnic leaders were far from demanding to be the sort of university which we have described. Rather timidly – but no doubt pragmatically – Barden and Booth reminded the Secretary of State that although universities were traditionally created by Royal Charter he 'need only exercise his powers under clause 1 (4) of schedule 7 of the Education Reform Act of 1988 to change the name of a polytechnic or college by order'.[33] At the same time it was within the minister's power to confer on polytechnics the right to award their own degrees. Finally, they were at pains to point out that 'it will take the polytechnics a further 20 or 30 years to attain parity of esteem with the universities'.[34] This was not exactly a clarion call to arms for the polytechnics to breach the walls of the university citadel. Perhaps it was more a case of Marx's plea (*tendence Groucho*) that 'he wouldn't want to join a club who would have him for a member'. In practice that was what was to happen: the nature of the university 'club' that polytechnics were seeking to join had already begun to change.

The 1988 Education Reform Act had radically altered the fiduciary relationship between the universities and the government. The arms length relationship between the UGC and the Treasury had been broken; increasing public accountability had made universities much less autonomous. As Kenneth Baker pointed out in his autobiography, 'the academic establishment was the first professional middle class group whose practices and interests were challenged by the Thatcher government'.[35] Although that government spoke a great deal about market forces, the 1988 Act continued the very considerable subsidy of higher education. With the income stream of universities coming largely from government sources it was now much easier for it to control costs, that is, drive them down. As Robert Stephens, quoting Simon Jenkins, points out, 'If a government cuts your income each year without cutting its expectations you not only run out of money, you run out of autonomy'.[36]

When the proposal to grant title came from John Major's Secretary of State, Kenneth Clarke – that 'bluff barrister with a rumpled Rumpole style'[37] – in the 1991 White Paper,[38] it was greeted by outside observers with a certain scepticism, at least as far as calling polytechnics universities was concerned. It proposed that the binary line be abolished and that polytechnics could have the university title 'if they wished to use it'. The CNAA was to be abolished and polytechnics could award their own degrees and diplomas. A unitary funding body for higher education was to be established, merging the UFC and the PCFC. Teaching and research were to be funded separately and a form of external quality control would be put in place; there would be a single admissions agency. Governing bodies were to continue to reflect the importance of the private sector in their make up, not something everyone agreed with.[39] The sting in the tail, as with the 1988 Act, was to increase the student participation rate, this time to 30 per cent by 2000. To many a Director of a polytechnic, but by no means to all, the Bill seemed to grant most of their wishes. Indeed, John Rear in a paper to the governors was able to conjure up as many as seventeen reasons why the reforms should be supported by Newcastle Polytechnic.[40] He also warned that the changes did not mean that some kind of level playing field had been created by the merger of the two systems.

One important academic observer, Martin Trow, thought the White Paper, which he was sent to comment on, some kind of mistake. There were so few pages of it: Was this all there was to government policy for higher education?[41] He called it 'a document of assertion, without much argument or evidence'.[42] It did not get rid of the dirigisme of the 1988 Act but it was clear that the State could no longer manage two systems. It did, however, herald the arrival, if a little belatedly, of mass higher education. In 1979 12 per cent of the relevant age group had gone into higher education; by 1991 this had reached 19 per cent. In the few years after 1988 full-time numbers rose by a remarkable 65 per cent, even part-time numbers increased by about a quarter. Trow had noted before that 'mass' was reached with a 15 per cent participation rate.

Naturally, Newcastle Polytechnic was anxious to exercise its option to adopt a university title and join the club that Rutherford College of Technology had been so anxious to join in the 1950s. Nonetheless, Clarke made it clear that he did not expect the mission of the 'new' university to be different from that of the 'old' polytechnic.

What's in a name?

Becoming a university was momentous enough; finding a name for it was just as exciting. The Academic Board and the governors were anxious for the words 'Newcastle' and 'city' to appear somewhere in the title.[43] Rightly, both bodies believed that the city had a magnetic attraction for students from outside the North East and abroad; for more locally based students it was their regional capital. It will be recalled that when a proposal to develop a major centre for further education in the late 1940s was put forward, its protagonists drew attention to the centrality and accessibility of Newcastle.[44] When the city was faced with reconstructing its economy in the mid-1980s, many pointed to the need to develop a positive urban image for Newcastle in order to help attract inward investment; higher education formed part of a modern, forward-looking city.

Any new name had to be approved by the Privy Council and despite the widespread support for the institution to be called 'Newcastle City University' this was opposed, not surprisingly, by the university on the other side of the Great North Road, and eventually, by the Secretary of State.[45] Clarke, in a speech to the Committee of Directors of Polytechnics had set the directors a puzzle: 'What do the following have in common? Amherst, Boston University, North Eastern University, the University of Massachusetts, Vassar College? That's right, you've got it. They are all famous and are all in the city of Boston', inferring that including the name of a geographical place was not essential to ensure success.[46]

These signals sent the Polytechnic back to the drawing board. The Staff Newsletter called for more suggestions and the local daily paper ran a competition for the most acceptable name. Altogether nearly forty names were submitted, including those associated with royalty (e.g. Queen's University, Newcastle), with the city (e.g. City of Newcastle University), with the region (e.g. the Great North University) and with the province of Northumbria (e.g. Northumbria University). All had their supporters and detractors: royalists, provincialists, regionalists, mythologists. One (the author of this chapter!), went so far as to describe the use of 'Northumbria' as 'redolent of transient ancient history, romantic daydreaming and the rural outback'.[47] In the end a compromise was reached that embraced 'Newcastle' and 'Northumbria', the *University of Northumbria at Newcastle*, soon reduced to its acronym, UNN; city and region were reconciled. This was probably the invention of John Rear who earlier in his career had served at the new University of Kent at Canterbury. Few people had an accurate idea of where Northumbria was or what its origins were. At best, it conjured up an image of the Christian kingdom, twixt Humber and Tweed and its fine Anglo-Saxon artistic contribution to early medieval European culture. 'Newcastle' complemented this with powerful images of coalmining, shipbuilding, a tradition of heavy industry and engineering and a football club of varying fortunes. Just as the first name may have had little appeal to largely ahistoric students, the latter's' more potent symbols were rapidly becoming obsolete as the local economy declined. However, both gave the public relations company hired to develop a new image for the new university, plenty to work on.

Acquiring university title was a momentous event and UNN was determined to celebrate it in fine style. Naturally, the day – 1 September 1992 – had to include elements of sumptuary display so a public procession from the City Campus through the streets of Newcastle to St Thomas' Church – the students' church – with Lord Glenamara, the Chancellor, capped and gowned at its head and led by the sword and mace bearers. A grand dinner was held in the evening at which roast saddle of venison, accompanied by a 1989 claret, was served, speeches made and commemorative pewter goblets distributed. The final confirmation came in 1995 when, at a cost of £5,600, the University acquired its coat of arms replete with its Latin motto, *Aetas discendi* – 'a lifetime of learning*.[48] Surely now the ladder had been climbed and paradise reached!

If it's a university, it ought to have professors

At the time of its inauguration the University of Northumbria at Newcastle already had quite a few professors, dating from 1977. Unlike Privy Council approval to use the title 'university', that of 'professor' needed no such sanction, it was open to anyone to use. Its use in universities came rather late in England principally following the enforced reforms of Oxford and Cambridge in the second half of the nineteenth century, when professors were appointed to teach, the fellows of colleges being somewhat less than proficient in the arts of the lecture hall. In some other countries it was usual to distinguish between those who held a chair (Greek, *cathedra*) and those for whom it was a title (French, *professeur titulaire*); it could simply mean 'teacher'. In Britain in the late twentieth century, however, it had become a status-loaded term signifying a certain level of academic achievement or recognition and was used rather more sparingly. Early in

---

*On a much earlier occasion, before even polytechnics were thought of, a waggish member of staff at the College of Commerce had suggested a quotation from Virgil's *Aeneid*, Book VI as the college motto: *Noctes atque dies patet atri*, which in Dryden's translation means 'The gates stand open night and day', not bad for a college dominated by part-time, evening class students. Unfortunately, Virgil was referring to the gates of Hell.

1994 Laing Barden, himself a professor, after taking soundings, decided that the newly created university should have more professors.

As a polytechnic Newcastle seems deliberately to have avoided appointing people to 'Chairs' and most of those appointed to be professors appear also to have held the more senior management positions such as Assistant Director, Head of a Faculty or a Head of Department. This is not to doubt their scholarly attributes in any way, of course, but it did seem to many that the title was associated with an office. In both universities and polytechnics it was usual to have some kind of appointment panel to approve of those applying to use the title.

Barden's reasons for having more professors are not clear. Perhaps he felt it necessary in order to raise the profile of Northumbria or to be part of other changes such as the use of the traditional university title of Vice-Chancellor as opposed to the more prosaic and industrial, Director, or it may have had more to do with the confirmation of power and authority on certain offices. In a paper he brought before Academic Board he stated that Heads of Department should be given a more prominent role in terms of academic leadership especially where research was concerned.[49] Barden argued that 'it would appear that the criteria for the appointment of a head of department include the criteria for the appointment of a professor', and that from this he proposed that all future appointments to the post of Head of Department should automatically take the title of Professor. Existing Heads of Department had already, by their very appointment, successfully demonstrated that they had the academic credibility and status to take the title Professor. They were Professors *de facto*, if not *de jure*. He wrote, 'the present situation disadvantages a number of our key academic leaders… UNN is a mature, self confident and powerful institution and should behave as such'.

What upset a number of members of Academic Board, and indeed large numbers of all staff, was that this would by-pass the existing professorial appointments panel, but Barden argued – and there seemed a certain logic in it – that the criteria for appointing Heads of Department and those describing the attributes of professors were essentially the same. In quantitative terms he thought his proposal modest; it would give UNN about forty professors compared to the University of Newcastle's 120 approximately. There followed a lengthy debate in the board in which 'members expressed disquiet' and 'the House divided'.[50] Those against the proposal had two arguments: one was, why not put every Head of Department who was not already a professor in front of the professorial appointments panel and test Barden's hypothesis on similarity of criteria? The second asked that Heads of Department on Academic Board should not be allowed to vote on this issue 'which might be deemed to be a matter of direct self-interest'. The Vice-Chancellor took the view that the opinion of the whole of the Academic Board was being sought, and in the end, that view prevailed. Ten Heads of Department and four Deans (who would also be able to claim the title under this proposal) attended Academic Board that day. Five Heads of Department were already professors under the old regulation, as were two of the Deans. The motion was carried by seventeen votes to ten, but there is no record of who voted 'for' and who 'against' the motion.

Because of the unease Barden felt it necessary to write to the *Staff Newsletter*.[51] He reiterated the arguments about the criteria and felt that these were rigorously observed at the board. On the issue of the declaration of interest, he added, 'there is no legal or constitutional statement to be observed... the proposal was accepted that members of Academic Board must be trusted to act professionally and to vote in what they perceive to be the best interests of the University'.

The matter was brought to the attention of a much wider audience by the dramatic resignation of his professorship by Dr Phil O'Keefe, a senior lecturer in the Department of Environment, on the occasion of his inaugural lecture. This became front page, headline news in the *Times Higher Educational Supplement* on 18 March 1994 with a picture of O'Keefe together with a human skull ('Alas, poor Yorick, I knew him, Horatio; a fellow of infinite jest...', the skull a metaphor for professorships perhaps). At the next Governors' meeting the Chair of NATFHE asked for the decision to be referred back to the Academic Board on the grounds of self-interest but the Governors supported the Vice-Chancellor and 'expressed disapproval of the action of staff in disagreeing with a decision of Academic Board, in raising these concerns through the media, rather than the internal processes of the University'.[52] A circular from seventy-four members of staff – the majority in the Arts and Social Sciences Faculties – had argued that Barden's proposals were tautological and based on a self-fulfilling prophecy. Their solution was to ask for all Heads of Department to be vetted by the professorial appointments panel. It is hard to see that this too would not have been self-fulfilling because of its composition. Despite the heated discussions, the Board's original decision stood. It only increased the number of professors by fourteen, from twenty-two to thirty-six, out of a total of 980 academic staff, or 3.7 per cent.

Some thought an alternative solution could have been used; others thought it gave UNN more of the trappings of a university. The opponents perhaps exaggerated the role and status of a professor, especially at this institution where it was nearly always a title and not a Chair. For many it was a lesson in realpolitik. Soon after, most of the new universities had professors – and some Chairs – but more significant was the reaction of older universities where, in the next few years, there was to be a rash of such appointments so that much of the 'exclusivity' of such titles was lost. Perhaps the word had reverted to its original meaning of 'teacher', the counter irony being, of course, that at UNN many of the professors did little teaching or none at all!

Satellite campuses: Carlisle and Longhirst

By the late 1980s it was clear, as student numbers rose rapidly, that the two main campuses would not be able to accommodate the predicted growth. The PCFC had made it abundantly plain, as had its predecessor NAB, that Newcastle Polytechnic was unlikely to receive much capital investment in new buildings. This was not solely due to the government stinginess referred to above but partly attributable to Newcastle's good fortune in having so many buildings from the 1960s and 1970s at both its sites. It is sometimes forgotten that many polytechnics had no such buildings, let alone campuses. Many had been forced to expand from their technical or art college origins into old Victorian schools, warehouses, and even in the case of one West Midlands polytechnic, into occupying space beneath the stands of the local football club. Elements of this were not entirely unfamiliar to the Polytechnic where St Dominic's and St Andrew's schools housed academic departments, a former British Road Service depot became a library and a former CIU social club was used for staff offices, if only temporarily.

If no capital was forthcoming from PCFC the Polytechnic had to look elsewhere. In the absence of a fully articulated accommodation strategy, two types of solution presented themselves to Brian Roper, the Assistant Director (Resources) who was responsible for the Polytechnic's estate. One was the time honoured *ad hoc*ism of acquiring property in close proximity to the Polytechnic as and when it could find it and afford it. The second was in developing partnerships with other organisations away from the existing sites. Here, two quite different opportunities presented themselves, both of which were associated with a local desire to spread higher education into the more distant corners of England.

The first of these was in Cumbria to the west of Newcastle. In the late 1980s the County Council had examined the feasibility of establishing higher education in the county.[53] The report found that despite having 'A' Level successes above the national average, the county had one of the lowest participation rates in higher education. However, about two thirds of the students surveyed said they would prefer to study in Cumbria rather then go elsewhere. This seemed to indicate a strong latent demand for the provision of university level education within the county. The report concluded that because of the capital cost and the scattered geography of the small amount of provision there was already, the best way forward was through a collaboration with the then Lancashire Polytechnic in Preston. This would involve franchising parts of its degree courses to local further education colleges. The emphasis would be on part-time study, mainly in the humanities and social sciences. The only purpose-built higher education facility in the county – the former teacher training college at Ambleside, Charlotte Mason College – was for a time taken over by Lancaster University but that was not to last. In any case, it was a monotechnic college though its specialism in outdoor education was highly regarded.

The north of the county did not suffer from the same degree of economic malaise as the industrial west coast and Carlisle believed it could provide a better service to its young people and its more successful local industries by developing its own, freestanding centre. It already had a flourishing art college and a large further education college. The City Council and its MP Eric Martlew approached the Polytechnic in Newcastle to explore the possibility of a joint venture, Newcastle's search for expansion complementing Carlisle's ambition. The initial aim was to use the city's further education college's HNDs and HNCs in Business Studies as part of a 'ladder of qualifications' to first and higher degrees and to transfer Lancashire's combined studies programme to Newcastle Polytechnic. The Polytechnic had no possibility of securing capital funds for any building but Carlisle City Council was prepared to invest heavily to supply teaching accommodation, 'a long term commitment promised on the assumption that the Polytechnic will establish a permanent basis in Carlisle'.[54] The PCFC agreed to support the plan with twenty FTE degree students, fifty FTE sandwich degree students and forty part-time FTE degree students. The Polytechnic planned to increase its complement to 450 students within 5 years. The focus would be on international business courses supported by IT and modern languages. A core of staff would be employed at Carlisle, with minimal commuting from Newcastle. A Head of Campus would be appointed equivalent to at least a Head of Department. The scheme was supported in principle by the governors but decisions on when and if to proceed 'would depend on a rigorous assessment of each… detailed proposal'.[55] The Academic Board had similar financial reservations but there was general support for this development at Carlisle.

Brian Roper was originally given responsibility for the Carlisle initiative but before much progress had been made he left Newcastle to become Deputy Director of Oxford Polytechnic. He was succeeded by Professor Tony Dickson, promoted after 2 years as Dean of the Faculty of Social Sciences. In a paper to the Academic Board he rehearsed the arguments for going ahead at Carlisle concerning student demand and likely numbers, the types of courses and the provision of facilities. The revenue he noted, 'will fall short of covering the costs of offering these courses', largely because of the high start-up costs but 'break even should be reached by 1993–94'.[56] This seemed optimistic given that courses could not start until September 1992.

For its part Carlisle City Council and its planners produced a most attractive scheme based on the conversion of listed and other buildings in a network of medieval streets in the Botchergate area between the cathedral and the castle, focussed upon the Tully House Museum. Around a tree-shaded quadrangle with the museum, a well-designed and sympathetic development of an old tea warehouse and adjacent buildings took place to provide attractive classrooms, library, computing and language laboratories and staff offices at a cost to the city of £1.5 million. There were even some Roman remains to provide the necessary degree of antiquity. The site had the air of a small Oxbridge college but *sans residences*. The Students' Union, known here as the Guild, was provided with excellent accommodation in a converted Scouts and Guides headquarters. A hall of residence was created from the former Carlisle state brewery buildings. The cathedral and its dean cooperated from the start. The inauguration of Carlisle Campus on Wednesday 7 October 1992 was held in the medieval splendour of the cathedral as were subsequent graduation ceremonies.

Everything looked set fair for what was soon to be the University of Northumbria at Carlisle, particularly when Professor Robin Smith was appointed as its permanent head. Much of Cumbria took the endeavour to its heart. As an example, local agencies helped fund and support a professorship in regional development to assist with economic regeneration. This was occupied by Dr Frank Peck, a geographer, originally of the Polytechnic's Department of Environment. To complement the courses in business and management studies, a modular programme in humanities and social sciences was introduced later, together with courses in tourism studies, a logical subject for the nearby Lake District.

However attractive the venue, however well taught and organised the courses, there was always a problem of reaching the target student numbers and securing PCFC/HEFCE support for them. When the government decided to restrain growth in higher education in 1993 it proved difficult for PCFC to assign anything other than 'fees only' funding for the Carlisle (and Longhirst) ventures.[57] Professor Dickson wrote to the chief executive of HEFCE setting out the case for both satellite campuses emphasising the economic impact of the projected growth to 600 FTEs at each site. This level of development would generate over £20 million of capital investment by the end of the decade, place additional revenue spending of £3 million into each of the two local economies and generate 400 extra jobs.[58] Despite his pleas which were supported by strong letters from Melvyn Bragg of Border Television and Lionel Chamberlain of British Nuclear Fuels, little additional funding was forthcoming. With the main University continuing to raise its staff-student ratio and needing to finance its activities by taking more and more students, the Carlisle branch had to take its share of the increasing burden. From the beginning it was seen as one means of increasing numbers in business and management but it became apparent that this buoyant field was not inexhaustible. Newcastle and Carlisle appeared to be competing for similar students. Numbers rose to 250 in 1993 but struggled to meet ever rising targets. As a result the element of subsidy from Newcastle inevitably rose. The funding body refused to allocate sufficient numbers to support both centres in business education, the same field that was also being developed at Longhirst. In the end it was these financial pressures that led to Northumbria University finally withdrawing from its Carlisle Campus in 2004. But all was not lost for higher education in Cumbria. The campus was taken over by the University of Central Lancashire. Perhaps one day Cumbria's hope for a university of its own – The University of the Lakes – will be realised, but it won't involve its neighbour in the North East.[59]

The second out of town project was to be in Northumberland, the large sprawling county adjacent to Newcastle but divisible into two parts: a highly urbanised south east corner originally based on coal mining, and a largely empty upland interior. The county had lost the few elements of higher education it once had with the closure of the colleges of education at Alnwick and Ponteland in the 1970s. Northumberland was seeking to restructure its economy after the collapse of mining and engineering in the mid-1980s. It had had a certain degree of success in attracting inward investment, especially in the pharmaceutical industries, but it needed to raise and diversify the skill content of its workforce. To this end it ran a successful Training and Enterprise Council (TEC).[60] If such councils could make surpluses from their projects and schemes, government was prepared to allow them to retain them for reinvestment.

Following what appears to have been rather clandestine discussions between members of the TEC and the Polytechnic about something rather curiously called the

Lindisfarne Project*, a paper was put before the Academic Board in the autumn of 1991.[61] Northumberland TEC approached the Polytechnic with a proposal to establish a high quality business and training centre in the county. It was to have three components: a management and training facility, a business innovation park especially for small and medium sized enterprises and a higher education facility in business and management studies. The TEC established a separate trading company to buy Longhirst Hall, a distinguished John Dobson building of 1826, to be the core of their development.[62] This was originally the country house of coal owners, first the Lawsons and then the Joblins, but which had languished for some time as an unused reform school, where, oddly, the Head of the Polytechnic's Department of Social Work had once served – as a member of staff of course, not as an inmate. This building was to house conference facilities, a restaurant and eventually, an hotel. To the rear would be built a large suite of classrooms for the use of the Polytechnic. The grounds, 42 acres, were to be landscaped, and on the large, lawned area to the front of the house, Morpeth Cricket Club would develop a most appealing ground, reminiscent of the Edwardian games once played there under country house rules. The TEC's planned investment for the site amounted to £800–900,000, plus £2.5 million of European Regional Development Fund support.

The Academic Board and the governors took a hard headed view of the proposal. The principal protagonist was Don Cassells, the newly promoted Head of the Newcastle Business School (NBS). He had the difficult job of persuading the Polytechnic to join the TEC in this venture; it was his School that would provide all the academic courses at Longhirst. Two things worried the governors and the Academic Board: the financial risk involved, and whether such a place would prove attractive to students. On this last point the board felt that a location in the countryside just outside the county town of Morpeth, 15 miles from Newcastle was, if not literally, a long way from the city's academic facilities and its night life. The joint venture hoped to solve this problem by building student accommodation on site, by providing sports facilities and a bar, together with a frequent bus service to Newcastle.

On the question of costs and revenue, an optimistic forecast was made. First, the company the TEC had formed would provide all the capital for the refurbishment of the hall and its grounds and for building the teaching accommodation. For its part the Polytechnic would pay the company a per capita fee based on student numbers. The Polytechnic's proposers, led by Professor Dickson for the Directorate, calculated that to provide similar accommodation in Newcastle would have cost at least £2 million. Revenue would be in deficit in 1993–94 by nearly £60,000 and in the following year by over £100,000 but by 1997–98 would produce a surplus of over £90,000.[63]

Despite these assurances the Academic Board was not convinced by this proposal to develop a satellite campus, confined to use by the Business School. The risks looked too great and the scheme was voted down by eleven votes to nine with six abstentions.

---

*This was a curious name for a project that sought to help modernise and transform the county's economy, signifiying as it does, monastic isolation.

This was a serious defeat for the Directorate and another meeting of Academic Board was especially convened to discuss it further, accompanied by a rather desperate instruction that 'attendance at this meeting is to be considered of the highest priority'. Don Cassells produced a new paper that set out the risks rather better. He assured members that 'retrenchment to the city site would be possible in a relatively short time scale' if the scheme failed but threatened that if it was not approved, he would not be able to expand in business and management areas as the plan for the Polytechnic required.[64] This time the proposal was carried *nem. con.*

For the governors, who were shortly to become university governors with considerable responsibility for income and expenditure and property, Longhirst proved one of their first important decisions. Their employment and finance committee had reported that 'despite a high level of demand for NBS courses, it will be important to assess how attractive the environment at Longhirst is likely to prove to students',[65] but recommended it on economic grounds, that is, the low charge per student and the low level of capital investment required. They also noted that Carlisle would have to be supported at the same time and it too was aiming for business students. However, one governor, Peter McKendrick, a partner in one of the city's leading estate agencies, later asked for his disagreement with the decision to be recorded.[66]

Although some other Departments were involved, the Longhirst Campus was largely the province of the Business School. They appointed a core of staff to posts at Longhirst but most of the teaching came from commuters from the city centre. Initially, a range of courses was offered but soon it became a locus for post-experience and postgraduate courses. In time many of the students were to come from overseas, living in the newly built accommodation. Staff found the Hall a useful place for 'away-days' and conferences, even playing the odd cricket match there, but the fears expressed by the Academic Board at the outset were soon realised. Longhirst was not a popular location for students and the predicted surpluses were never generated. In 2004 the University of Northumbria at Newcastle's involvement with Longhirst ceased.

Accommodation 1: some piecemeal solutions

Carlisle and Longhirst were all very well but even when their eventual target numbers were reached it was predicted that between them they would accommodate less than a thousand students. Eventually the University would need a bolder and more expansive strategy but in the meantime the 1992 plan had a piecemeal approach, seeking out a mixture of large scale and small scale areas and associated buildings for conversion. From a number of the larger ones that were given preliminary examination two front runners emerged. The Wills Tobacco Company had built in the 1950s a large cigarette and cigar factory on the Coast Road to supply the north British market. By the late 1980s the dangers of smoking were at last being recognised and it was scheduled for closure. The front offices consisted of a handsome art deco style block that was listed Grade II; the City Council were anxious to find a use for it without demolition. To the rear was the actual factory which could be knocked down to provide valuable land for new building. Professor Dickson and the governors gave serious consideration to acquiring and developing the site. Amongst its advantages was its proximity to the Coach Lane Campus. However, the cost of buying the site and converting the main office block proved prohibitive. Today, the 1930s style front block has been converted to expensive and exclusive apartments and a housing estate developed on the land to the rear.

The second possibility was even closer to Coach Lane, indeed, it was contiguous with it. Heaton Manor School might come onto the market as Newcastle Education Committee considered rationalising its secondary school provision against a background of falling rolls. In addition to 1960s style buildings that might convert to university use, the school had large playing fields adjacent to Coach Lane Campus. However, the City Council changed its mind about the sale and the school was taken off the market.

In addition to these two large scale possibilities, the University of Northumbria moved ahead with acquiring smaller properties as and when it could in the area immediately around the city centre site. The lease of the underused YMCA building was acquired for £175,000 a year and converted to use by the burgeoning Sports Studies degree courses. It was renamed the Wynne-Jones Building after a Chancellor of the Polytechnic*. Another block of attractive buildings nearby consisted of Burt Hall and the Riding School, usually known as the Drill Hall, on the south west corner of College Street and Northumberland Road. Burt Hall (1897) had been the home of the Northumberland Miners Association, later a branch of the National Union of Mineworkers and named after Thomas Burt, the Northumberland miners' leader and radical MP for Morpeth, another echo of the University's nineteenth century origins. It was bought at a cost of £300,000 and converted for use by the postgraduate courses in the conservation of fine art, one of the few such centres for this important work outside London. The Drill Hall – 'a dour utilitarian structure'[67] – was a John Dobson building of 1847. It was originally the indoor riding school for the Northumberland Hussars. Initially leased it was eventually bought from the city council for £375,000 and developed as an important IT centre and a set of lecture theatres and classrooms largely used by the Law School.[68] A second IT centre was developed from the redundant Baptist Trinity Church in Northumberland Road. We have seen that 21 Ellison Place was acquired for External Relations so that when the lease of its smaller neighbour, No. 22, became available it was logical to acquire it. The new Director of External Relations was able to obtain a generous grant from the James Knott Foundation Trust to help equip the building to a high standard. The University even looked into buying or leasing part of MEA House, a modernist building of the 1970s in Ellison Place which always looked as though it was part of the Polytechnic but was in fact the home of

---

* Lord Wynne-Jones was a distinguished chemist. Educated at the University College of Wales, Aberystwyth and Balliol College, Oxford he had been a professor at Dundee and Newcastle Universities. He was made a Life Peer in 1964. His first wife, Anne Drummond, was a Newcastle City Councillor.

voluntary social services. Durant Hall, a 1930s church building belonging to the Unitarians whose congregation was dwindling was considered too for possible acquisition. If these had been added to the University's portfolio another quadrangle might have been added to the city centre site, complementing those in Ellison Building and across Northumberland Road.

Another local project was for the development of the Salem Chapel site across the motorway, to the rear of Pandon Building. This was originally owned by a major city landowner, the St Mary Magdalene Trust, of mediaeval origin but run by the City Council since the nineteenth century. The plan was for a prestigious building for the Newcastle Business School but when the government announced a further brake on growth in higher education that scheme was dropped. It was a valuable site and instead a deal was done with Tolent Construction Company to develop it for student residences, now Lord Glenamara House, opened in 1995.

Just as the demand for more and better teaching space grew so did the need for more office accommodation for the administration. The row of houses in Ellison Place to the west of Ellison Building had been in their time amongst the most prestigious addresses in Newcastle. Among those who had lived there was the future Roman Catholic primate Cardinal Hume and G. L. Mounsel – a pioneer in reinforced concrete! The terrace was built by Richard Grainger and probably to designs by John Dobson. By the 1970s, like many properties affected by motorway proposals and general inner-city decline, they had fallen into a variety of uses. The former Lord Mayor's Mansion, No.1, was used as offices by the City Education Department. No. 2 was the Manors Social Club. As leases fell in and properties purchased the Polytechnic gradually acquired them, using them first of all as staff and tutorial rooms for the Department of Humanities. By the 1990s they were used as offices by the administration.

Accommodation 2: Coach Lane Campus

Such small scale additions to the University's building stock solved a few problems but the failure of the Wills/Heaton Manor School schemes showed there was a need for a proper well-articulated estate strategy to plan for future growth. While Professor Tony Dickson was a more than adequate champion of the University's physical expansion it became clear that for any concerted large scale development more professional help was required. In 1994 Colin Jackson was appointed as Head of Estates and Property, another addition to the University's growing band of technocrats. He brought a new dimension to planning to add to Nick Purdie's pioneering work in the estates office. He came to the University of Northumbria having held a similar position for IBM (UK).

When the Polytechnic merged with Northern Counties College of Education in 1976 it acquired considerable land on the eastern border of the city, on both sides of Coach Lane. The city planners had scheduled the easternmost part of the site as 'white' land with a view to its eventual development for industrial purposes. The University of Newcastle had already obtained a large land holding to the south of the University of

Northumbria's campus and developed it for the Henderson hall of residence and playing fields. It had also built sports fields to the north and east of Coach Lane. With a hall of residence further north still there was clearly something of a higher education 'quarter' emerging in Benton by the 1990s. It seemed logical for the University of Northumbria, then, to seek to undertake a large scale expansion in the same area to consolidate this pattern of land-use. Initially, the city's draft unitary development plan had classed the University of Northumbria's holdings as too small for industrial purposes and was considering other uses such as housing.[69] At about the same time the Secretary of State for the Environment was reconsidering administrative boundaries on Tyneside and a decision was taken to transfer the land to the east of Coach Lane to neighbouring North Tyneside. Once accomplished, planning permission to develop the site was soon granted subject to some changes to the road layout. Local residents were not entirely happy to have an expanded university on their relatively new doorsteps. Professor Dickson had to find ways to placate them. This done, the way was clear for contracts for the new buildings, sports facilities and landscaping to be let. It would not be completed until late 1996.

For existing staff and students at the University of Northumbria Coach Lane became synonymous with upheaval and a large measure of dissent. Who was to occupy these new buildings and the expanded campus? We have shown that there was considerable resistance to anyone moving form the city centre to Coach Lane. The same perceptions obtained in 1995 as they had some years earlier. This time one tenant, at least was known – the students and staff from the local college of health that merged with the University of Northumbria in 1995. The question remained of who was to join them. For many years it had always hoped that two faculties would be located there. As on the previous occasion the logical occupant was the Newcastle Business School. The School itself did not acquiesce, of course, putting up a spirited defence for remaining in central Newcastle, based mainly on the links between it and the city's businesses, a symbolic as well as a symbiotic location it was argued. Dickson did not agree and the Business School was scheduled to move. However, fate intervened, the merger with the nursing college bringing about the creation of a new faculty large enough to occupy the whole of Coach Lane.[70]

Enter the nurses – by boat!

On 31 March 1995 members of the Newcastle, Northumberland and Bede College of Health Studies sailed up the River Tyne to Newcastle's Quayside to celebrate the transfer of their college and their students to the University of Northumbria.[71]

This dramatic entry was the culmination of many years of negotiation with the Northern Regional Health Authority during which nurse education and training had gradually developed as a partnership between the hospital service, a variety of colleges of nursing on Tyneside and the Polytechnic. It was stimulated by pioneering courses at diploma level beginning in 1986 which enabled the nursing colleges and the Polytechnic to exploit common ground.

For the Polytechnic this was by no means its first venture into nurse education as we shall see. For nursing itself, the struggle for professional recognition had an even longer history.

It was not until the end of the nineteenth century that nurse training was put on a more formal footing. Essentially, it was highly vocational and centred on a narrow curriculum of skills nurses needed to carry out their duties, and little else. Through much of the twentieth century they were regarded as employees not students. Even in the first year of entry about 60 per cent of their time would be spent on the wards of hospitals, often carrying out quite menial tasks. For many it involved heavy work, long hours and low pay; studying came second, and on top of these duties.[72] Like the early history of teacher training described elsewhere (see Chapter 4) the training of nurses was largely 'on the job' with tuition coming from authoritative figures that were seen as the repository of all knowledge. There was little or no concern for the development of intellectual skills, little academic stimulation and very low levels of theoretical content. Trainee nurses were cast very much as apprentices learning from their 'elders and betters'.[73] By the 1980s the United Kingdom Central Council's (UKCC) Report highlighted the conveyor-belt like nature of training for nurses and their tutors alike. Often there would be six entries a year into a large hospital, sometimes with as many as one hundred in any cohort. Learning opportunities had to be accommodated with ward duties. The aim seemed to be to produce a controlled workforce armed only with functional knowledge. For many student nurses who had had a more liberal education in the sixth form, including 'A' Levels, the rigidity and poor quality of a highly convergent nurse training system must have been deeply disappointing. It was also very wasteful with 20 per cent of initial entrants not registering, many withdrawing before completion. Nurse tutors dominated the learning process, controlled discussion and fed the students on a diet of Gradgrindian 'facts'. This may have led to technical competence for some but it did little for the appreciation of the context of care, independent decision-making and the therapeutic process.

Any reform of nurse training had to find solutions to two dilemmas: reconciling 'service' (work) with 'education' (not training), and technical ability with intellectual autonomy. Many post-war reports had pointed to this need[74] but until the publication of the 1986 UKCC Report few real changes were implemented. By 1983–84 the number of nurses and midwives failed to grow for the first time since 1948. With birth rates falling and more young women staying on at school to take 'A' Levels, nursing had to compete with degree level higher education. At the same time many senior nurses, especially those dealing with education and training, also recognised the need to reform their own role. As the 1986 Report put it, the system had become 'inefficient, ineffective, unjust and in severe need of overhaul'.[75]

In the English NHS at that time there were 192 District Health Authorities grouped into fourteen regions. There were 168 Schools of Nursing and 152 Schools of Midwifery. There were nine degree courses in higher education institutions and twenty-two centres approved to train nurse tutors. Most of the training programmes were based in hospitals and while it would wrong to describe every course as different there was a quite confusing array of schemes.[76] For its part the Department of Health had already begun to question why such a large proportion of its hard pressed budget was being spent on 'education', not exactly its 'core business'.[77]

The profession recognised that entering upon degree or diploma level education for nurses might bring about a two tier structure with the graduate nurses forming an elite cadre. The UKCC's proposals addressed this by eventually aiming for an all graduate corps supported by nursing aides or auxiliaries. While attention was given to the creation of a much smaller number of larger colleges of nursing and of midwifery, the Report recommended closer liaison with higher education institutions and the development of a new university level diploma. Higher education centres would also be able to offer much better facilities for nurse tutor training and staff research. New entrants to nursing were to be treated as supernumeries (students) and not part of the work force; the cost of training would now be separated from service budgets.[78]

The proposed course would have a common foundation year followed by specialisation in one of four branches of nursing: mental illness, mental handicap, adult, child, and midwifery. The award would be a Diploma in Higher Education validated by a university or CNAA, to be piloted in six centres in England from 1986 onwards, including one in Newcastle Polytechnic.

Higher level nurse education in Newcastle was not new. As early as 1972 a degree course was submitted to CNAA and approved with a fifteen student entry.[79] This was led by Sheila Smith, herself a nurse, Head of the Department of Nursing and Welfare. Her newly created department had already run the London University external diploma in nursing as well as many specialist courses for district nurses and midwives.[80] Unfortunately, this pioneering degree courses did not survive, running into difficulties with a somewhat conservative professional body at that time.[81] It was not until the mid-1980s, and foreseeing the likely outcome of the UKCC report, that the Polytechnic ventured again into higher education for nurses.

In 1985 a pilot scheme between the Polytechnic and Sunderland Health Authority's School of Nursing was established with an entry of twenty-four nurses who would study for 3 years for a Polytechnic Diploma in Nursing Sciences that would also give them registered status. The first two terms would be spent in the Faculty of Social and Community Studies and the second year would be hospital-based.[82] This was soon succeeded by Project 2000 in which Newcastle Polytechnic collaborated with Newcastle and Northumberland Schools of Nursing to award CNAA's Diploma in Higher Education. In addition, the Polytechnic ran a part-time degree in nursing science and had validated a degree in midwifery in conjunction with Bede College.[83]

Most of the Polytechnic's input to these innovative courses came from Dr Don Watson's Department of Behavioural Sciences. Foreseeing the potential of tremendous growth in the field of nurse education, Watson succeeded in renaming his department to include health sciences. Some of his colleagues felt as he did and pressed for expansion; others, mostly psychologists, wished to continue to develop their particular field. A split was inevitable (see p.115), despite the best efforts by the Faculty of Social Sciences to retain this kind of work. As we have shown earlier this Faculty was simply becoming too large and unwieldy with much of its work located at Coach Lane. The Polytechnic had already established a Department of Health at Coach Lane to contain the 'professions allied to medicine' such as physiotherapy and occupational therapy led by Dr Jean Potts. Splitting Watson's department and uniting these two areas seemed a logical outcome. Eventually the Polytechnic established the Institute of Health Sciences to give proper recognition to this growing dimension to its portfolio. It grew to have over forty staff and entered into a formal partnership with the Newcastle and Northumbria College of Nursing and Midwifery and had a close working relationship with the Bede College in Sunderland. Professor Barden was determined to take the fullest advantage of collaboration with the health service.

The opportunity came in 1993 when Professor Rear reported to Academic Board on NHS/DES plans to integrate colleges of nursing into higher education.[84] The Newcastle and Northumbria College had over 200 staff spread over fifteen hospital sites, 1,500 student nurses and a budget in excess of £15 million. Bede College had nearly 700 students on four sites and a budget of £7.5 million. Clearly, any transfer was going to be on a massive scale, at least as large as the college of education mergers in the 1970s. The University of Northumbria, if it decided to bid for the contract, would have some difficulty absorbing this scale of activity, at a time when its own numbers were still rising rapidly.

A number of factors made that decision difficult. The first was that prior to joining, all the Tyneside colleges themselves had merged, spurred on by Project 2000. Mary Dunning had been appointed as Principal of the new college of Bede, Newcastle and Northumbria College of Health Studies (BNN). Secondly, the Northern Regional Health Authority was forced to amalgamate with the Yorkshire Health Authority, and the latter was very much against nurse education coming into the Polytechnic. The third challenge was just how was such a merger of higher education and NHS traditions to be brought about? It was important for the health college's staff and students to be fully integrated as members of the University.

A new fifth faculty

The University proposed to create a new, fifth faculty with a focus in community and professional studies; new buildings would be required. Preliminary estimates allowed for a total cost of over £6 million, providing 4,500 square metres of teaching accommodation.[85] Later calculations showed that as part of the wider estates strategy described earlier there was a need for 22,000 square metres of teaching space and for 900 student bed spaces, all at a cost of £20 million. The College of Health's share was likely to be £5 million.[86]

Meanwhile, Dr Royston Stephens, Deputy Dean of the Faculty of Health and Social Work at Anglia Polytechnic University was appointed as Dean as from 1 September 1994.[87] Stephens had a PhD in Welsh history from the University of California and had spent much of his academic career in the USA. Mary Dunning, Principal of BNN, was to become Deputy Dean but prior to the transfer agreed to be co-opted to the University of Northumbria's Academic Board*.

The new faculty, to be known as Health, Social Work and Education, would include the Institute of Health Sciences and BNN. The Academic Board recorded that, 'it is the view of the University that in order to reap the benefits of transferring nurse education into higher education, the College should be fully integrated'.[88] There was likely to be 1,200 pre-registration and degree nursing students. The College now had over 280 staff of which 200 were teaching staff but it was expected that about 150 would transfer. This would give the new faculty about 300 staff and 4,500 students, leaving Social Sciences with 2,700 students and 160 staff. Monica Shaw would remain as Dean of the Faculty which would now contain four Departments of Applied Social Sciences, Environment, Law and Economics and Government.[89]

The final proposal for the merger was agreed by the Board of Governors of the University of Northumbria on 13 March 1995 on the assumption that the bid to the regional health authority was successful.[90]

The end of an era

In November 1994 the Chairman of the Governors, Reay Atkinson, announced that Professor Laing Barden, the University's first Vice-Chancellor, was to retire. Barden told all who would listen that he did not want to go and asked if some way could be found for him to extend his period of office. But rules were rules and the teachers' pension scheme laid down that all had to go at sixty-five, irrespective of position. Professor John Rear, for so many years Barden's Deputy – and so much more than his right-hand man – was now sixty and he decided to retire too. Gordon Campbell was Pro Vice-Chancellor (Resources) and responsible for the University's finances since 1979 but agreed to remain until 1998. Just at that point in the University's history when yet further expansion and growth was underway, two senior figures were about to be lost. It was an occasion when the cliché is appropriate; it was truly the end of an era.

In Barden's case, a period of office from Deputy Director of the Polytechnic, appointed in his early forties, to leaving the Vice-Chancellorship of the University at sixty-five, was now coming to an end. But there was no standing still. The restless vigour that had characterised his leadership of the University and the Polytechnic had to be maintained. There was still much to be done.

---

* Mary Dunning had left school prior to taking 'A' Levels and had trained as a cadet nurse, achieving her SRN and winning a gold medal at University College Hospital, London. She trained as a midwife in Edinburgh. On returning to London she took a nurse tutor's teaching diploma and MEd at the Institute of Education, London University. She became senior tutor at St Bartholomew's Hospital before moving to Newcastle in 1983.

In November 1995 the Governors established the procedures for appointing his successor. An appointments committee was agreed and head hunters appointed. Atkinson was very open about the process, circulating all members of staff with details of how an appointment would be made and by whom. Over thirty applied for this prestigious post; after all, as a polytechnic Newcastle had been amongst the top three in the country; as a 'new' university it was rapidly emerging as a national leader in its class for teaching quality. It more than deserved the very strongest of applicants from home and abroad.

After 'due process' the Governors appointed Professor Gilbert Smith to succeed Barden. Smith was Deputy Director of Research for the National Health Service; he also held the Chair of Social Administration at the University of Hull. He was a graduate of Leeds and Essex Universities and held a doctorate from Aberdeen University. In addition to spending most of his academic career at Aberdeen, Glasgow and Hull, he had also been Chairman of the East Riding Health Authority. He had successfully combined scholarly activity and university administration with public life and service. Given developments in the newly created fifth faculty, his experience in the health service appeared to be of considerable benefit to the University of Northumbria. He was one of the growing number of social scientists to be appointed to a post traditionally held by engineers. Many challenges lay ahead not the least of which was for him and his colleagues to maintain the momentum of enhancing further the University of Northumbria's reputation.

The 8 year period covered by this chapter was perhaps the most energetic in the history of the institution. Student numbers had grown from more than 8,000 in 1988–89 to more than 22,500 in 1995–96. The budget had increased from £31 million in 1989 to £75 million at the end of our period. The economic impact of the University was greater than many conventional businesses in the city with a regional output of about £120 million and a contribution to the labour market directly and indirectly of over 5,000 jobs. The University was the city's fifth largest employer in 1996.[91] The Polytechnic had been created a corporation independent of its local authority in 1988 and four short years later was made a university. It had consolidated its physical presence in the centre of Newcastle and was about to embark on an exciting building programme at its second campus at Coach Lane. It had established two satellites at Carlisle and Longhirst. Its curriculum had been broadened and made more flexible by being unitised. It had added a new skills component to all its courses. It was beginning to weather the pressures brought about by the decline in demand for one of its traditional strengths, engineering, and had added new dimensions in design, media, business studies and nurse education. It had successfully embarked on a nationally determined quality assurance system. More and more students were coming to the University from overseas and the delivery of its programmes abroad was growing rapidly. The ladder had been scaled but by the end of the next decade, the University and the city in which it was set would change yet again.

Coach Lane Campus East

Epilogue

THE UNIVERSITY that Professor Gilbert Smith was appointed to lead in 1995 was the outcome of 125 years of rather variable progress.[1] For many of those years the amount of university-level work had remained relatively small and yet from the very beginning the hope for higher things was always there. It was not until the foundation of the Polytechnic in 1969 that degrees and diplomas proliferated. Prior to that date the work of the various colleges whose fortunes we have tried to trace was, for much of the time, involved in *further* education, much of it on a part-time basis. The city's original vision of having a university in Newcastle had been realised but through the College of Medicine, the College of Physical Science, Armstrong College, King's College – all predecessors of the University of Newcastle upon Tyne.

But what of the aspirations of John Hunter Rutherford and his 'ladder of opportunity'? What were the major processes that finally brought about the transformation from his School of Science and Arts of the 1870s to the University of Northumbria in the 1990s? Who were the principal actors in this long struggle? Was it simply the product of local energy and determination? Was it the inevitable and logical outcome of emerging national policies, especially since 1945? Although beginning as a local venture, did the later colleges become another example of the State provision of a service for the greater good, the common weal, for the welfare of its citizens? Was it an attempt to raise levels of output at a variety of geographical scales, regional and national, via the economists' beloved human capital theory? Or was the whole thing just a glorious accident, the unintended outcome of a series of loosely connected events, which like Topsy, just grew and grew?

What emerged does not appear to have been the product of any long-term plan. None of our research has revealed such a scheme neither from Whitehall mandarins nor local government officers. Certainly, there was much political aspiration but this ranged from Rutherford's hopes for working class advancement, to some kind of socialist planning, to business-like corporations. On balance it would seem that much of the success was attributable to the prescience of leading actors within the colleges complemented by the hard work and dedication of teachers determined to provide the best possible education for successive generations of students.

However, in the language of economics, these are supply-side factors. What of the rising demand for higher education over this long period? School students and their parents began to recognise the social and economic benefits from going to college. Particpation rates rose from 4 per cent of the relevant age group in the 1960s to over 40 per cent today. In all periods mature students sought better access on full- and part-time courses, often making up for missed opportunities earlier in life or enhancing their qualifications as they worked. One group above all who have continually pressed for better access has been women. From largely being excluded from higher education through much of the first 100 years of this history and having to settle for low status courses, women now make up more than 50 per cent of students in universities; at Northumbria nearly 60 per cent of full-time students are women. From the end of the Second World War the colleges began to take students from most parts of northern England, not just Tyneside. By the end of our period the University had almost one thousand students from overseas, a small measure of its growing internationalism.

One important theme that runs through this history is the debate of providing a useful education. Rutherford may have been a radical reformer but his educational ideas were not romantic; they were rooted in the principle of education for work, and thereby, social advancement. While this emphasis on vocational education was by no means exclusive or confined to this kind of college it remained a defining characteristic. Traditional universities have always offered courses related to certain professions such as law and medicine but their main driving force has been the transmission of culture, whether in the sciences or the arts. A second characteristic has been their responsibility for producing the next generation of scholars and academics; until very recently there were few polytechnic-trained teaching staff at Northumbria. Graduates of the colleges went, for the most part, into business, industry and public service; few went on to higher degree work upon graduating, largely because there was, to begin with, only a superficial research culture in the polytechnics and their successors, and virtually none in their predecessors. Until the 1950s many staff did not have degrees. Later, when more graduates joined the teaching staff, what was remarkable was how those from the more 'liberal' universities who came to work in teacher training, in engineering and in commercial education were able to leave behind their own earlier acculturations and help develop mainly vocational courses. There might be two explanations for this: either they brought with them industrial and business experience or perhaps they were a group of people who were dissatisfied with the higher education they had received and were determined to develop an alternative. What happened in more recent years was that staff trained in the conventional university apprenticeship system – that is, after gaining a first class degree, completing a PhD and undertaking post doctoral work – came into the polytechnics and, after 1992, the new universities, expecting to find the same culture as the one they were used to, with similarly motivated or qualified students and the same kind of facilities. This history has dealt with a different reality.

If the curriculum retained its vocational dominance over these many years, it changed radically its approach to teaching and learning. Further education through most of the twentieth century was characterised by a marked narrowness and convergence. The education and training of engineers, teachers and nurses was initially, and for many years, largely a style of learning handed down by the previous generation; students memorised material and learned to regurgitate it in examinations. There was little questioning of what they were taught and by teachers of the way to teach. Rote was everything until some time after the Second World War. This methodology, if it can be so described, was not helped by the professional bodies – the engineering institutes, the national body for nurses, the accounting organisations, even the Law Society. Only slowly, and often following government reports into education and training, were more liberal approaches introduced and 'education' began to replace 'training'. A parallel influence was the increasing intellectualisation of certain disciplines, usually in a traditional university environment, where a more sceptical, questioning view was *de rigueur*. Engineering, for example, in the 1960s became more and more orientated to engineering science; social work adopted critical, more holistic views of the social setting of their clients and their own profession; the new fangled BEds of the same period placed more emphasis on ways of learning than subject content and classroom techniques. These could all be interpreted as moves towards *higher* education, and away from their further education origins. In addition, the world of academe rated more highly the more abstract approaches being developed.[2] 'Doing' and 'making' were said to be poor substitutes for thought. Many of these subjects remained vocational but they lost their accepting, uncritical stances and adopted more liberal and questioning perspectives that reflected the changing world around them.

When subjects that were liberal by definition were introduced at about the same time into the world of the technical, commerce and art colleges – subjects such as fine art, the humanities, sociology and politics – they brought with them a new, more certain university-like atmosphere. Despite the fears of artists like Patrick Heron, painters and sculptors and later performance artists, brought a new and critical philosophy to the changing art school. Political science students exposed the ideologies that lay behind many government decisions about the future direction of higher education. Sociologists detected class, gender and ethnic bias in syllabuses and indirectly made the institution address its own prejudices via an Equal Opportunities policy. In Sport Studies, for example, a subject relatively new to British higher education, the emphasis shifted from sport practice to the social patterning of sport, examining its participants and its audience. In its more scientific aspects it increasingly adopted the philosophy and techniques of older disciplines, which, being more highly rated by the scientific establishment, began to direct the emphases of sport scientists. All these were, of course, part of wider shifts in the educational paradigm but their influence in restructuring what was taught, and how, was considerable.

Governments, meanwhile, continued to issue policies that were more narrowly cast, at least until the late 1980s. The view from Smith Square (Conservative Party HQ), Transport House (Labour Party HQ) or Elizabeth House (the Civil Service heart) was that the country needed more technical graduates because in some simple, but largely unproven way, there was a correlation between trained labour and the growth of gross domestic product. Luckily attempts by civil servants and others to impose manpower planning on the basis of this belief always foundered, but it took a long time for party leaders to appreciate that the education supply could not readily adjust to the needs of the labour market. Experience of wartime conditions and the consequent direction of labour may have shown that such strategies might have been possible then, but in peacetime, when choice was a readily exercised strategy, it would not work. Gradually, policy moved towards a form of higher education that produced the kind of critical, reflective practitioner who was adaptable and flexible in rapidly changing circumstances, supported by a range of transferable skills.

By the late 1980s the national system had become a *mass* system, moving perhaps towards a universal system. In 1988 there were 12,000 students in the Polytechnic. By 1995, a mere 7 years later, the University total had risen to 22,500. It would have been difficult, if not impossible, to educate this number along traditional university lines. Even traditional universities could not retain such methods as they too underwent an explosion in size. Economic costs alone dictated the inexorable rise in staff-student ratios from 10:1 to 15:1 to over 20:1. A new form of curriculum had to be adopted, the modular or unitised scheme, based on a simple industrial division of labour and neo-Fordist principles. But this was the outcome of rapid adjustment to changes post-1988. Before that Northumbria's more traditional academic and professional courses had served its students well. Newcastle Polytechnic proved that it excelled at these both approaches, scoring amongst the highest nationally in HMI and HEQC ratings for teaching through much of the 1980s and early 1990s. In the previous decade its growing autonomy from CNAA proved how well it could manage expansion and subject diversity.

It would be convenient to be able to state categorically that what happened at Northumbria was solely the product of national policies and the passionate concern of successive education ministers but the truth is that over most of our period higher education did not figure very prominently in their political landscape. The present features are not the outcome of some long-held dream but a much messier affair. Certainly, there were some long-term trends in educational policy that were significant; we have already pointed to the vocational emphasis of this kind of college and the belief of some politicians and civil servants that this would result in economic advancement for the nation. Similarly, there appears to be some evidence for public sector higher education being used to counterbalance the more traditional universities and their autonomy under the UGC and Treasury funding system that sidelined the Department of Education. We can also point to the colleges and the Polytechnic that preceded Northumbria University as being part of a national educational service delivered locally. Under the Thatcher/Joseph/Baker regime of the 1970s and '80s this was seriously undermined as central government sought to control and reduce the powers of local democracies. It could be argued that this eventually benefited Northumbria because the abolition of CNAA, the incorporation of the polytechnics by the 1988 Act and the creation of the new generation of universities after 1992, finally gave it the autonomy it had been working towards. However, this is to underestimate the generosity of treatment the colleges and the Polytechnic had received from their local authority. The city always had high aspirations for its local colleges from the adoption of Rutherford's original college after the Acts of 1902 and 1904 and the founding of the College of Art and Industrial Design in 1953. Even the half-hearted attempt to merge the technical college with King's College, Durham after the failure to secure CAT status, flowed from the best possible motives. Nowhere was this aspiration for high status, nationally recognised educational activity better summarised than in the development of the education precinct from the mid 1950s onwards. It may have been T. Dan Smith's strength of character that finally gave the city colleges their key site but the idea of a central location can be traced back to earlier statements of both political parties.

From about the early 1980s relations between central and local government shifted and it would be true to say that since that date there has been much more central direction of higher education – and since 1992, of older and newer universities alike. Once the old Advanced Further Education Pool was capped and then abolished and polytechnics funded directly and not via their local education authority, and once the long and intimate relationship between the UGC and the Treasury was broken, then central government, by controlling the purse strings, could dictate much more the style and tone of higher education. This has not, of course, been carried out in any crude way; it was more a case of 'smoke and mirrors', more of Lord Robbins's 'abracadabra'. As Whitehall and the various Secretaries of State insisted on value for money, accountability and certain visible standards and qualities, their indirect control became more apparent. None of their demands were unreasonable but their implementation resulted in a different kind of the autonomy from that once enjoyed by universities. British higher education throughout much of the post-war period remained generously funded, as did its students. There have, of course, been dramatic changes in the decade since 1995. Politicians may argue that they did not interfere directly with higher education, and certainly not with its content, and that decision-making remained in the hands of academic boards and governing bodies, but it was clearly a *constrained autonomy*. For the public sector under NAB and PCFC, and later under HEFCE, the emergence of an apparently contradictory tension between planning on the one hand and market-led competition on the other led to universities' own actions being severely limited. Some writers have observed that this has been most keenly felt by the older universities.[3]

Another theme that runs through this history is that of *merger*, a process that enabled the central institution to grow and diversify while rationalising local provision. It was, as is so often the case, usually accompanied by differentiation and specialisation so that as one college merged with another, then certain aspects of work were transferred to a third institution. This was the case with Rutherford College in the late 1950s, with the Colleges of Art and Commerce in the 1960s, the teacher training colleges in the 1970s and the nursing and health colleges in the 1990s. Such changes were mostly locally controlled even if the impetus came from national policy decisions. The long-term benefits from the creation of the Polytechnic in 1969 and the entry of nursing and other health service professions in the 1970s and more especially in the 1990s, were self-evident. The colleges of education mergers in the 1970s were rather bloodier, and some at Kenton Lodge and Northern Counties argued that not all was beneficial either to individuals or to the way teacher training developed. It was significant, however, that at Newcastle Polytechnic both management and unions sought, where they could, to create new opportunities for the more enterprising staff.

One important structural characteristic that must not be overlooked or taken for granted in this evolving history is the increasing professionalisation of the administration. In the early days support for the academic enterprise was indeed limited. Administrative and clerical work was largely carried out directly by the city's Education Department. As teaching and research became more sophisticated, and above all as numbers of students and staff increased, so as part of the growing autonomy of the colleges from the local authority, it became necessary for them to develop their own independent bureaucracy and administration. When the powers of academic boards and governors grew then decisions could be made in the colleges and not in the Town Hall or Civic Centre. Until the 1950s even college principals were more or less under the fairly direct control of the Education Committee. As the Polytechnic and University developed as a national, and not simply local institutions guided by Whitehall decisions rather than Town Hall ones, so a new cadre of well educated administrators had to be appointed and trained. Key figures in this process were the Registrars, the finance officers and property specialists. The role of this group was not restricted to the central effort of the institution because, as we have shown from the mid-1980s onwards, part of the energy had to be devoted to a stream of 'initiatives' to which funding was often attached, such as Enterprise, PICKUP and RAEs. Initially, much of the administration was devoted externally to the work with CNAA and other validating bodies, but in time it would grow into the vital fields of annual and longer term planning and financial, personnel and property management. Such complex and specialised tasks required a professional contribution supported by articulate and technically competent clerical staff. The idea that the 'collegium of scholars' could somehow have supplied this service to itself became ever more quaint. At times there may have been a tension between the essential academic management of the institution and the administrative delivery of its decisions but Northumbria was always fortunate in having an administration that saw its role as a service to students and academic staff. Like all bureaucracies in large organisations, it was not always possible to obtain full agreement on respective roles. There is some evidence that this led to the development of what we have referred to as a 'parallel' polytechnic.

We said at the outset that this was not to be a history of individuals who inhabited the various colleges that came to form Northumbria University; that might be the task of a future generation of historians. Our mission was to trace the development of the institution *qua* institution, the *making* of the university as in our sub-title. That being said, it is inevitable that certain people left a powerful impression on the University. The tone was set at the outset by Rutherford; in Chapter 1 his political and educational philosophy was explored together with his determination to provide accessible education as a means of social advancement for the working class. In the long period from the 1920s to the 1960s the colleges were led, as was the style at the time, by largely autocratic Principals. Unfortunately the record of their personalities and styles is silent. We have not been able to find much evidence in the form of letters or diaries; none wrote an autobiography or memoirs. The names are recorded – Ellis, Gaunt, Scarborough, Rotheram, Rowlands, Elliott, etc. – but of their personalities we know little. It is not until the formation of the Polytechnic in 1969 that the influence of certain figures becomes more discernable. From then on the archive is more complete and we have the benefit of the reminiscences of our interviewees, some of whom lived and worked through the earlier periods of our story.

Throughout this work the good relations the colleges had with the city and its Council has been commented upon. The key figure was always the Chairman of the Education Committee. Two men in particular stand out, interestingly from both parts of the political spectrum – Dr Cyril Lipman for the Conservatives and Derek Webster representing the Labour Party. Interestingly, neither men saw the Polytechnic as being subject to ideological treatment, perhaps because at a personal level they were friends, Webster being especially impressed by Lipman's commitment to the Polytechnic and his generous treatment of it following the death of his son in 1973.[4]

Professor John Clark and Peter Torode did much to navigate a position of national leadership and forge a unique relationship with CNAA. Ron Hopkinson played a key role in developing a sound administration for the Polytechnic. Professor John Rear in the 1980s and 1990s laid the foundations and then built upon them the principal structures for modern academic self-management and improvement, introducing new patterns of teaching and learning, a different academic calendar, fostered enterprise and ensured high standards of quality in all parts of the University. The University's leading position as a teaching institution owes much to his efforts. Richard Bott as Secretary guided at least two generations of Governors through the murky waters of incorporation and university status. In their midst, helping Chairmen like Webster and Atkinson, sat Lord Glenamara, Chancellor of the University since 1983 who brought his experience from his many years in local politics, the House of Commons, the Cabinet, Party leadership and the House of Lords to bear on the Governors' deliberations. And what graduating student could forget his perorations at their awards congregation, often against prevailing government policy?

For more than 25 years, one man did so much to direct the fortunes of, first, Newcastle Polytechnic and then the University of Northumbria at Newcastle – Professor Laing Barden. Although he was not always able to articulate it, he usually knew what he wanted from the institution and where it was headed. If he had a long-term plan he never wrote it down but he was a marvellous opportunist, a man who knew how to take advantage of emerging situations, a man of action. He came, as he readily admitted, having little knowledge of the world of local authority higher education but he retired as one of the consummate leaders of the maturing polytechnics and newer universities. But Northumbria was not the product of his energies alone. Because he inspired loyalty and was generally 'canny' in the appointment of his immediate assistants, he had able and experienced staff to support him. As in any major institution, relations may have been strained at times but rarely to breaking point; he acknowledged contrasting views and listened to and was guided by his Academic Board. This was due in part to his personal charm and humour which in turn attracted this loyalty, it brought out the best in others at all levels, a key feature of a good leader. His strong strategic instinct for what was required as government priorities shifted may have made him appear ruthless occasionally but his efforts were always directed towards the betterment of the Polytechnic and the University. Naturally he mellowed over time, the firebrand Assistant Director became the more accommodating Vice-Chancellor. When he retired in 1995 he had held office for longer than anyone in a similar position nationally, a longevity that will probably never be repeated. Newcastle and Northumbria were fortunate to have his services.

Many have helped make 'Rutherford's Ladder' and thousands of students have climbed it but whether it has made the benefits of higher education as accessible to the working class as he had hoped, is questionable. Over time it has developed an enviable reputation for offering wider opportunities and access to higher education. In its earlier guises its students were mainly part-time and evening students but paradoxically, the huge growth of higher education in more recent years has seen the gap between working and middle class people attending university in Britain widen. Higher education has become the province of children of the middle classes, mostly attending full-time. This history has shown Northumbria to be a leading university of its type. It is ironic that success and the sheer growth of the institution may have thwarted one of Rutherford's founding principles. While much of the present day rhetoric is directed towards the aspirations the early pioneers, the fact is, his revolution remains unfinished.

Notes

Preface

1. R. J. Buswell, 'Old Stones and the Laburnum Tree: the University as place', unpublished Inaugural Professorial Lecture, University of Northumbria at Newcastle, 29 November 1995. See also M. Barke and R. J. Buswell (eds.), *Newcastle's Changing Map*, Newcastle upon Tyne, 1996.

2. Joan Allen has published work on politics and the press in the Victorian period with special reference to the north-east of England. For example, see J. Allen and O. R. Ashton (eds.), *Papers for the People. A Study of the Chartist Press*, London, 2005.

Introduction

1. 'The Robbins principle' as cited in Alan Matterson, *Polytechnics and Colleges*, London, 1981, p.61.

2. *Ibid.*, p.183. The Robbins Committee 'had no difficulty justifying its recommendations in terms of both egalitarian principle and of national economic benefit'. See also Harold Silver, *Education as History*, London, 1983, p.213, who states that Crosland 'preferred a binary system to a 'ladder' hierarchy'.

3. Harold Silver, *A Higher Education, The Council for National Academic Awards and British Higher Education 1964–1989*, London, 1990, p.65.

4. *Ibid.*, p.66; See also A. H. Halsey, *Decline of Donnish Dominion. The British Academic Professions in the Twentieth Century*, Oxford, 1992, p.111 who cites Robbins' reaction in 1965: 'If I had known that anything so reactionary and half baked as the binary system was going to be propounded I certainly would have suggested adding a few paragraphs to the report dealing with this as it deserves'.

5. Silver, *Education as History*, pp.213–14.

6. For a discussion of 'academic drift' see J. Pratt, *The Polytechnic Experiment, 1965–1992*, Buckingham, 1997.

7. *Higher Education, a New Framework*, London, 1991, p.6.

8. Note the clumsy reporting of league tables at the end of the 1990s. For example, see 'Good University Guide', *Daily Telegraph*, 17 February 1999. Even now the British press finds it difficult to resist drawing unhelpful comparisons.

9. Mission Statement, Northumbria University, 2005.

10. Rutherford's belief in an educational 'ladder' is discussed in chapter 2.

11. Speech made by Joseph Cowen, 30 December 1873 and provided in *Speeches on Public Questions and Political Policy By Joseph Cowen Esq., MP*, Newcastle upon Tyne, 1874, p.18. It is interesting to find Beveridge's famous mantra for the 1947 National Health Service being articulated so precisely some seventy years or so earlier.

12. Ann M. Garnham, 'Education for Industry. The Newcastle Experience, 1889–1902', unpublished University of Sussex MPhil thesis, 1978, p.29.

13. W. B. Stephens, *Education in Britain*, Basingstoke, 1998, p.12. See also Silver, *Education as History*, p.65.

14. Tyrrell Burgess and John Pratt, *Policy and Practice: The Colleges of Advanced Technology*, London, 1970.

15. Silver, *A Higher Education*.

16. Brian Simon, *The State and Educational Change*, London, 1994, p.100. Simon quotes Claus Moser's warning (1990) that 'major deficiencies' in education provision would have 'dire consequences' and observed that neither the government nor the Labour opposition were 'attempting to make the required 'leap' in priority, quality and vision'.

17. Halsey, *Decline of Donnish Dominion*.

18. Simon, *State and Educational Change*, pp.4–5.

Chapter 1

1. Dr John Hunter Rutherford (1826–1890) was a Congregationalist preacher who established Bath Lane School (founded in 29 June 1870), the School of Science and Art (1877) and several branch schools at Shieldfield, Heaton, Gateshead and Byker. Rutherford Memorial College (1892) was dedicated to his memory, as was a memorial fountain which still stands in Newcastle's Bigg Market. For biographical details of his life and career see W. Maw, *The Story of Rutherford Grammar School*, Gateshead, 1964. See also R. Welford, *Men of Mark 'Twixt Tyne and Tweed*, London and Newcastle, 1895; G. D. H. Cole, *A Century of Co-operation*, Manchester, 1944, pp.161–165.

2. Welford, *Men of Mark 'Twixt Tyne and Tweed*, London and Newcastle, 1895. The fountain with the inscription 'Water is best' was originally located adjacent to St Nicholas Cathedral.

3. Maw, *The Story of Rutherford Grammar School*, p.47.

4. For details of Rutherford's involvement in North East Co-operation see Joan Hugman, 'Joseph Cowen and the Blaydon Co-operative Store: A North East Model', in Bill Lancaster and Paddy Maguire (eds.), *Towards a Co-operative Commonwealth*, Loughborough, 1996.

5.   H. J. Rutherford (ed.), *The Bible Defender*, 5 vols. London, 1856–58. Volume 1 was published 'for the free discussion of great religious and social questions'.

6.   *Ibid.* Also see Maw, *The Story of Rutherford Grammar School*, p.11.

7.   For a discussion of the 1870 Act see W. B. Stephens, *Education in Britain 1750–1914*, Basingstoke, 1998, chapter 5. Rutherford was elected to serve on the Newcastle upon Tyne School Board on 25 January 1871, *Chater's Diary and Local Remembrancer for 1872*, Newcastle upon Tyne, 1872, p.11.

8.   Stephens, *Education in Britain*, p.7. The Revised Code enabled Government to provide funding only to those schools which were clearly successful at providing a basic elementary education.

9.   Gillian Sutherland, 'Education', in F. M. L. Thompson, *The Cambridge Social History of Britain 1750–1950*, 3 vols. Cambridge, 1990, vol. 3, pp.141–142.

10.   D. G. Paz, *The Politics of Working Class Education in Britain 1830–50*, Manchester, 1980, p.3.

11.   For instance, see Rosemary O'Day, *Education and Society, 1500–1800*, London, 1982, pp.xii, 239–259.

12.   Mary Carpenter addressing the National Association for the Promotion of Social Science in 1861, as cited in Harold Silver, *Education as History*, London, 1983, p.41.

13.   Michael Sanderson, *Education, Economic Change and Society in England, 1780–1870*, Basingstoke, 1983, p.13.

14.   Stephens, *Education in Britain*, p.4. See also J. F. C. Harrison, *The Common People*.

15.   O'Day, *Education and Society*, p.256.

16.   David Wardle, *Education and Society in Nineteenth-Century Nottingham*, Cambridge, 1971, p.43.

17.   Stephens, *Education in Britain*, p.5.

18.   In 1851 Sunday school enrolment in Northumberland was 12.1%. See T. W. Lacquer, *Religion and Respectability: Sunday Schools and Working Class Culture 1780–1950*, New Haven, 1976, p.52.

19.   *Census Report*, London, 1854, p.xv.

20.   Peter King, 'The Rise of Juvenile Delinquency in England, 1780–1840: Changing Patterns of Perception and Prosecution', *Past & Present*, 1998, pp.116–166.

21.   Raymond Williams, *The Long Revolution*, London, 1961, p.157.

22.   Norman McCord, *North East England. The Region's Development 1760–1960*, London, 1979, p.101. See also TWAS.MS.E/NC 42 for information on Dame Allans School.

23.   P. Corder, *The Life and Times of Robert Spence Watson*, London, 1914; R. Sansbury, *Beyond the Blew Stone. 300 Years of Quakers in Newcastle*, Newcastle upon Tyne, 1998.

24.   Stephens, *Education in Britain*, p.10.

25.   Sansbury, *Beyond the Blew Stone*, chapter 8, especially pp.195–196.

26.   Corder, *The Life of Robert Spence Watson*, p.135.

27.   The Newcastle upon Tyne Literary and Philosophical Society was established in 1793, and promoted an interest in science and the arts through lectures and papers as well as by providing reading material and laboratories. See Stephen Harbottle, *The Reverend William Turner: dissent and reform in Georgian Newcastle upon Tyne*, Newcastle, 1997. A mechanics' institute modelled on the Edinburgh School of Arts (1821) was founded in 1824. For a useful discussion of the role of mechanics' institutes in education see Gordon

W. Roderick and Michael D. Stephens, *Education and Industry in the Nineteenth Century*, London, 1978, chapter 4; J. F. C. Harrison, *Learning and Living, A Study in the History of the English Adult Education Movement*, London, 1961.

28. R. J. Morris, *Class, Sect and Party The Making of the British Middle Class, Leeds, 1820–50*, Manchester, 1990.

29. Joseph Cowen, 1829–1900, a leading Radical and Republican activist was Liberal MP for Newcastle upon Tyne from 1874 to 1886. He had extensive business interests in the city, most notably as proprietor of the *Newcastle Chronicle*, and served on the Town Council. He collaborated closely with J. H. Rutherford on a range of campaigns, particularly educational reform. For details of his life and political career see J. Hugman 'Print and Preach': The Entrepreneurial Spirit of Nineteenth-Century Newcastle', in Robert Colls and Bill Lancaster (eds.), *Newcastle upon Tyne. A Modern History*, Sussex, 2001; J. Hugman 'Joseph Cowen of Newcastle and Radical Liberalism', unpublished University of Northumbria PhD thesis, 1993. See also N. Todd, *The Militant Democracy*, Whitley Bay, 1990.

30. *Annual Report of the Northern Union of Mechanic's Institutes*, vol. 1, 1855–56.

31. Stephens, *Education in Britain*, p.71.

32. Michael Gordon and Roderick Stephens, *Education and Industry in the Nineteenth Century: The English Disease*, London, 1978, p.64. See also table 4.3, p.65 which shows that in 1880 there were 894 Science and Arts students in Northumberland and 1,387 in Durham, many of whom were taking classes in mechanics' institutes.

33. *Annual Report of the Northern Union of Mechanics' Institutes*, vol. 1. 1856–1857, p.17. For a history of the University of Durham, see C. E. Whiting, *The University of Durham 1831–1932*, London, 1932.

34. *Annual Report of the Northern Union of Mechanics' Institutes*, vol. 1, p.17.

35. Later this became the Royal College of Art while its provincial counterparts 'came under the auspices of the Department of Science and art'. See Thomas Kelly, *A History of Adult Education in Britain*, Liverpool, 1970, p.129; Stephens, *Education in Britain*, p.135.

36. Wardle, *Education and Society in Nineteenth-Century Nottingham*, p.124.

37. 'Newcastle Fifty Years ago', *Newcastle Weekly Chronicle*, 18 August 1883.

38. W. Minto (ed.), *Autobiographical Notes on the Life of William Bell Scott and Notices of his Artistic and Poetic Circle of Friends, 1830–1882*, London, 1887, p.173. Also see C. Frayling, *The Royal College of Art, One Hundred and Fifty Years of Art and Design*, London, 1987, p.12. Following the establishment of the School of Design in 1837 'a network of branch schools' was set up in most of the major industrial cities and towns including Manchester, Birmingham, Glasgow, Leeds and, of course, Newcastle upon Tyne.

39. Paul Usherwood, 'Art on the Margins from Bewick to Baltic', in Colls and Lancaster (eds.), *Newcastle upon Tyne*, p.253.

40. Frayling, *The Royal College of Art*, p.9.

41. Minto, *Autobiographical Notes*, p.179.

42. *Ibid.*, p.188.

43. Frayling *The Royal College of Art*, pp.32–34. Wornum was lecturer in the History of Ornamental Art and heavily criticised by the *Journal of Design* for the 'esoteric' content of his lectures.

44. P. W. Musgrave, *Society and Education in England since 1800*, London, 1968, p.25.

45. David Cannadine, *G. M. Trevelyan: a life in history*, London, 1992.

46. W. E Armstrong began his career as a solicitor but made his name and fortune from, first of all, the manufacture of hydraulic machinery and later, armaments. McCord, *North East England*, pp.133–138; K. Warren, *Armstrong's of Elswick: Growth in Engineering and Armaments to the Merger with Vickers*, London, 1989.

47. For instance, a number of colliery works' schools were set up in the north east of England.

48. Stephens, *Education in Britain*, p.11.

49. TWAS. MS. E/NCIS/1/1. Elswick Works' School Log Book, 28 April 1869 – 11 December 1885.

50. TWAS. MS. E/NCI3/1/2. Elswick Works' Girls School Log Book 1888–1908. The Girls school was also established in 1866 but there are no log books for the earlier period. After 1888 the school seems to have had a progressive Headmistress who was keen to introduce science and drawing into the curriculum but was thwarted at every turn. See entries dated December 1890, August 1891 and October 1891.

51. TWAS. MS. E/NCIS/1/1, entry dated 31 March 1871. It is notable that while the school was also open to girls (taught separately) maintaining records of their progress seems to have been a lesser priority.

52. J. F. Clarke, Edwin Allen and Norman McCord (eds.), *The North-East Engineers' Strike of 1871: The Nine Hour League*, Newcastle upon Tyne, 1971.

53. TWAS. MS. E/NCIS/1/1. For example, see entries dated 24 July 1871, 12 January 1872, 13 December 1872.

54. Stephens, *Education in Britain*, p.80. Stephens points out that because the dual system placed so much control in the hands of local providers 'the quality of education consequently varied very considerably not only between voluntary and board schools, but between the schools of some boards and others. *Ibid.*, p.93.

55. TWAS. MS. D253 (Joseph Cowen Papers). Speech at Bewick Street Schoolroom, 23 January 1871. For details of Cowen's campaign 'knowledge is power' see Joan Allen, 'Resurrecting Jerusalem: The Late Chartist press in the North East of England, 1852–1859', in Joan Allen and Owen R. Ashton (eds.), *Papers for the People. A Study of the Chartist Press*, London, 2005.

56. *Newcastle Daily Chronicle*, 25 November 1869; Stephens, *Education in Britain*, pp.78–79.

57. Gordon and Stephens, *Education and Industry in the Nineteenth Century*, p.17.

58. See J. S. Hurt, *Elementary Schooling and the Working Classes, 1860–1918*, London, 1979, chapter 4.

59. TWAS. MS. D253, 23 January 1871.

60. Hurt, *Elementary Schooling*, p.94.

61. Cowen, Rutherford and Spence Watson were all elected together with George Luckley and Isaac Lowthian Bell. In addition, the new School Board included four 'Church' candidates, three Wesleyans, two Presbyterians, one 'Independent Churchman' and one Primitive Methodist. See *Chater's Diary and Local Remembrancer*, p.11.

62. Evan Rowland Jones, *The Life and Speeches of Joseph Cowen, MP, London, 1885*, p.301. Speech in the House of Commons by Joseph Cowen, 5 August 1876.

63. Francis Adams, *History of the Elementary School Contest*, London, 1882. Reprinted with an introduction by Asa Briggs, Sussex, 1972, p.xlvi.

64. Quoted in Silver, *Education as History*, p.87. Briggs notes that despite Morley's diatribe he did not advocate free higher education. See Adams, *History of the Elementary School Contest*, p.xlvi.

65. *Newcastle Daily Chronicle*, 29 June 1870. Lord Amberley was the son of Earl Russell.

66. *Newcastle Daily Chronicle*, 30 June 1870.

67. *Ibid.*

68. Maw, *Rutherford Grammar School*, pp.34–46.

69. *Newcastle Daily Chronicle*, 21 November 1877.

70. TWAS. MS. E/NC8. Bath Lane Day Schools Minute Book, minutes dated 14 November 1877.

71. Cole, *A Century of Co-operation*, p.164. Cole notes that while Rutherford was 'animated no doubt by the highest intentions' his finances were 'outrageously faulty'.

72. TWAS. MS. E/NC8, minutes dated 1 March 1878.

73. *Ibid.*

74. *Ibid.*, minutes dated 1 March 1878.

75. *Ibid.*, minutes dated 27 May 1878, 29 May 1878.

76. *Ibid.*, minutes dated 13 September 1878.

77. *Ibid.*, minutes dated, especially 24 January 1879, 7 June 1879. It is notable that Maw's official history glosses over his ignominious departure and instead claims that the death of his wife was the key factor in his removal to Lanarkshire. See Maw, *Story of Rutherford Grammar School*, pp.18–19.

78. Maw, *Story of Rutherford Grammar School*, pp.18–19.

79. *Ibid.*, pp.20–21.

80. TWAS. MS. E/NC8, minutes dated 27 February 1880.

81. *Ibid.*, minutes dated 30 July 1880. By this stage the Committee had also secured premises for another elementary school in Byker.

82. *Ibid.*, minutes dated 30 June 1881.

83. *Ibid.*, minutes dated 13 April 1883.

84. *Ibid.*, minutes dated 13 November 1883.

85. *Ibid.*, minutes dated 13 November 1883, 22 February 1884.

86. *Ibid.*, Financial Statement, 25 August 1885.

87. The British and Foreign School Society (BFSS) was the principal non conformist society and a substantial provider of voluntary school places. See Hurt, *Elementary Schooling*, p.4.

88. *Royal Commission on the University of Durham Report*, London, 1935, pp.88–89. See also E. M. Bettenson, *The University of Newcastle upon Tyne, A Historical Introduction 1834–1971*, Newcastle upon Tyne, 1971, pp.21–29. Notably, Bettenson ascribes no role to Cowen in these fundraising efforts.

89. TWAS. MS. E/NC8, minutes dated 27 January 1888; Bettenson, *The University of Newcastle upon Tyne*, p.25; *Royal Commission Report*, 1935, p.88.

90. TWAS. MS., Newcastle Council Educational Sub-Committee Minutes, minutes dated 8 April 1886, 23 February 1888, 8 March 1888.

91. TWAS. MS. E/NC8, 27 January 1888.

92. Roderick and Stephens, *Education and Industry*, p.70. One former Whitworth scholar went on to become Chair of Engineering and Mathematics at Newcastle College of Physical Science.

93. 'The Grievances of a Modern Schoolgirl', *The Magazine of the Science and Art School*, Volume 3, May 1888.

94. *Nineteenth Century*, 24 July 1888, as cited in Garnham, 'Education for Industry', p.10.

Chapter 2

1. Brian Simon, 'David Reeder's 'alternative system': the school boards in the 1890s', in Robert Colls and Richard Rodger (eds.), *Cities of Ideas. Civil Society and Urban Governance in Britain 1800–2000*, Aldershot, 2004, p.187.

2. *Ibid.*, p.181.

3. For example, W. B. Stephens notes that the system 'was lacking in homogeneity and geographically patchy, with responsibilities divided untidily between school boards and technical instruction committees'. See Stephens, *Education in Britain*, p.102.

4. *Newcastle Daily Chronicle*, 22 April 1890.

5. TWAS. MS. E/NC8. Bath Lane Day Schools Minute Book 1885-1936, minutes dated 28 March 1890.

6. TWAS. MS. ENC 14/4/9/4 (4), Preface, List of Subscribers for Rutherford College.

7. TWAS. MS.E/NC8, minutes dated 18 April 1890, 23 May 1890.

8. TWAS. MS. ENC14/4/9/2 (9), Proceedings of the City Engineers and Town Surveyors Office, 21 April 1890.

9. TWAS. MS. E/NC8, minutes dated 26 November 1890; TWAS. MS. ENC14/1/9/2, *Rutherford College Calendar, 1903–4*, p.20 states that Blaydon, Newcastle and Newcastle Wholesale Society each gave £100, while fifty-seven other Co-operative societies gave smaller donations. See also Cole, *A Century of Co-operation*.

10. Roderick and Stephens, *Education and Industry*, pp.72–73; Maclure, *Educational Documents*, pp.121–127, especially pp.122, 125.

11. TWAS. MS. E/NC8, minutes dated 24 November 1890, 30 January 1891, 27 February 1891.

12. *Newcastle Daily Chronicle*, 5 May 1891, notes that the Council allocated £900 to Bath Lane Schools for technical instruction.

13. TWAS. MS. E/NC8, minutes dated 28 August 1891. For instance, fees at Bath Lane were reduced from 3 shillings per month (Standard VI) to *2s 2d*.

14. TWAS. MS. ENC14/4/9/3(2) Prospectus, November 1892. For a list of subscribers, see TWAS. MS. ENC14/4/9/3(4); *Newcastle Daily Chronicle*, 16 April 1891.

15. TWAS. MS. ENC14/1/9/2, *Rutherford College Calendar 1903–4*, p.25; *Newcastle Daily Chronicle*, 6 October 1892.

16. TWAS. MS. E/NC8, minutes dated 16 March 1894; Local Studies, Newcastle City Library, (hereafter LS/NCL) *Rutherford College Brochure*, 5–7 April 1894; Maw, *Rutherford Grammar School*, pp.61–64.

17. LS/NCL. *Rutherford College Brochure*, 5–7 April 1894. The cost of furnishings and fittings was estimated at £5,000. The architects were Oliver and Leeson of Mosley St. Newcastle and the acclaimed Newcastle artist and sculptor Ralph Hedley supplied the ornamental woodwork in the hall and entrance.

18.   *Ibid.*, p.11. Negley Harte observes that in the nineteenth century London University 'in its Mark II form was notoriously a "mere examining board"', see N. Harte, *The University of London 1836–1986*, London, 1986, p.23. See also *Ours. The Magazine of the School of Science and Art*, volume 2, June 1890 which included a lengthy article on the London University Matriculation Examination which was to begin at the school for the first time.

19.   *Ours, The Magazine of the School of Science and Art*, Vol. 1, May 1890. See also Maw, Rutherford Grammar School, pp.27–34.

20.   TWAS. MS. E/NC8, minutes dated, 27 April 1894. Other members of the thirty-three strong committee included six representatives for Durham and Northumberland County Councils and the five trustees of Rutherford College (*ex officio*).

21.   G. A. N. Lowndes, *The Silent Social Revolution: An Account of the Expansion of Public Education In England and Wales 1895–1965*, Oxford, 1969, p.59, notes that in 1902 many authorities were not spending their 'whiskey money'.

22.   Other applications were made to Newcastle Dispensary and Edinburgh Life Insurance. See TWAS. MS. E/NC8, minutes dated, 25 October 1895, 28 February, 24 April 1896.

23.   *Ibid.*, minutes dated 30 August 1895.

24.   *Ibid.*, minutes dated 27 March 1896, 29 May 1896.

25.   *Ibid.*, minutes dated 12 June 1896, 7 August 1896.

26.   *Ibid.*, minutes dated 28 March 1896. The Church retained the right to use the hall on Sundays.

27.   *Ibid.*, minutes dated 26 March 1897.

28.   *Ibid.*, minutes dated 27 August 1897, 24 September 1897.

29.   *Ibid.*, minutes dated 5 March 1897.

30.   The DSA wanted all classes to have a maximum of forty whereas the college wanted to teach up to sixty.

31.   Fitch, the former Principal of a 'leading training college' was a highly regarded inspector who had served on a number of commissions and enquiries. See Simon, 'Reeder's Alternative System', p.180.

32.   Sir Joshua Fitch, *Report on Technical Education*, 8 February 1897, pp.19, 24.

33.   The former Newcastle College of Physical Science was renamed Durham College of Science after 1883. After 1904 it became known as Armstrong College. See E. M. Bettenson, *The University of Newcastle upon Tyne A Historical Introduction 1834–1971*, Newcastle, 1971, p.80.

34.   For information about the Durham members of the Committee, and more generally on the development of the Durham College of Science, see C. E. Whiting, *The University of Durham 1832–1932*, London, 1932, especially pp.200–207.

35.   TWAS. MS. E/NC8, minutes dated 27 November 1896, 28 May 1897, 15 June 1897.

36.   *Ibid.*, minutes dated 27 August 1897, 29 October 1897, 17 December 1897.

37.   *Ibid.*, minutes dated 28 January 1898.

38.   TWAS. MS. ENC14/4/9/2(2). Most staff were educated to degree standard. For instance, the new science master appointed in August 1899 had a BSC from Edinburgh University; the German master, Dr Schunemann was from Leipzig; the French master, Msr. Chibourg, was from Paris; the music Mistress had a diploma from the Royal Academy. See also Maw, *Rutherford Grammar School*, chapter 7.

39. TWAS. MS. E/NC8, minutes dated 16 February 1898, 23 March 1898.

40. *Ibid.*, minutes dated 25 February 1898.

41. Lowndes, *Silent Social Revolution*, p.47.

42. TWAS. MS. E/NC8, minutes dated 28 October 1898.

43. Voluntary Aid Associations were created under the 1897 Voluntary Schools Act and were empowered to disperse 5*s* per pupil. See P. W. Musgrave, *Society and Education in England since 1800*, London, 1969, p.70.

44. The grant due was £186 16*s* 8*d* and the costs of the additional inspection had to be borne by Rutherford Council. See TWAS. MS. E/NC8, minutes dated 25 November 1898, 16 December 1898, 27 January 1899, 24 March 1899, 30 September 1899.

45. *Ibid.*, minutes dated 29 July 1899.

46. TWAS MS. Council Minutes, Newcastle upon Tyne, 23 February 1900, show that Rutherford College received £1,150 whereas Durham College of Science were awarded £1,650. The under spend in 1898 was £1,123 17*s* 3*d* and in 1900, £1,117 18*s* 10*d*.

47. Roderick and Stephens, *Education and Industry*, p.73 claim that 92% of the whisky money was spent on education but this clearly was not the case in the North east of England. They do, however, accept that there was wholesale confusion about funding arrangements; see also Stephens, *Education in Britain*, pp.90–94.

48. TWAS. MS. E/NC8, minutes dated 26 August 1899, 24 November 1899.

49. *Ibid.*, minutes dated 1 September 1999.

50. *Ibid.*, minutes dated 30 August 1900, 25, October 1900.

51. See generally, Theodore K. Hoppen, *The Mid-Victorian Generation 1846–1886*, Oxford, 1998; Jose Harris, *Private Lives, Public Spirit*, London, 1994.

52. TWAS. MS. E/NC8, minutes dated 30 August 1900, 25 October 1900.

53. TWAS. MS. E/NC8, minutes dated 26 April 1901, records the following donations: Cornforth and Coxhoe CS: 5 guineas; DMA: £5.00; Wallsend CS; £5.00; Bookbinders' Union: 10*s*; Shiremoor CS: 2 guineas; Pegswood CS: 2 guineas; Amble CS: 2 guineas; Haswell CS: 2 guineas.

54. Lowndes, *Silent Social Revolution*, pp.47–48 notes that there were 70,000 prosecutions for non-payment of rates and resistance was particularly strong in Wales.

55. *Ibid.*, p.48.

56. Brian Simon makes a strong case for the contribution of the School Boards, describing the Act as 'vandalism', 'Reeder's 'Alternative System'', pp.204, 206. See also, Philip Gardner, 'There and not seen': E.B.Sargent and educational reform, 1884–1905', *History of Education*, vol. 33.6, 2004, pp.609–635, especially p.612. Sargent set up Field School in Hackney in 1884 as a 'working-class private school'.

57. TWAS. MS. E/NC8, minutes dated 24 April 1902.

58. For example, see *Newcastle Daily Journal*, 29 September 1903.

59. TWAS. MS. E/NC10. Bath Lane Day Schools Minute Book 1904–1936, minutes dated 13 March 1905.

60. *Ibid.*, minutes dated 2 December 1904.

61. *Ibid.* A full breakdown of the College finances is lodged with the minutes; *Northern Echo*, 13 September 1907.

62. TWAS. MS. E/NC10. Secondary Day School: 708; Science and Arts: 312; Evenings and Saturdays: 1,243.

63. TWAS. MS. E/NC10. Transfer Statement, 2 December 1904.

64. Maw, *Rutherford Grammar School*, pp.97–98.

65. *Newcastle Journal*, 22 August 1907.

66. *Newcastle Daily Chronicle*, 14 August 1907; TWAS. MS. ENC14/4/9/5(1), Minutes, Newcastle Council, 7 February 1907.

67. Note: Durham College of Science was renamed Armstrong College in 1904 as a memorial to Lord Armstrong College. See Bettenson, *The University of Newcastle upon Tyne*, p.29.

68. Matterson, *Polytechnics and Colleges*, p.44.

69. TWAS. MS. MD/NC/65/1, Rutherford College Council Minute Book, minutes dated 3 September 1908.

70. Maw, *Rutherford Grammar School*, p.72; see also TWAS. MS. ENC14/4/9/3(4); TWAS. MS. ENC14/5/1, Minutes, Newcastle Council, 22 September 1910.

71. TWAS. MS. MD/NC/62 /2, Rutherford College Sub-Committee Minutes, minutes dated 12 November 1913, 5 December 1913, 22 December 1913.

72. *Ibid.*, minutes dated 26 March 1914.

73. TWAS. MS. MD/NC/62/2, minutes dated 22 January 1914, 27 February 1914, 26 March 1914.

74. Geoffrey Sherrington, *English Education, Social Change and War, 1911–1920*, Manchester, 1981, chapter 2, especially p.19 which refers to the Report of the Consultative Committee of the Board of Education on Practical Work in Secondary Schools, 1912. See also Matterson, *Polytechnics and Colleges*, p.50, who argues that the South Kensington system 'eschewed the encouragement of aspirant artists'.

75. TWAS. MS. MD/NC/62 /2, minutes dated 26 June 1914, 30 July 1914.

76. *Ibid.*, minutes dated 28 August 1914.

77. *Ibid.*, minutes dated 27 November 1914.

78. Sherrington, *English Education, Social Change and War*, pp.44–45; see also chapter 2 which discusses educational initiatives between 1911 and 1914.

79. *Ibid.*, p.46.

80. *Ibid.*, pp.51–2.

81. TWAS. MS. MD/NC/65/3, Newcastle Education Committee Minutes, 1915–1916, minutes dated 26 November 1915.

82. Pamela Horn, 'Ministry of Labour female training programmes between the wars, 1919–1939', *History of Education*, vol. 31.1 (2002), pp.71–73.

83. TWAS. MS. MD/NC/65/3 minutes dated 20 December 1915.

84. For example, classes were held at Armstrong's Walker Yard.

85. TWAS. MS. MD/NC/65/3 minutes dated 2 June 1916, 1 December 1916, 29 December 1916.

86. *Ibid.*, minutes dated, 27 January 1917, 2 March 1917.

87. *Ibid.* Supervisory Sub-Committee, minutes dated 4 April 1917, 27 April 1917, 6 July 1917.

88. *Ibid.* Advisory Committee for Disabled Soldiers and Sailors, minutes dated 2 November 1917, 30 November 1917, 17 December 1920.

89. TWAS. MS. MD/NC/61/6, Higher Education Sub-Committee Minutes, minutes dated 13 December 1920.

90. *Ibid.*, minutes dated 21 February 1921, 29 April 1921, 30 April 1921, 29 July 1921.

91. *Ibid.*, minutes dated 26 March 1923.

92. *Ibid.*, minutes dated 23 July 1923, 24 September 1923, 29 October 1923, 1 August 1924.

93. *Ibid.*, minutes dated 30 December 1924.

94. Natasha Vall, 'The emergence of the post-industrial economy in Newcastle, 1914–2000', in Robert Colls and Bill Lancaster (eds.), *Newcastle upon Tyne. A Modern History*, Chichester, 2001, p.55.

95. TWAS. MS. MD/NC/61/6, 26 July 1927, 22 May 1928.

96. *Ibid.*, minutes dated 29 January 1923, 29 June 1926.

97. Gordon Hogg (ed.), *The Professional Education of Teachers at the University of Newcastle upon Tyne 1890–1990*, Newcastle upon Tyne, 1990, p.2.

98. Matterson, *Polytechnics and Colleges*, p.45.

99. Newcastle City Library. Proceedings of the Newcastle City Council, 1921–2, p.220.

100. TWAS MS. T195/53, *Prospectus*, Northern Counties College, 1901.

101. TWAS MS. T195/117, Correspondence of the Northern Counties College, 1911–1913.

102. Horn, 'Ministry of Labour', p.72.

103. I. Rowland, 'The History and Development of Northern Counties College', brochure published for the opening of the new College in the grounds of Manor House, 8 July 1963.

104. TWAS. MS. MD/NC/56/5, Newcastle Upon Tyne Education Committee Minute Book, 1934–1935, minutes dated 27 November 1934, 30 April 1935.

105. TWAS. MS. MD/NC/56/5, minutes dated 8 December 1935.

106. TWAS. MS. MD/NC/ 56/9, Newcastle City Council Minutes, Reports, Speeches, 1939–40. Board of Education Circular, 29 September 1939.

Chapter 3

1. Raymond Williams, *The Long Revolution*, London, 1961, p.11. Williams argued that 'the aspiration to extend the active process of learning, with the skills of literacy and other advanced communication, to all people rather than to limited groups, was comparable in importance to the growth of democracy and the rise of scientific industry'.

2. G. A. N. Lowndes, *The Silent Social Revolution. An account of the expansion of public education in England and Wales 1895–1965*, Oxford, 1969, pp.190–191. See also P. H. J. H. Gosden, Education in the Second World War, London, 1976, chapter 1; Roy Lowe, *Education in the Post-War Years: A Social History*, London and New York, 1988, p.4.

3. Lowndes, *The Silent Social Revolution*, p.219.

4. *Ibid.*

5. Lowe, *Education in the Post-War Years*, p.6. See also, Harold Silver, *Education as History*, London, 1983, p.264.

6. TWAS. MS. MD/NC/56/10, Newcastle upon Tyne Education Committee Minutes, vol. XXXVII, 1939–1940, minutes dated 28 November 1939, 23 January 1940.

7. *Ibid.*, minutes dated 28 November 1839, 9 April 1940, 11 June 1940.

8. TWAS. MS. MD/NC/56/11, Newcastle upon Tyne Education Committee Minutes, vol. XXXIX, 1940–1941, minutes dated 17 December 1940, 21 January 1941, 20 May 1941.

9. TWAS. MS. MD/NC/56/12, Newcastle upon Tyne Education Committee Minutes, vol. XXXX, 1941–1942, minutes dated 21 July 1942. On this occasion, Alderman Scanlon insisted that his vote against the concession should be recorded but allowing married women to continue to teach became a regular occurrence. For example, see TWAS. MS. MD/NC/56/13, Newcastle upon Tyne Education Committee Minutes, vol. XXXXI, 1942–1943, minutes dated 20 July 1943.

10. *Ibid.*, minutes dated 19 December 1943.

11. TWAS. MS. MD/NC/56/14, Newcastle upon Tyne Education Committee Minutes, vol. XXXXII, 1943–1944, minutes dated 17 January 1944, 16 May 1944, 19 September 1944; TWAS MS MD/NC/56/15, Newcastle upon Tyne Education Committee Minutes, vol. XXXXIII, 1944–1945, minutes dated 19 November 1944.

12. *Ibid.*, minutes dated 20 March 1945.

13. Lowndes, *The Silent Social Revolution*, p.327.

14. Glynn Williams and John Ramsden, *Ruling Britannia. A Political History of Britain 1688–1988*, Harlow, 1990, p.411.

15. White Paper on Educational Reconstruction (1943); J. Stuart Maclure, *Educational Documents: England and Wales 1916 to the present day*, London, 1979, p.206.

16. *Ibid.* p.226 (The Percy Report).

17. *Ibid.*, p.226n.

18. Alan Matterson, *Polytechnics and Colleges*, London, 1981, p.57.

19. Lowndes, *Silent Social Revolution*, p.346.

20. Percy Report, Section 6 (Chairman's note), pp.25–6, and reprinted in Maclure, *Educational Documents*, p.229.

21. Barlow Report, pp.8–9, and reprinted in Maclure, *Educational Documents*, p.231.

22. W. A. C. Stewart, *Higher Education in Postwar Britain*, Basingstoke, 1989, p.78.

23. Lowe, *Education in the Post War Years*. pp.66–67.

24. David Cannadine, *In Churchill's Shadow*, London, 2003, p.36.

25. Speech given on 18 January 1956, as cited in Lowndes, *The Silent Social Revolution*, p.334.

26. Percy Report, pp.25–26. See also Matterson, *Polytechnics and Colleges*, p.58.

27. Tyrrell Burgess and John Pratt, *Policy and Practice: The Colleges of Advanced Technology*, London, 1970, p.85.

28. Harold Silver, *A Higher Education, The Council for National Academic Awards and British Higher Education 1969–1989*, London, 1990, p.21.

29. *Ibid.*, p.87.

30. Carswell, *Government and the Universities*, p.20.

31. *Ibid.*, p.39. The other CATs were London, Battersea, Chelsea, Northampton College, Birmingham, Bradford, Cardiff, Loughborough and Salford, Bristol, 1960 and Brunel, 1962.

32. *Report of the Education Committee (City and County of Newcastle upon Tyne), May 1956–May 1957*, p.12.

33. *Report of H.M. Inspectors on the Rutherford Technical College*, London 1935, p.21. The Authority had already decided to build a new technical college to cope with the growing demand. Also see chapter 2.

34. D. H. Thomas, unpublished 'Memoir', 1980, p.2.

35. *Ibid.*, p.3.

36. *The Journal*, 16 April 1960.

37. T. Dan Smith, *An Autobiography*, Newcastle upon Tyne, 1970, p.41.

38. The question of whether his uncompromising stance re the educational precinct was justified has proved controversial. As one commentator observes, without his intervention 'higher education facilities would have been pushed out to green field sites'. See Archie Potts, 'T. Dan Smith – The Man and the Legend', *Bulletin*, North East Labour History Society, 28, 1994, p.13.

39. *Ibid.*

40. Northumbria University, unattributed newspaper clipping from a scrapbook of local newspaper cuttings and ephemera produced by an unknown member of the College of Art and Design (hereafter Northumbria University 'scrapbook').

41. See also D. Byrne, 'The Disastrous Impact of a Liberal Authoritarian Moderniser', *Bulletin*, North East Labour History Society, 28, 1994, pp.19–26.

42. *Report of the Education Committee*, May 1956–May 1957, p.13.

43. *Ibid.*, p.12.

44. *Newcastle Evening Chronicle*, 11 November 1957.

45. Silver, *A Higher Education*, London, 1990, p.14.

46. John Carswell, *Government and the Universities in Britain: programme and performance 1960–1980*, Cambridge, 1985, p.38. Carswell, Secretary to the Robbins Committee, drew his comments from a speech in the House of Lords, 11 December 1965. See *Hansard*, vol. 253, p.1211.

47. *The Years of Crisis; Report of the Labour Party's study group on higher education*. The Taylor Report, 1960.

48. Labour Party Conference Report, 1963, p.133.

49. Gordon W. Roderick and Michael D. Stephens, *Education and Industry in the Nineteenth Century: The English Disease?* Harlow, 1978, chapter 7 offers a detailed critique of failure to invest in research and training and notes that the need to explain the decline in British industrial strength particularly exercised economic historians in the 1940s and 1950s.

50. Maclure, *Educational Documents*, p.241.

51. *Report of the Education Committee, May 1959–May 1960*, p.13.

52. *Report of the Education Committee, May 1960–May 1961*, p.15.

53. *Report of the Education Committee, May 1961–May 1962*, p.16.

54. See chapter 2.

55. Matterson, *Polytechnics and Colleges*, p.50.

56. *Programme* for the Official Opening of Newcastle upon Tyne College of Art and Industrial Design, 14 October 1955. The college was opened by Sir David Eccles MP who was then Minister of Education.

57. *Newcastle Evening Chronicle*, 12 November 1952.

58. *Ibid.*

59. Anon., *The First Five Years: The College of Art and Industrial Design*, July 1959, p.2. Although it was anonymous the promotional nature of the leaflet suggests that it was probably penned by C. H. Smith who was College Principal at the time.

60. *Principal's Report*, College of Art and Industrial Design, 1959, p.1.

61. *Ibid.*

62. Northumbria University 'scrapbook'.

63. *Prospectus. College of Art and Industrial Design, 1955–56*, p.31.

64. C. H. Smith, *Art Education: Past, Present and Future*, Newcastle upon Tyne, 1957.

65. *Ibid.*, p.9.

66. Newcastle upon Tyne Education Committee, *The Training of Graduate Handicraft Teachers and Designers for Industry*, Newcastle, 1957.

67. *Ibid.*, This brochure was produced and published by the College of Art and Industrial Design, School of Printing.

68. *Report of the Education Committee*, May 1957–May 1958, p.13.

69. For example, the Northern Bedding Company provided 'The Lunarest' award (£25) for the most promising student of furniture design. College of Art and Industrial Design, *Prospectus* Session 1960–61.

70. *The Journal*, 17 February 1959, 18 May 1960.

71. Matterson, *Polytechnics and Colleges*, p.50.

72. *Ibid.*, p.51.

73. *Report of the Education Committee, May 1960–May 1961*, p.17.

74. *Newcastle Journal*, 27 June 1963.

75. *The Guardian*, 8 May 1963; *The Journal*, 31 May 1963. The reference to 'Beeching' reflected contemporary criticism of his (Beeching's) rationalisation of the railways.

76. *Newcastle Evening Chronicle*, 18 April 1962.

77. *The Sunday Times Magazine*, 29 April 1962; *Newcastle Evening Chronicle*, 5 May 1962.

78. Interview by Joan Allen with Professor Tom Bromley, 12 March 1999.

79. Marion Scott, 'Post war developments in Art in Newcastle: Was it a golden age?', *Northern Review. A Journal of Regional and Cultural Affairs*, vol. 4, winter 1996, pp.37–41; E. M. Bettenson, *The University of Newcastle upon Tyne: An Historical Introduction 1834–1971*, Newcastle, 1974.

80. *Report of the Education Committee*, May 1964–May 1965, p.36.

81. *Ibid.*

82. Interview by Joan Allen with Lord Glenamara, 20 November 1998.

83. *Report of the Education Committee*, May 1957–May 1958, p.11.

84. *Ibid.*

85. Burgess and Pratt, *Policy and Practice*, p.84 noted that even in 1966 only 27% of students at the CATS were in residence.

86. *Education Committee Minutes, City of Newcastle upon Tyne*, 2 December 1964, pp.638–651.

87. Speech by A. Crosland, *Hansard*, House of Commons 1964-65, vol. 707.391: 'they [the Government] are actively considering the possibility of creating... a completely new technological university in the north east'.

88. Silver, *A Higher Education*, p.38.

89. *Ibid.*

90. *Ibid.*, p.42. British technology graduates, as a percentage of all first degrees in science and technology, was estimated at 36%, compared with Germany (68%), Canada (65%) and USA (49%). See also Stewart, *Higher Education in Postwar Britain*, p.107.

91. Burgess and Pratt, *Policy and Practice*, p.43.

92. Stewart, *Higher Education in Postwar Britain*, p.109.

93. Silver, *A Higher Education*, p.39.

94. Speech by A. Crosland at Woolwich Polytechnic, 27 April 1965, quoted in Pratt, *The Polytechnic Experiment*, p.1.

95. Bettenson, *The University of Newcastle upon Tyne. A Historical Introduction 1834–1971*, Newcastle upon Tyne, 1974, p.64ff.

96. *Proceedings*, Newcastle Council, 2 December 1964, p.867.

97. Burgess and Pratt, *Policy and Practice*, p.174.

98. *Ibid.*, p.179.

Chapter 4

1. *Hansard*, House of Lords, 11 December 1965, vol. 253,1267. Lord Robbins, 'Debate on higher education'.

2. *Hansard*, House of Commons, 1965-66, vol. 725,631ff. 'Debate on technical education'. In 1977 Prentice was to cross the floor of the House and join the Tories.

3. C. Price, 'Elegant and democratic values; how will the new English universities gel?', *Higher Education Quarterly*, 46.3, Summer 1992, pp.243-251.

4. J. Pratt, *The Polytechnic Experiment* 1965-1992, London, 1997, p.8.

5. 'Some 40 towns up and down the country – Scarborough I seem to remember was among them, and Perth and Inverness – had launched university promotion committees. Country houses with ample parks were everywhere on offer.' See J. Carswell, *Government and the Universities in Britain; programme and performance 1960-1980*, Cambridge, 1985, p.57, and quoting Robbins. Carswell was Secretary to the Robbins Committee.

6. Obituary of Sir Edward Britton, *The Guardian*, 11 January 2005.

7. Carswell, *Government and the Universities*, p.67.

8. Susan Crosland, *Tony Crosland*, London, 1982, p.158, and quoting her husband.

9. *Hansard*, House of Lords, 1 December 1965, vol. 270, 1258-9.

10. *Ibid.*, 1266.

11. As cited in Pratt, *The Polytechnic Experiment*, p.19.

12. F. Robinson (ed.), *Post-industrial Tyneside: an economic and social survey of Tyneside in the 1980s*, Newcastle, 1988, p.13.

13. H. Silver, *A Higher Education: the Council for National Academic Awards and British Higher Education 1964-1989*, London, 1990, p.39.

14. *Ibid.*, p.56.

15. *Ibid.*, p.61.

16. E. Robinson, 'Cinderella has grown up', *Higher Education Quarterly*, 42.1, winter 1988, p.93.

17. HMSO, *Committee on manpower resources for science and technology*, London, 1966.

18. Newcastle Polytechnic, *Interim report from the academic board to the Board of Governors*, September, 1969.

19. Newcastle College of Art and Industrial Design, Governors' Papers, 6 June 1967.

20. *Ibid.*, 26 November 1968.

21. S. Cornock, 'Celebrating the achievement of the art schools: a new resource' (nd). See www.fineart.ac.uk/collection/html/stoud.html

22. *The Guardian*, 20 July 1970.

23. *The Guardian*, 12 October 1971.

24. *The Guardian*, 18 October 1971.

25. Joan Allen interview with Professor Tom Bromly, 12 March 1999.

26. Municipal College of Commerce Governors' Papers, 6 March 1968.

27. M. Watson (ed.), 'Information and library management 2000+', University of Northumbria Department of Information and Library Management, 2000, p.3.

28. Lord Hives, of Rolls-Royce, was the first Chairman of the National Council for Technological Awards.

29. *Evening Chronicle*, 29 June 1970.

30. Joan Allen interview with Professor Monica Shaw, 21 October 1999.

31. Newcastle Polytechnic Academic Board *Annual Report*, 1971–72, p.33.

32. Carswell, *Government and the Universities*, p.49.

33. *Hansard*, House of Commons, 25 March 1965, vol. 709, 784.

34. Carswell, *Government and the Universities*, p.73.

35. Pratt, *The Polytechnic Experiment*, p.163.

36. Newcastle Polytechnic Academic Board *Annual Report*, 1969-70.

37. T. Hinde, *An Illustrated History of the University of Greenwich*, London, 1996.

38. Joan Allen interview with Ron Hopkinson, 29 March 1999.

39. *Proceedings*, Newcastle City Council, 5 January 1966, p.810.

40. *Ibid.*, 6 September, 1967, p.369.

41. This notion of devolved budgeting for the Polytechnic was not acceptable to all the city's officers who thought its freedom to allocate funds internally created anomalies and dissatisfaction elsewhere in the LEA. See *Times Higher Education Supplement*, 22 April 1977, p.9.

42. Richard Buswell interview with Derek Webster, 28 April 2005.

43. Newcastle Polytechnic Council Papers, March 1973.

44. Newcastle Polytechnic Council Papers, October 1973.

45. Richard Buswell interview with Derek Webster, 28 April 2005.

46. Joan Allen interview with Professor Tom Bromly, 12 March 1999, and brochure produced by City of Newcastle Education Committee to commemorate the opening of Squires Building.

47. Newcastle Polytechnic Academic Board *Annual Report*, 1972-73, p.4.

48. HMSO, *Teacher Education and Training* (The James Report), London, 1972.

49. HMSO, *Teachers and Youth Leaders* (The McNair Report), London, 1944.

50. Richard Crossman, *The Diaries of a Cabinet Minister*, (3 vols. London, 1975-77), vol. 1, Minister of Housing 1964-66, p.136.

51. Carswell, *Government and the Universities*, p.66.

52. HMSO, *Half our future*, (The Newsome Report of the central advisory committee for education – England), London, 1963.

53. D. Hencke, *Colleges in Crisis; the reorganization of teacher training, 1971-77*, Harmondsworth, 1978, p.30.

54. *Ibid.*, p.48.

55. Hencke, *Colleges in Crisis*, p.37.

56. *Ibid.*, p.42.

57. *Ibid.*, p.43.

58. *Hansard*, House of Commons, 1972-73, vol. 851, 41-167.

59. B. Simon, *Education and the Social Order, 1940-1990*, London, 1991, p.597 (Table 14a).

60. Hencke, *Colleges in Crisis*, p.51.

61. *Hansard*, House of Commons, 1972-73, vol. 851, 41-167.

62. *Ibid.*, vol. 859, 107-166.

63. *Ibid.*, 160.

64. Hencke, *Colleges in Crisis*, p.62.

65. City of Newcastle Education Committee, minutes dated June 1969.

66. *Ibid.*, minutes dated December 1969.

67. Correspondence from Lesley France and Dr Michael Sill to Richard Buswell.

68. Personal communication from Clive Sowden to Richard Buswell.

69. HMSO, *Colleges of education (Compensation) regulations* 1975. DES Circular 6/75, London, 1975. To benefit a member of staff's conditions of service had to have been 'materially worsened due to amalgamation'.

70. J. Lynch, *The Reform of Teacher Education in the UK*, Guildford, 1979, pp.1, 2.

71. Newcastle Polytechnic Academic Board *Annual Report, 1973-74,* p.4.

72. Silver, *A Higher Education*, p.4.

73. Newcastle Polytechnic Council papers, December 1973.

74. Peat, Marwick, Mitchell and Co., *Newcastle Polytechnic: a survey of the organisation of non-teaching staff*, Newcastle, 1976. Filed with Polytechnic Council papers for that year.

75. *Ibid.*

76. Newcastle Polytechnic Academic Board, *Annual Report, 1976-77.*

77. Newcastle Polytechnic Council Papers, 13 December 1978.

78. Newcastle Polytechnic Council Papers, December 1973.

79. Newcastle Polytechnic Council Papers, 12 December 1979.

80. *Education*, 12 January 1979, p.28, and Richard Buswell interview with Derek Webster, 28 April 2005.

Chapter 5

1. In an editorial for the *Higher Education Quarterly* in 1991 Maurice Shattock, former registrar of the University of Warwick, wrote 'One cannot be so certain of the polytechnics... we may be sure... that although in the future individuals may ascend the yellow brick road to university status, the conversion of the polytechnics will be the last great wave of university creations for at least a generation.' See also L. Frank Baum, *The Wonderful Wizard of Oz* (Chicago, 1900) in which Dorothy followed the yellow brick road to the City of Emeralds where Oz lived; only he could transport her back to Kansas, but as one of the witches pointed out, the land of Oz had never been civilized.

2. Numbers in polytechnics rose from 144,068 in 1970-71 to 177,801 in 1975-76. Approximately 45 per cent were part-time students in 1975-76 but there had been over 70 per cent in the constituent colleges in 1966-77. See J. Pratt, *The Polytechnic Experiment 1965-1972*, London, 1997, p.32 (Table 3.4).

3. All this data is taken from various tables in *Ibid.*, chapter 3.

4. H. Silver, *A Higher Education: the Council for National Academic Awards and British Higher Education*, 1964-1989, London, 1990, p.40.

5. *Ibid.*, p.144.

6. These procedures are described in detail in Newcastle Polytechnic, *Mid term report to CNAA on the operation of the Polytechnic's internal validation and review procedures through the work of the course coordination and course review committees*, 1979.

7. Silver, *A Higher Education*, pp.176-181.

8. CNAA, *Developments in partnership in validation*, 1979.

9. CNAA, *Newcastle upon Tyne Polytechnic Institutional Quinquennial Review*, June, 1981.

10. *Evening Chronicle*, 14 January 1982.

11. Joan Allen interview with Peter Torode, 11 March 1999.

12. *Ibid.*

13. *Ibid.*

14. Newcastle Polytechnic, *Developments in partnership in validation; the response from Newcastle upon Tyne Polytechnic to the Council for National Academic Awards*, March, 1980, p.24.

15. N. Lindop, *Academic validation in public sector higher education: report of the Committee of Inquiry*, London, 1985.

16. *Ibid.*, p.6.

17. P. Cosgrave, *Margaret Thatcher: a Tory and her party*, London, 1978, p.32.

18. DES, *The Development of Higher Education into the 1990s*, London, 1985 (Cmnd 9254).

19. Pratt, *The Polytechnic Experiment*, p.234.

20. Joan Allen interview with Peter Torode.

21. CNAA, *Future strategy; principles and operation*, February 1987.

22. For a detailed account see M. Halcrow, *Keith Joseph – a single mind*, London, 1989.

23. S. Jones, 'Reflections on a capped pool', *Higher Education Review*, 17,1 (1984), pp.5-18.

24. B. Salter and T. Tapper, *The State and Higher Education*, Ilford, 1994, p.141.

25. Pratt, *The Polytechnic Experiment*, p.254.

26. C. Urwin, *Fitness for Purpose: essays in higher education by Christopher Ball*, London, 1985.

27. Newcastle Polytechnic Council Papers, 29 January 1980.

28. *Ibid.*, 8 February 1981.

29. *Ibid.*, 10 December 1980, 21 January 1981.

30. Newcastle Polytechnic Academic Board, 8 February 1981.

31. Newcastle Polytechnic Council Papers, 24 June 1981.

32. *Ibid.*, 25 November 1981.

33. HMSO, *White Paper on Expenditure*, London, March 1982 (Cmnd 8494-II).

34. Newcastle Polytechnic Council Papers, 16 December 1982.

35. *Hansard*: House of Lords, vol. 254, 19 January 1983, 1416-1424.

36. *Ibid.*, 1417.

37. Newcastle Polytechnic Council Papers, 31 October 1984.

38. *Ibid.*, 20 November 1985.

39. *Ibid.*, additional paper.

40. *Ibid.*, 25 June 1986.

41. Pratt, *The Polytechnic Experiment,* p.256.

42. Richard Buswell interview with Derek Webster, 28 April 2005.

43. DES, *Higher Education: meeting the challenge,* London, 1987 (CM 114).

44. R. Stevens, *From University to Uni*, London, 2004, pp.58-59.

45. Salter and Tapper, *The State and Higher Education*, p.146.

46. *Hansard*, Parliamentary debates, House of Lords, vol. 495, April 18-19, 1988, 1211-1349, 1362-1474.

47. *Ibid.*, 1437.

48. *Hansard*, Parliamentary debates, House of Commons, vol. 123, 1987-88, 779.

49. *Ibid.*, 838.

50. Richard Buswell interview with Derek Webster, 28 April 2005; Evening Chronicle, 23 May 1989.

51. Joan Allen interview with Reay Atkinson, 19 August 1999.

52. Briefing papers for Polytechnic Council.

53. Pratt, *The Polytechnic Experiment*, p.262.

54. Newcastle Polytechnic Council Papers, 26 March 1990.

55. Salter and Tapper, *The State and Higher Education*, p.133.

56. Richard Buswell interview with John Rear, August 2004.

57. Newcastle Polytechnic Council Papers, 25 June 1986.

58. *Ibid.*

59. Richard Buswell interview with John Rear, 24 August 2004.

60. Newcastle Polytechnic Council Papers, 17 December 1987.

61. Newcastle Polytechnic Academic Board Papers, 25 May 1988.

62. Newcastle Polytechnic Council Papers, 23 March 1989.

Chapter 6

1. 'The ladder from the technical colleges to paradise which Robbins had left leaning against the wall.' See J. Carswell, *Government and the Universities in Britain; programme and performance 1960-1980*, Cambridge, 1985, p.67.

2. G. Williams, 'An honest living or dumbing down?', in G. Williams (ed.), *The Enterprising University*, Buckingham, 2003, p.4.

3. R. Barnett and S. Bjarnason, 'The reform of higher education in Britain', in D. C. B. Teather, *Higher Education in a Post-Binary Era*, London, 2003, p.90.

4. Filed as background paper with Newcastle Polytechnic Governors' Papers, 28 November 1988.

5. Freda Tallentyre had a first class degree in English from University College, London, had taught at Dame Allen's School in Newcastle and came to Enterprise from a background in continuing education in the WEA and at the Polytechnic. She went on to be Pro Vice-Chancellor at the University of Derby.

6. P. Wright, 'Learning through enterprise: the Enterprise in Higher Education Initiative', in R. Barnett (ed.), *Learning to Effect*, Buckingham, 1992.

7. Newcastle Polytechnic Executive Papers. Memorandum from Freda Tallentyre to the Executive, 'The future of enterprise in higher education', 6 June 1991.

8. Newcastle Polytechnic Governors' Papers, 28 November 1988. Letter from Kenneth Baker to Sir Ron Dearing.

9. DES, *The English Polytechnics: an HMI commentary*, London, 1989.

10. Newcastle Polytechnic Governors' Papers, 19 November 1990.

11. DES, *Higher Education: a new framework*, London, 1991, p.28 (CM 1541).

12. R. Williams, 'Quality assurance and diversity: the case of England', in J. Brennan, P. de Vries and R. Williams, *Standards and Quality in Higher Education*, London, 1997, pp.104-118.

13. *Ibid.*

14. University of Northumbria at Newcastle (UNN) Academic Board, *Quality Assurance at the University of Northumbria at Newcastle*, pp.79-80 (Annex 4 to Appendix K).

15. *Ibid.*, p.61 (Appendix I).

16. Higher Education Quality Committee (HEQC), *University of Northumbria at Newcastle: quality audit report*, June, 1994, p.28.

17. DES, White Paper, 1991, p.24.

18. D. Green, 'What is quality in higher education? Concepts, policy and practice', in D. Green (ed.), *What is Quality in Higher Education?*, Buckingham, 1994, pp.3-20.

19. UNN Governors Papers, 22 March 1993. 21 Ellison Place was initially leased for £40,000 per annum.

20. J. Pratt, *The Polytechnic Experiment, 1965-1992*, London, 1997, p.119. It should be remembered that, at about the same time, Newcastle Polytechnic was receiving almost the same ratio of applications to places for its programme of largely traditional single and combined subject honours degrees.

21. UNN Governors' Papers, 20 November 1995. Letter from Professor John Rear to Dr Malcolm Levy 18 October 1995.

22. *Ibid.*

23. DES, *Report on the Review of the Academic Year* (Flowers Report), London, 1993.

24. UNN Executive Papers, 18 October 1995. Letter from the Branch chair together with the resolution.

25. This was confirmed by CNAA's Quinquennial Review in 1988. See Newcastle Polytechnic Council Papers 30 June 1988.

26. Municipal College of Commerce Governors' Papers, 8 November 1967.

27. CNAA, *Resources for research in polytechnics and other colleges* (The Rochester report), London, 1974.

28. UNN Academic Board Minutes, 21 October 1992.

29. UNN Academic Board Papers, 25 November 1992.

30. *Times Higher Educational Supplement*, 17 December 1992.

31. *Hansard*, House of Lords, 2nd reading of the 1988 Education Reform Bill, vol. 495, April 18-19 1988, 1211-1349, 1362-1474.

32. L. Barden and C. Booth, 'Polytechnics or Universities? The case for allowing freedom of title', December 1989, Committee of Directors of Polytechnics.

33. *Ibid.*

34. *Ibid.*

35. K. Baker, *The Turbulent Years: My life in politics*, London, 1993, p.147.

36. R. Stevens, *From University to Uni,* London, 2004, p.60.

37.   *Ibid.*, p.68.

38.   DES, *Higher Education: a new framework*, London, 1991 (CM 1541).

39.   As Lord Beloff stated, 'Apparently they (new universities/ex polytechnics) are to be judged by businessmen who run some of the less efficient institutions in this country, as our trade figures frequently remind us.' See *Hansard*: House of Lords, vol. 352, 21 November 1991, 1056.

40.   Newcastle Polytechnic Governors' Papers, 24 June 1991.

41.   M. Trow, 'Thoughts on the White Paper of 1991', *Higher Education Quarterly*, 46, 3, 1992, pp.213-226.

42.   *Ibid.*, p.216.

43.   Newcastle Polytechnic Academic Board Papers, 24 June 1991; Governors' Papers, 24 June 1991.

44.   'Advanced education in Art, Commerce and Technology can only be conducted near a transport centre. Trains and buses for the whole of Tyne side centre upon Newcastle.' See Education Committee City of Newcastle, *A scheme for further education, submitted to the Ministry of Education*, Newcastle, 1949.

45.   Newcastle Polytechnic Governors' Papers, 25 November 1991.

46.   Newcastle Polytechnic Governors' Papers. K. Clark speech to Committee of Directors of Polytechnics, 17 September 1991.

47.   Newcastle Polytechnic Academic Board Papers, 23 October 1991.

48.   UNN Governors' Papers, 26 July 1993.

49.   UNN Academic Board Papers, 16 February 1994.

50.   *Ibid.*, 25 May 1994, 16 February 1994.

51.   UNN Staff Newsletter, 2 March 1994.

52.   UNN Governors' Papers, 20 June 1994.

53.   Cumbria County Council, *Cumbria higher education research project (CHERP)* Report, 1989.

54.   Newcastle Polytechnic Governors' Papers, 24 June 1991.

55.   *Ibid.*, 24 July 1991.

56.   *Ibid.*, 25 March 1991.

57.   UNN Executive Papers, 13 September 1993. Letter from Professor A. R. Dickson to executive and governors, 24 August 1993.

58.   UNN Executive Papers, 11 October 1993. Letter from Professor A. R. Dickson to HEFCE 20 September 1993.

59.   D. Campbell-Savours, *The Case for a University of the Lakes*, (n.p. n.d.) p.158, published before Northumbria's withdrawal.

60.   For example, see R. Bennett, P. Wicks and A. McCoshan, *Local Empowerment and Business Services: Britain's experiment with training and enterprise councils.* London, 1994.

61.   Newcastle Polytechnic Academic Board Papers, 23 October 1991.

62. T. Faulkner and A. Greg, *John Dobson, Newcastle Architect,* 1787-1865. Newcastle, 1987, pp.24-26.

63. Newcastle Polytechnic Academic Board, *op cit.,* 23 October 1991.

64. Newcastle Polytechnic Academic Board Papers, 6 November 1991.

65. Newcastle Polytechnic Governors' Employment and Finance Committee Papers, 9 October 1991.

66. UNN Governors' Papers, 26 July 1993.

67. Faulkner and Greg, *John Dobson,* p.88.

68. UNN Governors' Papers, 19 June 1995.

69. Newcastle City Council, *Draft unitary development plan,* May 1991, p.41.

70. Details of the two major estate strategies of 1992 and 1995 can be found with UNN Academic Board Papers, 17 May 1995.

71. Richard Buswell interview with Professor Mary Dunning, 18 February 2005.

72. D. O'Brien and D. Watson, 'Nurse education - a social and historical perspective', in J. Reed and S. Proctor (eds.), *Nurse Education: a reflective approach,* London, 1993.

73. S. R. Jowett, 'A longitudinal study with Project 2000 students; their views and experience during and after the course', unpublished Kings College, University of London PhD thesis, 1995.

74. For example, see Department of Health, *Report of the Committee on Nursing* (the Briggs Report), London, 1972 (Cmnd 5115).

75. United Kingdom Council for Nursing, Midwifery and Health Visiting, *Project 2000: a new preparation for practice,* London, 1986, p.9.

76. *Ibid.,* p.27.

77. Department of Health, *Education and training,* Working Paper no. l0. London, 1990.

78. *Ibid.,* p.62.

79. Newcastle Polytechnic Annual Report, 1971-72, p.36.

80. *Evening Chronicle,* 26 June 1970.

81. Newcastle Polytechnic Academic Board Papers, 23 April 1980.

82. Newcastle Polytechnic Council Papers, 26 June 1985.

83. Richard Buswell interview with Professor Mary Dunning, 18 February 2005.

84. UNN Academic Board Papers 24, February 1993.

85. *Ibid.*

86. UNN Governors' Papers, 21 November 1994.

87. UNN Academic Board Papers, 29 June 1994.

88. *Ibid.,* 16 February 1994.

89. *Ibid.*

90. UNN Governors' Papers 13 March 1995 which include a copy of the proposal highlighting the benefits of the merger to both parties.

91. I. Lincoln, I. Stone, A. Walker, P. Braidford and A. Oswell, *Local impact of the University of Northumbria: a study based on an audit of university-community linkages,* Newcastle, 1996.

Epilogue

1. In 1995-96 there were 22,500 students of which 14,000 were full-time and sandwich students and a further 8,500 were part-time. The crude staff-student ratio was 24:1. 55% of students were on degree courses, 34% on sub-degree courses and 12% at postgraduate level. 69% came with A Levels or their equivalent, 14% had a variety of access qualifications. 62% of full-time students were women. Most of the students (65%) came from northern England, 42% from the northern region. Health, Social Work and Education was the largest Faculty with over 30% of all students; the Business School had 20%, Engineering Science and Technology less than 20%. There were over 2,250 staff: 41% academic and managerial, 31% administrative, 20% manual and only 8% technical. While 55% of all staff was female only 33% lecturing and research staff were women, whereas 68% of the administrative staff were women. About three quarters of the staff were under 50 years of age. The total income of the University was £64.5 million of which 81% came from public sources. Two thirds of expenditure went on salaries. Statistics extracted from Northumbria University *Facts and Figures*, 1995–96, Newcastle, 1996.

2. The apocryphal story amongst academic engineers at the time was of the tutor who berated his student who was demonstrating a machine with the words, 'I don't want to know how it works in practice, I want to know how it works in theory'.

3. Lipman gave many generous donations to the Polytechnic including the ceremonial sword and mace, and furniture. The Lipman Building was, of course, named after him, not something that all members of the Labour group appreciated. Richard Buswell interview with Derek Webster, 28 April 2005.

4. In place of the traditional University was 'Baker's concept of a work-orientated, vocational, commercial institution, run more like an externally accountable public corporation than a collegium of scholars... the universities had become polytechnics'. See S. Jenkins, *Accountable to none: the Tory nationalisation of Britain*, London, 1995, pp.151-152.

Appendix I

Interviewees

THE FOLLOWING people very kindly agreed to be interviewed for this project. Interviews were conducted between 1999 and 2005. The authors would like to thank all those who generously gave their time.

Reay Atkinson	Professor Mary Dunning	Professor Alan Newall
Professor Laing Barden	John Frost	Professor John Rear
Sir Jeremy Beecham	Lord Glenamara	Professor Monica Shaw
Professor Tom Bromly	Ron Hopkinson	Peter Torode
Gordon Campbell	Sue Lawson	Derek Webster
		Professor John Wilson

Appendix II

Key players, reformers and educationalists

Reay Atkinson CB

Chairman, Board of Governors, Newcastle Polytechnic, 1990–92.

Chairman, Board of Governors, University of Northumbria at Newcastle, 1992–96.

Hon Fellow, University of Northumbria at Newcastle, 1987.

Hon DCL, University of Northumbria at Newcastle, 1998.

Professor Laing Barden CBE

Deputy Director, Newcastle Polytechnic, 1972–76.

Director, Newcastle Polytechnic, 1976–92.

Vice-Chancellor and Chief Executive, University of Northumbria at Newcastle, 1992–96.

Hon DCL, University of Northumbria at Newcastle, 1996.

George Bosworth CBE

Director, Newcastle Polytechnic, 1968–76.

Hon Fellow, University of Northumbria at Newcastle, 1982.

Professor John Clark

Assistant Director (Academic), Newcastle Polytechnic, 1974–1984.

Hon Fellow, University of Northumbria at Newcastle, 1987.

Joseph Cowen

Joseph Cowen (1829-1900), Radical Reformer, Liberal MP for Newcastle and proprietor of the *Newcastle Chronicle*.

Professor Tony Dickson

Assistant Director, Pro Vice-Chancellor, Deputy Vice-Chancellor, University of Northumbria at Newcastle, 1991 to date.

Lord Glenamara

Chancellor, University of Northumbria at Newcastle, 1983–2005.

Hon DLitt, University of Northumbria at Newcastle, 1990.

Hon Fellow, University of Northumbria at Newcastle, 1979.

Dr Cyril Lipman

Chairman, Newcastle Polytechnic Council, 1970–73, 1979–81.

Hon LLB, University of Northumbria at Newcastle, 1990.

Hon Fellow, University of Northumbria at Newcastle, 1977.

Irene Rowlands

Principal, Northern Counties College of Domestic Science and Cookery.

Reverend Dr John Hunter Rutherford

Congregationalist preacher, leader of the Cooperative movement and educational reformer.

Founder of Northumbria University.

Professor John Rear

Professor and Head of Faculty of Professional Studies, Newcastle Polytechnic, 1980–85.

Deputy Director, Newcastle Polytechnic, 1985–92.

Pro Vice-Chancellor and Deputy Chief Executive, University of Northumbria at Newcastle, 1992–96.

Derek Webster

Chairman, Newcastle Polytechnic Council 1976–79, 1981–89.

Lord Mayor of Newcastle, 1988–89.

Director of External Relations, University of Northumbria at Newcastle, 1992 to date.

Hon MA, Newcastle Polytechnic, 1989.

Appendix III

Well-known alumni and honorary graduates

Tony Blair

Prime Minister
Hon DCL, 1995

Dorothy Blenkinsop CBE

Vice-Chairman, Board of
Governors, Newcastle
Polytechnic, 1986–92
Hon MSc, 1990

Martin Corry MBE

England RFU captain
BA (Hons) Sports Studies, 1997

Steve Cram MBE

Athlete and broadcaster
BA Sports Studies, 1983
Hon DCL, 2003

Mike Figgis

Film director
Hon DCL, 1996

Leo Finn

Ex-CEO Northern Rock
BA (Hons) Business Studies, 1983
PGDip History of Ideas, 1985

Dr Adam Hart-Davis

Writer and broadcaster
Hon DCL, 2002

Scott Henshall

International fashion designer
BA (Hons) Fashion, 1987

Cardinal Basil Hume

Spiritual leader
Hon DCL, 1992

Jonathan Ive

Vice-President of Industrial
Design, Apple (designer of the
iMac/iBook/iPod MP3 Player)
BA (Hons) Design for Industry,
1989
Hon DCL, 2000

Robson Green

Actor
Hon DCL, 1998

Alexey Mordashov

CEO Severstal-Group
MBA, 2001
Hon DCL, 2003

Sir Claus Moser CBE

Government adviser, academic
and polymath
Hon DCL, 1994

Bruce Oldfield

International fashion designer
Hon DCL, 2001

*Princess Sirindhorn
of Thailand*

Hon DCL, 1998

*Elizabeth, Dowager Duchess
of Northumberland*

Hon DLitt, 1992

Queen Sonya of Norway

Hon DCL, 1996

Eva Schloss

Step-sister of Anne Frank and a
founder member of the Anne
Frank Educational Trust
Hon DCL, 2001

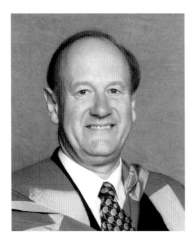

**_Lord Stevens of
Kirkwhelpington_**

Commissioner of the
Metropolitan Police, 2000–2005

Hon DCL, 2001

**_Gordon Sumner (Sting)
CBE_**

Cert Teaching, 1974
Hon DMus, 1992

Appendix IV

Scrapbook

Rutherford College: A.M. Ellis and some of his staff, 1893-94
l. to r. back row: R. Thomson, C.H. Innes, D. Campbell, Dr. V. H. Rutherford, J. Greenfield,J. H.
Oliver, D. Smith, Miss E. Simpson,J. Jeffrey, W. Elliott, J. D. Best, W. Lee, G. T. Easten.
l. to r. back row: R. Chilbourg, Miss A. Hope, J. Moore, G. Smith, F. Armstrong, A. M. Ellis
(Principal), F. Maher, Dr. R. H. Jude, W. T. Carr, Miss Mary Bolam, W. D. Oliver.

THE CITY WITH HUNDREDS OF PERFECT WIVES

IF you want a perfect wife, go to Newcastle. There are hundreds of them there, thanks to a local vicar and a college principal.

THE VICAR is Canon D. H. S. Mould, Vicar of Benwell, who is so worried by "Hollywood marriage," which he considers the main reason for the country's soaring divorce rate, that he has invited newly-weds and engaged couples to go to his church to talk over ways they can make their marriages work.

Canon Mould, plans to hold six meetings at which young men and women will be told about loyalty, marriage, partnership, children, sex life and "Christian marriage."

"I believe," he says, "that if decent people made it known that they will have none of the Hollywood standards of divorce and marriage, the divorce rate would be reduced."

TEACHING THEM YOUNG

THE COLLEGE PRINCIPAL is Miss T. Rowland, of the Northern Counties Training College of Domestic Science.

Her latest idea has been to take a 31-roomed house at Longbenton, on the outskirts of Newcastle, which is run as a model home by the students.

Each of the 110 girls at the college will have three weeks there, spending seven days at each of the jobs of cook, parlourmaid and in charge of budgeting.

The girls will be called upon to entertain with afternoon teas or intimate little dinners.

In the college, they are taught dressmaking, upholstery, and cookery.

When they finish their three-years course, they will be fully qualified schoolteachers.

But Miss Rowland admits ruefully that there is one snag.

Most of the students, aged 18 to 21, make such perfect wives that most of them get married within a year or so of completing the course at the college.

Northern Counties Training College of Domestic Science, 6 February 1939.

Newspaper article dated 16 February 1947.
Source: *unknown.*

Miss Adelaide Retford, Principal, 1932-1935, with Miss P. Henderson, Bursar at the Official opening of the Hexham Wing of the Northern Counties Training College of Domestic Science.

'Its a great scene', Newcastle upon Tyne Polytechnic advertisement.
Source: The Journal, *Tuesday 17 August 1971.*

Fenwick Lawson (Former Northumbria Head of Sculpture) and his The Risen Christ.

Gymnasium, Northern Counties College
Source: Programme of Official Opening of Northern Counties College, *8 July 1963.*

Advanced Chemistry Laboratory, Northern Counties College
Source: Programme of Official Opening of Northern Counties College, *8 July 1963.*

Reay Atkinson (Chairman, Board of Governors) and Professor Laing Barden (Director) celebrating University status, 1992.

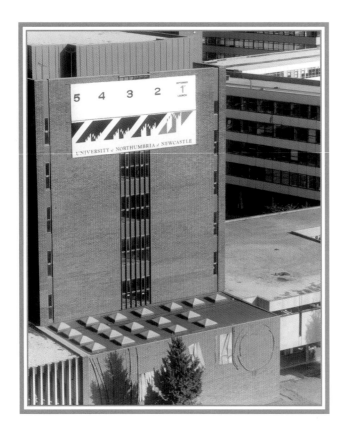

Countdown to University status in September 1992.

Her Grace the Duchess of Northumberland and Chancellor Lord Glenamara at the inauguration of the University of Northumbria at Newcastle, September 1992.

Student nurses celebrate Northumbria's perfect QAA score for Nursing in 2000.

The official opening of the Northumbria Solar Project, 19 January 1995. From left, Professor Bob Hill, Director of NPAC, Professor Laing Barden and Ian Taylor MP, Under Secretary of State for Trade and Technology.

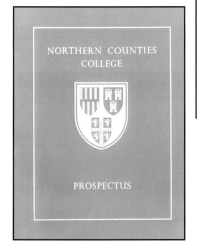

Awards Congregation December 2004. From left, Gavin Black, Chairman, Board of Governors and Pro-Chancellor; Professor Kel Fidler, Vice-Chancellor; Haydn Biddle, Deputy Chairman, Board of Governors and Pro-Chancellor. Seated, Lord Glenamara, Chancellor.

Select Bibliography

Baker, Kenneth, *The Turbulent Years: My life in politics*, (London: Faber & Faber, 1993).

Barke, M. and Buswell, R. J. (eds.), *Newcastle's Changing Map*, (Newcastle: Newcastle City Library and Arts, 1992).

Barnett, Ronald, *Learning to Effect*, (Buckingham: SRHE & Open University Press, 1992).

Becher, Tony, *British Higher Education*, (London: Unwin Hyman, 1987).

Becher, Tony and Kogan, Maurice, *Process and Structure in Higher Education*, (London: Heinemann, 1980).

Bettenson, E. M., *The University of Newcastle upon Tyne 1834–1971*, (University of Newcastle upon Tyne, 1971).

Bishop, A. S., *The Rise of a Central Authority for English Education*, (Cambridge: Cambridge University Press, 1971).

Brennan, J., de Vries P. and Williams, R., *Standards and Quality in Higher Education*, (London: Jessica Kingsley, 2003).

Briggs, Asa (ed.), *A History of the Elementary School Contest in England by Francis Adams, 1882/The Struggle for National Education by John Morley, 1873*, (Sussex: Harvester, 1972).

Burgess, Tyrell and Pratt, John, *Policy and Practice: The Colleges of Advanced Technology*, (London: Penguin, 1970).

Campbell-Savours, D., *The Case for a University of the Lakes*, (n.p., n.d).

Cannadine, David, *In Churchill's Shadow*, (London: Penguin Books, 2003).

Carswell, J., *Government and the Universities in Britain; programme and performance, 1960–1980*, (Cambridge: Cambridge University Press, 1985).

Chase, Malcolm and Dyck, Ian (ed.), *Living and Learning. Essays in Honour of J. F. C. Harrison*, (Aldershot: Scolar Press, 1996).

Cole, G. D. H., *A Century of Co-operation*, (Manchester: Cooperative Union Ltd., 1944).

Colls, Robert and Rodger, Richard, (eds.), *Cities of Ideas; Civil Governance and Urban Governance in Britain, 1800–2000*, (Aldershot: Ashgate, 2004).

Colls, Robert and Lancaster, Bill (eds.), *Newcastle upon Tyne. A Modern History*, (Sussex: Phillimore, 2001).

Cosgrave, P., *Margaret Thatcher, a Tory and her Party*, (London: Hutchinson, 1978).

Crosland, S., *Tony Crosland*, (London: Jonathon Cape, 1982).

Crossman, R., *The Diaries of a Cabinet Minister vol 1. Minister of Housing, 1964–66*, (London: Hamish Hamilton and Jonathon Cape, 1975).

Daiches, David (ed.), *The Idea of a New University*, (London: Ebenezer Baylis & Son, 1964).

Eggins, Heather (ed.), *Restructuring Higher Education*, (Milton Keynes: Open University Press, 1988).

Ellis, R. (ed.), *Quality Assurance for University Teaching*, (Buckingham: SEHE & Open University Press, 1983).

Faulkner, T. and Greg, A., *John Dobson, Newcastle Architect 1787–1865*, (Newcastle: Tyne and Wear Museums Service, 1987).

Flowers, A. and Histon, V. (eds.), *Water under the Bridges: Newcastle's Twentieth Century*, (Newcastle: Tyne Bridge Publishing, 1999).

Frayling, Christopher, *The Royal College of Art; One Hundred and Fifty Years of Art and Design*, (London: Barrie and Jenkins, 1987).

Gosden, P. H. J. H., *Education in the Second World War*, (London: Methuen, 1976).

Green, D. (ed.), *What is Quality in Higher Education?*, (Buckingham: SRHE & Open University Press, 1994).

Gurney, Peter, *Co-operative Culture and the Politics of Consumption in England, 1870–1930*, (Manchester: Manchester University Press, 1996).

Halcrow, M., *Keith Joseph – A Single Mind*, (London: Macmillan, 1989).

Halsey, A. H., *Decline of Donnish Dominion: The British Academic Professions in the Twentieth Century*, (Oxford: Clarendon Press, 1992).

Harrison, J. F. C., *Learning and Living 1790–1960. A study of the History of the English Adult Education Movement*, (London: Routledge and Kegan Paul, 1961).

Harte, Negley, *The University of London, 1836–1986*, (London: Athlone Press, 1986).

Hencke, D., *Colleges in Crisis: the reorganisation of teacher training, 1971–77*, (Harmondsworth: Penguin, 1978).

Hinde, T., *An Illustrated History of the University of Greenwich*, (London: James and James, 1996).

Hurt, J. S., *Elementary Schooling and the Working Classes, 1860–1918*, (London: Routledge, 1979).

Jepson, N. A., *The Beginnings of English Adult Education: Policy and Problems*, (London: Michael Joseph Ltd., 1973).

Kelly, Thomas, *A History of Adult Education in Great Britain from the Middle Ages to the Twentieth Century*, (Liverpool: Liverpool University Press, 1962).

Lapping, B., *The Labour Government, 1964–70*, (Harmondsworth: Penguin, 1970).

Laqueur, T. W., *Religion and Respectability: Sunday Schools and Working Class Culture, 1780–1850*, (New Haven: Yale University Press, 1976).

Locke, M., Pratt J. and Burgess T., *The Colleges of Higher Education, 1972–1982*, (Croydon: Critical Press, 1985).

Lowe, Roy, *Education in the Post-War Years: A Social History*, (London: Routledge, 1988).

Lowndes, G. A. N., *The Silent Social Revolution: An Account of the Expansion of Public Education in England and Wales, 1865–1965*, (Oxford: OUP, 1965).

Lynch, J., *The Reform of Teacher Education in the UK*, (Guilford: SRHE, 1979).

McCann, Philip (ed.), *Popular Education and Socialization in the Nineteenth Century*, (London: Methuen & Co. Ltd, 1977).

McCord, Norman, *North East England. The Region's Development 1760–1960*, (London: Batsford Ltd., 1979).

Maclure, J. Stuart, *Educational Documents, England and Wales, 1816–1967*, (London: Methuen & Co. Ltd., 1968).

Matterson, Alan, *Polytechnics and Colleges, Control and Administration in the Public Sector of Higher Education*, (London: Longman, 1981).

Maw, W., *The Story of Rutherford Grammar School: formerly Rutherford College, Newcastle upon Tyne*, (Gateshead: Rutherford History Publication Committee, 1964).

Minto, W. (ed.), *Autobiographical Notes on the Life of William Bell Scott and Notices of his Artistic and Poetic Circle*, (London: J. R. Osgood, McIlvaine and Co., 1887).

Morgan, K. O., *The People's Peace. British History 1945–1989*, (Oxford: OUP, 1990).

Morris, R. J., *Class, Sect and Party. The Making of the British Middle Class, Leeds, 1820–50*, (Manchester: MUP, 1990).

Musgrave, P. W., *Society and Education in England since 1800*, (London: Methuen, 1969).

O'Day, Rosemary, *Education and Society, 1500–1800*, (London: Longman, 1982).

Paz, D. G., *The Politics of Working-Class Education in Britain, 1830–50*, (Manchester: MUP, 1980).

Pratt, John, *The Polytechnic Experiment, 1965–1992*, (Buckingham: SRHE & Open University Press, 1997).

Reed, J. and Proctor S., *Nurse Education – a reflective approach*, (London: Arnold, 1993).

Robinson, Eric, *The New Polytechnics*, (London: Penguin Books Ltd, 1968).

Robinson, F., *Post industrial Tyneside*, (Newcastle: Newcastle City Libraries and Arts, 1988).

Roderick, Gordon and Stephens, Michael, *Education and Industry in the Nineteenth Century*, (London: Longman, 1978).

Salter, B. and Tapper, T., *The State and Higher Education*, (Ilford: Woburn Press, 1994).

Sanderson, Michael, *Education and Economic Decline in Britain, 1870 to the 1990s*, (Cambridge, Cambridge University Press, 1999).

Sanderson, Michael, *Education, Economic Change and Society in England, 1780–1870*, (Basingstoke: Macmillan, 1983).

Sanderson, Michael, *The University in the Nineteenth Century*, (London: Routledge, 1975).

Sanderson, Michael, *The Universities and British Industry, 1850–1970*, (London: Routledge, 1972).

Shattock, Michael, *The UGC and the Management of British Universities*, (Buckingham, SRHE, 1994).

Sherington, Geoffrey, *English Education, Social Change and War, 1911–1920*, (Manchester: MUP, 1981).

Silver, Harold, *Education as History*, (London: Methuen, 1983).

Silver, Harold, *A Higher Education: The Council for National Academic Awards and British Higher Education, 1964–1989*, (London: The Falmer Press. 1990).

Silver, H. and Teague, S. J. (eds.), *The History of British Universities (excluding Oxford and Cambridge), 1800–1969*, (London: SRHE, 1970).

Simon, Brian, *Education and the Labour Movement, 1870–1920*, (London: Lawrence and Wishart, 1965).

Simon, Brian, *Education in Leicestershire, 1540–1940*, (Aylesbury: Leicester University Press, 1968).

Simon, Brian, *Education and Social Order, 1940–1990*, (London: Lawrence and Wishart, 1991).

Smith, D. and Stephens, M., *A Community and its University: Glamorgan 1913–2003*, (Cardiff: University of Wales Press, 2003).

Smith, T. D., *Dan Smith, an Autobiography*, (Newcastle Upon Tyne: Oriel Press Ltd, 1970).

Stephens, W. B., *Education in Britain 1750–1914*, (Basingstoke: Macmillan, 1998).

Stevens, R., *University to Uni: the politics of higher education in Britain since 1944*, (London: Politico's, 2004).

Stewart, W. A. C., *Higher Education in Postwar Britain*, (Basingstoke: Macmillan, 1989).

Sutherland, Gillian, *Policy-Making in Elementary Education, 1870–1895*, (Oxford: OUP, 1973).

Tapper, T. and Salter, S., *Oxford, Cambridge and the Changing Idea of a University*, (Buckingham, SRHE and Open University Press, 1992).

Teather, D. C .B. (ed.), *Higher Education in a Post-Binary Era*, (London: Jessica Kingsley, 2003).

Todd, Nigel, *The Militant Democracy*, (Whitley Bay: Bewick Press Ltd., 1989).

Urwin, Dorma (ed.), *Fitness for Purpose, Essays in Higher Education by Christopher Ball*, (Surrey: SRHE & NFER-Nelson, 1985).

Venables, Peter, *Higher Educational Developments: The Technological Universities, 1956–1976*, (London: Faber & Faber, 1978).

Wardle, David, *Education and Society in Nineteenth-Century Nottingham*, (Cambridge: CUP, 1971).

Watson, M. (ed.), *Information and Library Management 2000+*, (Newcastle: Department of Information and Library Management, UNN, 1997).

Williams, Gareth (ed.), *The Enterprising University*, (Buckingham: SRHE and Open University Press, 2003).

Williams Glynn and Ramsden, John, *Ruling Britannia. A Political History of Britain 1688–1988*, (Harlow: Longman Press, 1990).

Williams, Raymond, *The Long Revolution*, (London: Penguin, 1975).

Index